MURDER
AND
MADNESS

BLITZ EDITIONS

Published by Blitz Editions
an imprint of Bookmart Ltd
Registered Number 2372865
Trading as Bookmart Ltd
Desford Road
Enderby
Leicester LE9 5AD

ISBN 1 85605 143 9

This material has previously appeared in *The Encyclopedia of True Crime*.

Every effort has been made to contact the copyright holders for the pictures.
In some cases they have been untraceable, for which we offer our apologies.
Special thanks to the Hulton-Deutsch Collection, who supplied the majority of pictures,
and thanks also to the following libraries and picture agencies:
Robert Hunt, Imperial War Museum, Marshall Cavendish,
Midsummer Books, Popperfotos, Press Association, Frank Spooner Pictures,
Syndication International, Topham Picture Source.

The Author
Allan Hall is the American correspondent for a major U.K. newspaper.
He has written several books on crime, the paranormal and the unexplained.

Designed by COOPER WILSON DESIGN

MURDER
AND
MADNESS

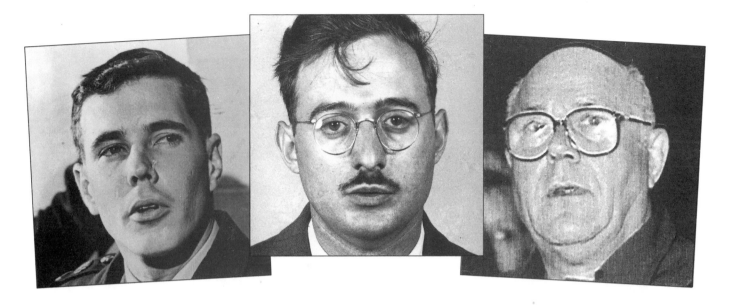

MURDER AND MADNESS

Most of humanity has a dream, or at least an idea, of a decent and orderly society. We try to live so that our own lives, and the lives around us, are at least secure, if not happy. But this dream is continually broken by both individual and mass acts of appalling cruelty and trickery.

Sometimes, a madness overtakes a group or a nation, and unbelievable horror stalks the land as gangs of sadists and killers take over. In our own time, we have witnessed the grotesque evil of the concentration camps in Nazi Germany. We have seen the carnage of thousands of gentle peasants in Cambodia, and the plains of Argentina have been littered with the mass graves of teachers, intellectuals and children.

There have also been instances of men and women, apparently united by the power of love, but in reality drawn together to form evil partnerships of depravity and perversity. These twosomes become grotesque in their mutual evil. They will maim and kill children, they will risk the security of their countries. There is no end to the evil they inspire in each other.

But when society itself turns to crime, when the law – designed to protect us, the good and innocent – itself is dubious, we have much to fear. Why do certain situations distort justice? Does the tragic suffering of a nation justify a mindless witch-hunt? Does the anger and frustration of a country beset by terrorists justify the victimisation of innocents by that country's legal system?

This book explores the kinds of stresses and tensions that drive individuals and institutions into the madness of injustice, treachery and murder. The twentieth century is rich in these dreadful cases of crime and miscarriages of justice. We need to explore the causes and motives behind these seemingly incomprehensible acts. The psychology and historical context behind such behaviour must be understood and analysed if we are to avoid further instances of murder and madness in our midst.

Contents

PARTNERS
IN CRIME

BONNIE & CLYDE
A Killing Love

The true story of Bonnie and Clyde is far more sinister than the movie. He was a homosexual and she a nymphomaniac, both were obsessed with guns and violent death and thrived on the publicity that surrounded them, even sending pictures of themselves to newspapers. Their small-time hold-ups were only an excuse for an orgy of killing.

Few villains achieve, in their own lifetime the status of folk hero. Robin Hood of Sherwood Forest was one who did, and in our own times, so has Ronnie Biggs, the Great Train Robber whose bravado and contempt for the law has earned him a certain popular respect. However, time adds lustre to even the most vicious criminals, and their evil is forgotten as myth gives them the glamour of brave individuals, outsiders who defy the constraints imposed by those in power.

Two such misplaced criminals are the professional thieves and murderers Bonnie Parker and Clyde Barrow, who went on the rampage during the Great Depression in America. Although they were ruthless killers, they have been immortalised in film, song and popular legend. They weren't very good robbers – most of their thefts were from gas stations, grocery stores and small-town diners. But they displayed a brutality and worked with a wild audacity that has earned them a place ias heroes in the myth of folk-lore.

Semi-literate and wholly without compassion, they roamed the Great Plains states of Missouri, Kansas and Oklahoma in their quest for easy cash. They loved their guns and their violent acts, cloaking themselves in the mystique of their 'mission' and recorded themselves for posterity in photographs.

With Buck Barrow, Clyde's brother, and other bandits, they formed the Barrow Gang, a nomadic outlaw tribe that criss-crossed state-lines, terrorising the small businessmen and farmers who were every bit as much victims of the Great Depression as themselves.

Their relationship was an odd one, for Barrow was a homosexual, Parker virtually a nymphomaniac. Together they found a kind of love, a bond between misfits, focussed on firearms and violent death.

Clyde was born on 24 March, 1909 into extreme poverty in Teleco, Texas. One of eight children, his older brother Buck – who would later take orders from him – taught Clyde how to steal and hot-wire cars. After petty crime as a juvenile, and time spent in a boys' reform school, Clyde graduated to robbing roadside restaurants and small, country filling stations.

Often there was no more than a handful of dollars and some loose change to steal from these places but Clyde reasoned they were safer to rob than banks. His brother was sent to prison in 1928 after he was caught on a raid on a diner. With the heat

Above: *The shattered Ford V8 in which the gangster pair met their death.*

Opposite: *Bonnie Parker and Clyde Barrow have passed into folklore as glamorous outlaws but they were really vicious killers.*

on him Clyde drifted to Texas. In January 1930, feeling peckish while wandering around Dallas, he dropped into a cafe called Marco's and was served a hamburger by a vivacious and pretty waitress. Her name was Bonnie Parker.

Parker, born on 1 October, 1910, was the daughter of a bricklayer, a petite blonde package of boredom – 'bored crapless' as she confided to her diary at the time. She listened to the tall tales that the customer spun her about life on the road. Later that night she met him for a date, but there was no sexual interest on his part. Rather, they fuelled their friendship with each other through tales of robbery and mayhem. Parker, married to a convict serving ninety-nine years for murder, moved into a small furnished apartment in Dallas with Barrow.

Guns became the consuming passion of this strange pair. Parker was thrilled by the pistols that her beau wore holstered beneath his coat, and they took regular trips to the farmland outside Dallas for target practice with revolvers, rifles and sub-machine guns. Soon Parker was every bit as good a shot as he was. Parker undoubtedly saw in her trigger-happy new friend the means of escape from the life of menial work that bored her so much.

They soon took to robbery, she driving the getaway car – despite the fact that

Clyde was a much better driver – while Clyde ran into the stores and cleaned them out at gunpoint. He would then run back to the car, jump on the running board and cover them as the car raced away. The thrill of these escapades was almost sexual for Parker, who could never find satisfaction with Barrow. He had confessed that he became homosexual in the reform school and she satisfied her considerable sexual needs with a series of one-night stands and with the men who would later drift in and out of the Barrow Gang.

Three months after they teamed up Clyde was behind bars, having left his fingerprints all over the scene of a burglary in Waco, Texas. He was arrested at the Dallas apartment and sentenced to two years, but he didn't stay to complete his sentence. His brother Buck had broken out of jail and Clyde wrote a coded letter to Bonnie asking her to spring him. Together, she and Buck travelled to Waco, with

Parker wearing a .38 police issue revolver strapped to her thigh. She escaped the attentions of prison guards due to an incompetent search and contrived to slip the weapon to Clyde. He managed to break out that same night and rode freight trains across the plains states to Ohio.

Clyde Barrow stayed free for just a week before he was arrested again and this time sent to Eastham Jail, the tough Federal penitentiary from which his brother had

beaten with a whips and made to perform exercises until he dropped. He also killed a man, Ed Crowder, a cellblock informer, with a lead pipe, but authorities at the penitentiary did not credit him with the killing until after Clyde's death.

Parker was the next to go to prison after they stole a car and were pursued by police. Clyde escaped after crashing into a tree and running across fields, but Parker was caught and sentenced to two months. While she was inside, Clyde continued to rob the small-town stores and highway gas stations. In Hillsboro, Texas, he murdered sixty-five-year-old John Bucher in his jewellery store after taking just ten dollars from the till. It was when Bonnie was released that their wild and cold-blooded-killing spree began in earnest.

On 5 August, 1932, Clyde murdered two lawmen, Sherrif Charles Maxwell and his deputy Eugene Moore. He intended to rob the ticket seller at a barn dance in Atoka, Oklahoma, when the lawmen saw him loitering suspiciously. 'You better come out into the light boy, so I can see you better,' said Sherrif Maxwell, the last words he ever spoke. Clyde lifted up his overcoat and shot the two men at point-blank range with two automatic weapons.

A BUNCH OF NUTTY KILLERS

The bizarre couple then began their deadly odyssey across America. They robbed an armoury in Texas of an arsenal of sub-machine guns, ammunition, small arms and rifles. They fired indiscriminately into a dozen state troopers who had set up a road-block in Texas, wounding several. They held up liqour stores, gas stations and grocery outlets, all for a few dollars. They even kidnapped a sherrif, stripped him and dumped him on the roadside with the parting words: 'Tell your people that we ain't just a bunch of nutty killers. Just down home people trying to get through this damned Depression with a few bones.'

On the road they lived like old-fashioned outlaws, sleeping by camp fires, surviving on wild fowl they shot and peanut butter sandwiches. At night they would get drunk on bootlegged bourbon whiskey and Parker would write turgid romantic poetry that bemoaned their lot in life – that they were persecuted by the establishment and that in

escaped. His mother Cummie Barrow deluged the state governor with pleas for leniency; pleas which were answered on 2 February, 1932, when he was released on parole. The prison was a crucial turning point in his life – after experiencing it he vowed to Parker, who waited to greet him at the gates, that he would rather die than ever go back inside. He had been tortured in the jail dubbed 'The Burning Hell',

Above: *Clyde cuddling his beloved firearms. The pair often sent photographs of themselves to the press for they delighted in their notorious fame.*

HE REGULARLY SLEPT
WITH BONNIE... AND WITH
CLYDE. THIS BIZARRE
TRIANGLE SEEMED TO SUIT
THEM ALL.

reality they were a new breed of hero. A sense of foreboding hung over the two of them; both sensed that they were not long for the world and that they would die young and die violently.

In the autumn of 1932, Bonnie and Clyde headed for New Mexico with gunslinger Roy Hamilton who joined them

house in Dallas for another robber, were gunned down when Clyde turned up instead. And together they kidnapped gas station attendant turned apprentice-robber William Jones, who was to travel with them for the next eighteen months. This fellow traveller would later give lawmen many details of the criminals' life.

Above: *Those in authority were appalled by the public's interest in Bonnie and Clyde. The pair were written about in popular magazines, their images were in all the papers. Here, 'souvenirs' of their vagabond life are assembled – stolen car plates, clothing and baggage.*

but they decided that pickings were not as rich there as Texas, so headed back. Hamilton, an accomplished robber, was also as perverted as the duo he now allied himself with. He regularly slept with Bonnie... and with Clyde. This bizarre triangle seemed to suit them all.

They killed indiscriminately and often. Clyde murdered a butcher with eight bullets when the man lunged at him with a cleaver after Clyde had stolen $50 from his store. He murdered Doyle Johnson in Temple, Texas, when he tried to stop them stealing his car. Two lawmen, staking out a

Like gypsies, they criss-crossed the southwest, continuing to hold up shops and garages. They picked up brother Buck again, together with his wife Blanche, and the robberies increased. In Kansas they robbed a loan company office where Bonnie saw her wanted poster for the first time. She was so excited that she and Clyde were 'celebrities', she fired off a dozen letters to prominent newspaper editors complete with snapshots of her and Clyde they had taken on the road. She perpetuated the myth that they were fighters against authority – authorities like the banks that were foreclosing on poor farmers and businessmen. She made no mention, of course, of the pathological delight they both took in killing.

At this time she was working on a turgid, autobiographical poem, 'The Story of Suicidal Sal' that would later reach the newspapers.

We, each of us, have a good alibi,
For being down here in the joint.
But few of them are really justified,
If you get right down to the point.
You have heard of a woman's glory,
Being spent on a downright cur,
Still you can't always judge the story,
As true being told by her.

As long as I stayed on the island,
And heard confidence tales from the gals,
There was only one interesting and truthful,
It was the story of Suicide Sal.

Now Sal was a girl of rare beauty,
Though her features were somewhat tough,
She never once faltered from duty,
To play on the up and up.

She told me this tale on the evening,
Before she was turned out free,
And I'll do my best to relate it,
Just as she told it to me.

I was born on a ranch in Wyoming,
Not treated like Helen of Troy,
Was taught that rods were rulers,
And ranked with greasy cowboys...

The poem was interrupted at this point due to a police raid on a hideout they used in Joplin, Missouri. Bonnie and Clyde, Buck and Blanche, fired more than one thousand machine gun bullets at the cops coming to get them, killing two of them. Later she finished the poem and mailed it.

Then I left my home for the city,
To play in its mad dizzy whirl,
Not knowing how little of pity,
It holds for a country girl.
You have heard the story of Jesse James,
Of how he lived and died,
If you are still in need of something to read,
Here's the story of Bonnie and Clyde.
Now Bonnie and Clyde are the

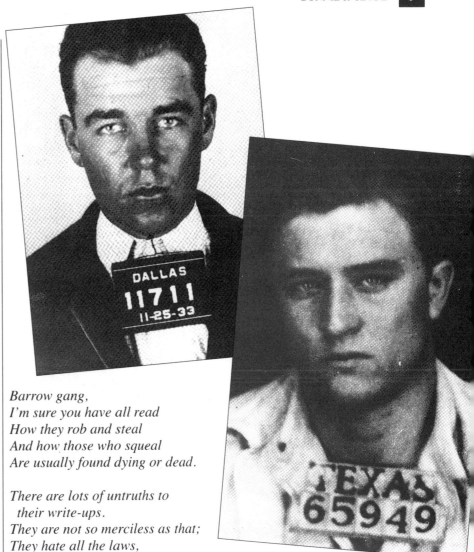

Barrow gang,
I'm sure you have all read
How they rob and steal
And how those who squeal
Are usually found dying or dead.

There are lots of untruths to
  their write-ups.
They are not so merciless as that;
They hate all the laws,
The stool pigeons, spotters and rats.
If a policeman is killed in Dallas,
And they have no clues to guide,
If they can't find a fiend,
They just wipe the slate clean,
And hang it on Bonnie and Clyde.

If they try to act like citizens,
And rent them a nice little flat,
About the third night they are invited
  to fight
By a sub-machine gun rat-tat-tat.

A newsboy once said to his buddy:
'I wish old Clyde would get jumped,
In these awful hard times,
We'd make a few dimes,
If five or six cops would get bumped.'

They class them as cold-blooded killers,
They say they are heartless and mean,
But I say this with pride,
That once I knew Clyde,
When he was honest and upright and clean.
But the law fooled around,

Above, left: *W.D Jones and Henry Methvin (above) were part of the Barrow Gang but both were to betray Bonnie and Clyde.*

SHE WAS SO EXCITED THAT SHE AND CLYDE WERE 'CELEBRITIES', SHE FIRED OFF A DOZEN LETTERS TO NEWSPAPER EDITORS.

Kept tracking them down,
And locking them up in a cell.
Till he said to me
'I will never be free
So I will meet a few of them in hell.'

The road was so dimly lighted,
There were no highway signs to guide,
But they made up their minds,
If the roads were all blind,
They wouldn't give up till they died.
The road gets dimmer and dimmer,
Sometimes you can hardly see,
Still it's fight man to man,
And do all you can,
For they know they can never be free.

They don't think they are too tough or
  desperate,
They know the law always wins,
They have been shot at before
But they do not ignore
That death is the wages of sin.

From heartbreaks some people have
  suffered,
From weariness some people have died,
But take it all and all,
Our troubles are small,
Til we get like Bonnie and Clyde.

Some day they will go down together,
And they will bury them side by side,
To a few it means grief,
To the law it's relief,
But it's death to Bonnie and Clyde.

Below: *Relatives of the Barrow Gang on trial for harbouring the criminals. Bonnie's mother is third from left, Clyde's mother third from right. The rest are sisters or sisters-in-law.*

Below: *Her family gave Bonnie a fine funeral ill-suited to a killer.*

The robbing went on. They switched mostly to small banks, in the rural towns of Indiana, Minnesota and Texas. A marshall was killed in cold blood outside the town of Alma and a two-hundred-strong possee set off after the gang. They were holed up in a rented log cabins at a country park near Platte City in Missouri but the manager became suspicious when they paid the rental in small change – the loot from several of their nickel-and-dime gas station hold-ups. The manager of the Red Crown Cabin Camp alerted police who, upon hearing the description of the guests, assembled a small army to lay siege to the rented cabin. It was 24 July, 1933.

In the ensuing confusion they escaped, leaving three officers dead. But Blanche had taken a slug in her leg, Clyde was grazed on the head, Bonnie was grazed with a bullet on her ribs and Buck... Buck was dying from a rifle bullet in his head.

NO PLACE TO GO

They escaped to a woodland area between Dexter and Refield in the rural state of Iowa where they did their best for Buck. But because they were always on the road, and without a network of contacts like those used by contemporary gangsters such as Ma Barker and John Dillinger, there was no place to hole up and get the medical attention Buck badly needed.

They were debating how to leave the wounded Buck when Clyde intuitively sensed a movement in the trees. Suddenly bullets began to rain down on their campsite. They returned fire with rifles and machine guns, even the mortally wounded Buck fired more than one thousand rounds at the lawmen. Bonnie and Clyde managed to bolt into thick undergrowth and escape but Buck was riddled with bullets. The posse found Blanche prostrate across his corpse, weeping inconsolably.

With the heat on, the duo headed back to the north and Minnesota, reasoning that

they do.' The following month Bonnie and Clyde drifted back to Texas for a meeting with his mother at a roadside picnic spot. But the pair barely escaped with their lives – his mother had been followed by a sherrif's posse who ringed the site. Once again alerted by some kind of sixth sense, Clyde drove straight past the rendezvous site. The back of the car was stuck by bullets and both he and Bonnie were wounded in the legs but not seriously.

After pulling off a few more small robberies, they teamed up again with Hamilton – after springing him from a jail

there would be less trouble in a state where they had committed relatively few crimes. They were practically bums now, stealing washing from clothes-lines and foraging for scraps of food. Jones, the kidnapped garage attendant, was with them and he later told police: 'This was not the life I expected when I joined up with them. We was nothing better than hobos.'

In October, fed up with his diet of raw vegetables stolen from fields, Jones hopped a freight train back to Texas, was arrested, and told police about the antics of the gang making sure he disassociated himself from the killings. 'It's them two,' he said. 'I ain't never seen anyone enjoy killin' as much as

with minor thugs Joe Palmer and Henry Methvin – and the Barrow Gang was back to strength once more. The FBI, because of the murders and the transportation of weapons and stolen cars across state lines, was now in on the hunt and the officers were instructed to shoot-to-kill and ask questions afterwards. J. Edgar Hoover, celebrated head of the FBI warned his G-men that Clyde was a 'psychopath – he should be killed like a rattlesnake'. Even other gangsters, knowing about their bloodlust, decided that there should be no honour among thieves. Charles Arthur 'Pretty Boy' Floyd, the gangster, was furious when he learned that the psycho-

Above: *Police hold a distraught Blanche Barrow after they shot dead her husband, Buck Barrow.*

pathic pair had entered territory that he regarded as his own in the Cookson Hills, northern Minnesota. 'Don't feed them and don't give them shelter,' he ordered his cohorts and criminal associates. 'Stick the law on them if you can. They are vermin and have nothing to do with our people.'

Public opinion was rapidly turning against them. The banks they robbed were forced to close because they were suffering in the hard times, as were the businesses they raided. Soon the newspaper readers who had adored her romantic poem realised that there was nothing Robin-Hood-like about their exploits. They were simply greedy and ruthless killers.

KNOW THINE ENEMY

Soon only Methvin was left with the gang. Hamilton had argued with Clyde and gone his own way, Palmer dropped out with chronic stomach ulcers. The heat was on like never before, particularly in Texas, where a lawman called Frank Hamer, who had gunned down sixty-five notorious criminals during his career, was given the task of hunting down Bonnie and Clyde.

Hamer analysed every move they made, drew up maps and charts of all their movements over the previous years and discerned a pattern of sorts in the type of places they hit and the routes they took. 'I wanted to get into their evil minds,' he said. 'Know thine enemy was my maxim and I learned it well.' Several times during the early months of 1934 Hamer and his men came upon campsites that the duo had abandoned just hours before, but he was determined to stay on their trail.

In April that year, after hiding out on a farm in Louisiana, they returned to Texas to see Bonnie's relatives and hopefully lie low. But, as they neared the outskirts of the town of Grapevine, motorcycle police Ernest Wheeler and Harold Murphy rode past them. When they crested a rise in the road in front, Clyde pulled the car over and stopped. The motorcycle cops, their suspicions aroused, turned around and came back towards them. As they drew level with the car Clyde murdered them both with both barrels of a shotgun. Two weeks later in Oklahmoa, when their car got stuck in mud, they were approached by two police officers. One died with a

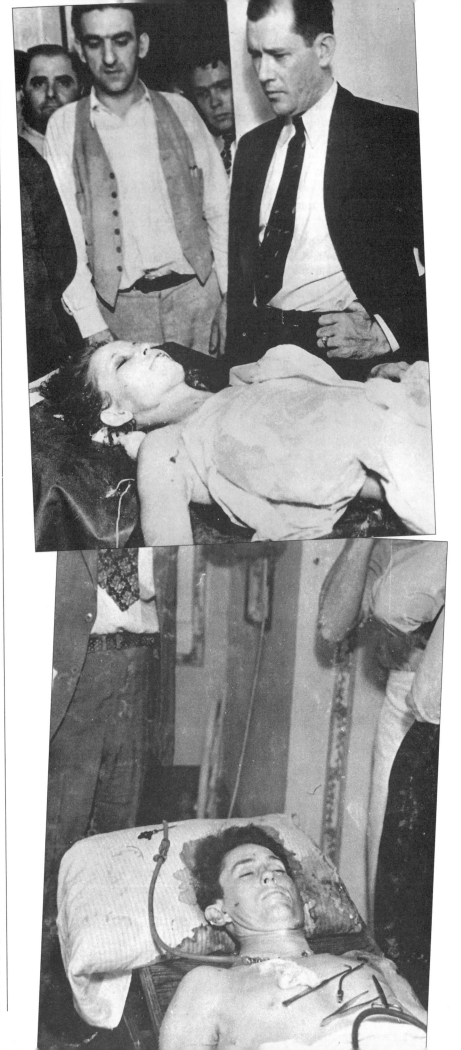

revolver bullet in the chest, the other was luckier - he was slightly wounded.

The key to capturing the outlaws lay with Methvin, who was still running with them. His father Ivan offered to help trap them if Hamer would agree to granting his son a pardon. Hamer, needing Bonnie and Clyde more than him, agreed to the deal. Henry Methvin, seeing a way out for himself, agreed to co-operate with his father when he next contacted him. Henry slipped away from a hideout shack in Shreveport, Louisiana, which was promptly surrounded by Hamer's armed Texas Rangers. Soon a posse had hidden themselves along the road leading to the shack; they were armed with Browning machine guns, high-powered rifles and numerous grenades and tear gas bombs.

At 9.15am on 23 May, 1934 the V8 Ford which the couple had been using for the past week – they changed licence plates every day – crested a rise in the road leading from the hideout. Clyde was at the wheel, his shoes off, driving with bare feet. He wore sunglasses against the strong spring sunshine. Next to him sat his deadly moll in a new red dress she had bought with stolen loot some weeks previously. Stashed in the car were two thousand bullets, three rifles, twelve pistols and two pump-action shotguns.

A FRIGHTENED DECOY

Methvin Snr has agreed to be a decoy. His truck was parked at the edge of the road and Clyde drew level with it. Clyde asked him if there had been any sight of his son. Methvin, almost quaking with fear, saw a truckful of black farm labourers coming down the road and he panicked, diving for cover beneath his own vehicle. A sherrif with the posse named Jordan suddenly yelled for the duo to surrender. But this was like a red rag to a bull for this homocidal pair. In one swift motion Clyde had his door open and a shotgun in his hand, Bonnie was equipped with a revolver.

This time there was no escape. A murderous rain of fire battered the car. More than five hundred bullets slammed into the bodies of the gangsters and they were literally ripped to pieces. Clyde was slumped backwards, his foot off the clutch pedal. The car was still in gear and it

Opposite: Pictures of the dead desperadoes were circulated all over the United States. The public could not get enough to read about the gruesome lives and bloody deaths of Bonnie and Clyde.

Below: Bonnie Parker at peace at last after a wild and dangerous life.

inched ahead, coming to a halt in a ditch. The posse of lawmen continued to pour fire into the wreck for four whole minutes after it had come to a stop.

As newspaper headlines around the world shouted the news of their deaths, local residents were charged a dollar a head to view the mangled corpses on a morgue slab. Thousands paid to look.

Ray Hamilton, the robber who ran with them, was eventually executed less than ten years later for other murders. Just before his death, he accurately described Bonnie and Clyde.'They loved to kill people, see blood run. That's how they got their kicks.

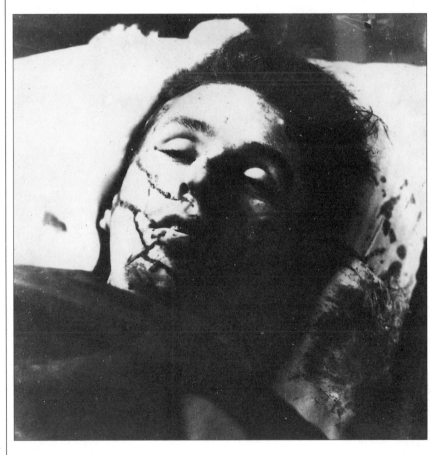

'THEY WERE DIRTY PEOPLE. HER BREATH SMELLED AWFUL AND HE NEVER TOOK A BATH. THEY SMELLED BAD ALL THE TIME. THEY WOULD STEAL THE PENNIES FROM A DEAD MAN'S EYES.'

There was many times when they didn't have to kill, but they did anyways. They were dirty people. Her breath smelled awful and he never took a bath. They smelled bad all the time. They would steal the pennies from a dead man's eyes.'

The Parker family tried its best to paint Bonnie in a different light. The horribly-inaccurate inscription on this murderer's tombstone reads thus: 'As the flowers are all made sweeter, by the sunshine and the dew, so this old world is made brighter, by the likes of folk like you.'

GOTTI & GRAVANO
A Broken Honour

John Gotti murdered and lied his way to the top of New York's Mafia empire yet the FBI could not make their charges stick to the 'Teflon Don'. That is until 1992 when 'Sammy the Bull' Gravano, the man who had killed nearly forty people in Gotti's name betrayed him in a spectacular courtroom drama.

John Gotti, Capo di Tutti Cappi – Boss of Bosses of all the Mafia families in America – made just one mistake in his rise to the top of the $16 million per-year crime empire. He trusted Salvatore 'Sammy the Bull' Gravano and chose him to become his underboss. It was a mistaken decision that would send John Gotti to prison for the rest of his life.

Gotti's rule came to an end in 1992 when Sammy Gravano broke the code of *omerta*, the Mafia code of secrecy and silence, to betray the Godfather Gotti. Sammy's testimony also broke the power of the Gambino clan, Gotti's mob 'family'.

To his admirers, Gotti was a generous guy who wore $4,000 silk suits and kept the drug-dealing scum away from ordinary, decent folk. Every year, without fail,he held an annual fireworks display on America's 4 July Independence Day, releasing thousands of dollars worth of rockets to the delight of the neighbourhood.

On the street well-wishers tugged at his pure cashmere coat, others called out respectful greetings,as he made his way to the Ravenite Social Club – a nondescript tenement in the heart of Little Italy.

It was behind these doors – fitted with alarms, armoured and locked – that John Gotti, Capo di Tutti Cappi, held court. It was here that the veneer of philanthropist. was dropped. This was the office of the Dapper Don, as he was known. Gambling, corruption, liqour sales, prostitution, drugs and murder were his business and he did it well. So well, in fact, that he earned another title: the FBI called him the 'Teflon Don' as no indictment they threw at him ever stuck to this criminal.

That was hardly surprising as he had a finger in every illegal pie. And he was protected by witnesses and associates who

were too afraid of the consequences to tell the truth. These people believed that they would meet a horrible death if they testified against John Gotti, the ruthless and arrogant leader if the powerful Mafia.

THE NAUGHTY BUT NICE IMAGE

The FBI task force that concentrates solely on Gotti and his Gambino crime family, were determined his naughty-but-nice image would not save him from justice when he was seized in 1990. He is languishing now in jail.

Above: *The law came to take Gotti away, but he belived he was immune from the ordinary rules of society.*

Opposite: *John Gotti ruled a criminal empire based on fear and terror.*

Thanks to the testimony of his former sidekick Sammy the Bull, he was convicted of numerous murders, including the 1985 assasination of Paul 'Big Paulie' Castellano, the Gambino Godfather whose assassination he masterminded in order to take over the organisation. Even as the paramedics were trying to save Castellano's life after the shooting in 1985, John Gotti was being sworn in as the new Capo di Tutti Cappi in a ceremony that has all the solemnity of a Vatican mass. But in 1990 when he was arrested for the fourth and final time, the FBI were determined that it was time for the spell to be broken.

Gotti was born on 27 October, 1940, the fifth of thirteen children and their first son, to dirt-poor John and Fannie Gotti. The family were squashed into a townhouse in the South Bronx – then, as now, New York's toughest neighbourhood. Gotti came to despise the Bronx so much that when he was at the peak of his power, it was the one borough where he refused to do business.

He quickly decided that violence was more fun than studying. His father, who had come from Naples as a child, worked sixteen hours a day as a sanitation worker and John Gotti realised then that the work route to success was for schmucks – you had to take what you wanted.

GOTTI WAS KNOWN AS 'FAST FISTS'

When he was twelve, the clan moved to the Brownsville section of Brooklyn – still a predominantly Italian neighbourhood, but one that seethed with ethnic tension. There were dozens of white street gangs which clashed regularly with the black community on the fringes of Brownsville and the strapping, muscular Gotti was known as 'Fast Fists' to his admirers. By the time he was sixteen, he led the feared Fulton-Rockaway Boys Gang. .On 15 May, 1957 came Gotti's first arrest when he was nabbed for disorderly conduct but the charges were dropped.

Mostly, Gotti and his cronies were coffee bar thugs who inhabited the storefront clubs popular among the Italian immigrants. Gotti was a frequent visitor at a club run by Carmine Fatico, then a '*Capo*', or captain, in the crime family headed by Albert Anastasia and nicknamed 'Murder Inc' by the Feds. Inside Fatico's

Below: *This is the public face of John Gotti, the smiling, benevolent philanthropist.*

club, smug, hard men with ready cash and fancy clothes lounged around all day and were treated with the same brand of obsequious respect that Gotti would one day command on his own turf.

His formal schooling ended at sixteen when he dropped out of the Franklin K. Lane High School in Brooklyn and he drifted into dead-end jobs. He worked as a garment presser on Seventh Avenue, the city's fashion district, and as a trucker's helper. But his thrills came from hanging out with the tough guys at the storefront cafes where old men heard of his prowess with his fists and his quick-thinking mind.

Gotti became a numbers runner for the illegal bookmakers and performed small chores for the local hoods – running money to bent cops on the mob's payroll and stealing cars for heists. At seventeen he started his criminal record – a probation

HE QUICKLY DECIDED THAT VIOLENCE WAS MORE FUN THAN STUDYING.

term for burglary. In 1959 he was working in the garment factory by day and running errands for the hard men at night. Around this time he met Victoria DiGiorgio, a petite woman with dark hair and classical Italian features and was won over by her serene charm and her quiet nature.

A SOLDIER IN CRIME

Over her parents' objections, she married him in April 1960 and they had their first

child, Angela, a year later. The year was significant too for another reason – Gotti had been accepted part-time into the ranks of the mob as a 'soldier' in the Gambino crime family. Here he was to meet Salvatore Gravano, nicknamed 'Sammy the Bull' because of his muscular frame which was always squeezed and closely-packed into too-tight suits.

Over the next three decades, John Gotti rose up the ranks; and with him he took along Sammy the Bull. Sammy came from the same background as himself and, lacking Gottis' ambition, was more than willing to be a loyal underboss. So blindly loyal to Gotti was he that he would later say at his boss' trial: 'John Gotti was my master and I was his dog. When he said "bite", I bit.' But the dog was to turn.

As Gotti rose in rank, the mobster king himself, Albert Anastasia, failed to read the

*Above: **John Gotti with his son, John Jnr. A devoted family man, Gotti was well regarded by his neighbours. They did not know how many men he had laid in unmarked graves.***

writing on the wall. He surrounded himself with too many ambitious men and not enough loyal servants. By the time he was ready to change things just a little, it was too late. The head of Murder Inc was killed by Carlo Gambino's thugs. With Anastasia shot to death in a Manhattan barber shop, Gambino became the boss and demanded loyalty from the 'soldiers' who previously worked for Anastasia. Gotti, sensing the main chance, swore his allegiance to the Sicilian, now the powerful Godfather.

Gotti quit the garment factory and took another job with a trucking firm where he learned the rudiments of hijacking and warehouse raids. At night he and Sammy hung out in pool halls and bars, hustling for information on lucrative truck-loads that he could pass on to his 'crew' capo – the revered Carmine Fatico. The Capo in the Mafia hierachy commands a team of 'soldiers', around two hundred and fifty, who swear life-allegiance to the family under whom they operate.

Because of his loyalty to Gambino, he was singled out by Fatico – nicknamed 'Charley Wagons' because of his speciality of hijacking trucks – for a special task. He was sent with Sammy to rough up the proprietor of one of Fatico's 'chop shops' – garages where stolen cars were dismantled, reassembled in different combinations of parts and re-sold.

THE SLOW CLIMB TO POWER

His nocturnal activities put a heavy strain on his marriage and led to a short separation from Victoria, who by 1963 had given birth to two more children, daughter Victoria and John Jnr. Then Gotti went to prison for twenty days for stealing a car in 1963. In 1966 he was jailed again for four months for attempted theft and this time lost his job at the trucking company where he had been able to provide so much inside information for Gambino's hijacking crews. By 1969 he had become a full–time hijacker and had a flash car and house in the suburbs on Long Island. He was

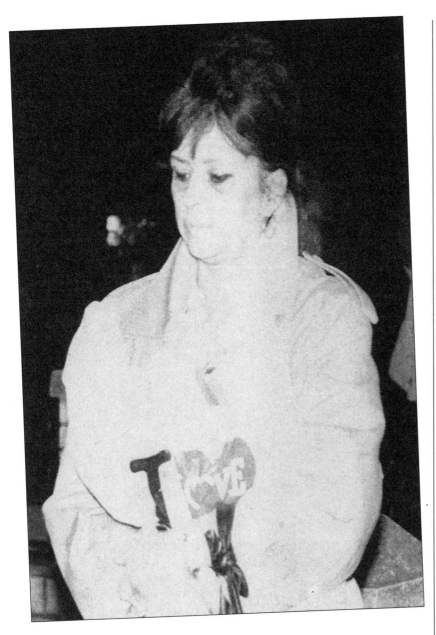

As Sammy became ever more enthusiastic about killing, so gambling became the chronic drug for Gotti. He had no weakness for wine or women and worked eighteen-hour days but he could never refuse a roll of the dice, a bet on a ball game or a long poker session. It left him forever chasing money which he made up for by taking on more and more dirty work for the mob. This also involved loansharking, and earning fat commissions from Gambino underbosses, to shake up businesses where the kickbacks were not fast enough coming through. Luck ran out, however, that same year when an FBI sting set up at New York's Kennedy Airport snared Gotti and several other Gambino associates as they robbed a warehouse on the airport complex of women's clothing worth $7,641. John Gotti was sentenced to three years in jail – and jail is the natural finishing school for any ambitious mobster.

When Gotti emerged from prison, the traditional order among the Mafia clans had not changed in New York. The city's rich pickings remained divided between his chosen tribe the Gambino family, and the Bonnano family, the Luchese family, the Genovese and the Colombo families. The structure of these criminal warlord societies was the same: the boss, followed by the underboss and then the *consiglieri*, or trusted counsellor, who relayed instructions to the capos in charge of the soldiers in their crews. The Gambino family had some twenty crews, each with their quota of 'made' men and numerous associates who shared their booty with the capos who, in turn, channelled profits to the top three leaders in the family.

While Gotti was in jail his capo, Carmine Fatico, moved the gang's HQ from East New York to a dismal storefront in the city borough of Queens at a club called The Bergin Hunt and Fish Social Club, which quickly became known to the underworld just as 'The Bergin'.

A TEST OF LOYALTY

In 1972, after three years inside, thirty-one-year-old John Gotti came out to a promotion. He had served his time 'honourably' inside, so the Gambino underboss Aniello Dellacroce gave the former hijacker and muscleman his capo's

committed to the mob by this time and he dreamed of having the kind of ruthless power that Carmine Fatico wielded.

Salvatore was his closest pal now. Sammy was becoming something of a legend in mob ranks. He was completely dispassionate when ordered to 'whack' somebody – mob parlance for executing an enemy. One day he was sitting at home watching the movie M*A*S*H with his family when his dog came in with a human hand in its mouth – the hand belonged to a member of his own family who had crossed Gotti. And Sammy had whacked him as if he was of no more consequence than a fly, buried him on a local rubbish tip and thought no more of him until his dog, foraging for scraps, had had the good fortune to disinter his remains.

Above: *The faithful wife, Victoria Gotti, has always stood by her man and remains silent when asked what her husband does for a living. She says simply: 'He provides. He puts food on the table.'*

job, putting him in charge of the Bergin crew. Dellacroce had befriended Gotti before he went in to jail and was impressed with his cool, his intelligence and his deep respect for Cosa Nostra traditions.

In his new job, Gotti concentrated on organising and consolidating the Family's white-collar rackets – the pay-offs from rigging contracts, waste-disposal kickbacks, protection money from the entertainment industries. But it was the Don, Gambino himself, who set the ultimate test of John Gotti's loyalty and bravery. The ageing Godfather was stricken with grief a year after Gotti's release when his nephew Emmanuel was kidnapped and murdered. Gambino was beside himself with sorrow and pledged 'great things' for the *capo* John Gotti if he could track down the killer and revenge the boy's death.

GOTTI PULLED OUT A SNUB NOSED .38 REVOLVER

The word went out on the street immediately and the net was cast among hit men, five-and-dime killers and rival gangs, like the Irish Westies who often took on the contracts that the Mob refused to carry out. Gotti, with two others, was happy to learn that stick-up man turned contract killer, James McBratney, had been identified as the kidnapper and murderer.

On 22 May, 1973, Gotti went with his accomplices to Staten Island's Snoopes Bar and Grill where McBratney was drinking alone. Witnesses saw Gotti swagger up to him and pull out a card – it turned out later to be a fake ID for a New York police detective. There was a scuffle as McBratney realised the trouble he was in. He was reaching into his inside pocket when Gotti reached into his own shoulder holster and pulled out a snub nosed .38 police issue revolver and opened fire.

A dozen bullets from Gotti's gun and those of his accomplices made sure that the job was done. However, it was a sloppy 'hit' and too many people got too good a look at Gotti and his sidekicks. Gotti and one other, his old friend Angelo Ruggiero, were arrested within seventy-two hours to face charges of murder.

A grateful Gambino made certain that money bought the best lawyer in the shape of John Cohn for Gotti and his accomplice.

Hottest of New York's hotshot lawyers, he negotiated a remarkable deal with the Staten Island district attorney's office. In exchange for reduced charges of attempted manslaughter, they both pleaded guilty and each received maximum terms of four years at state penitentiaries.

The tentacles of the mob reached far into the jail. Although apparently in good health, he was taken on three, one-hundred-and-twenty mile round trips from his cell at the Greenhaven Correctional facility in upstate New York to Brooklyn – allegedly for examinations by a private physician. In reality, Gotti had bribed guards to take him to his home for meetings with his wife Victoria and to restaurants where he ate hearty Italian meals with his cronies before being transported back to jail.

Carlo Gambino died in 1976 while Gotti was still inside. By normal rights of succession the underboss – and mentor to Gotti – Dellacroce should have moved into the top slot. But before his death Gambino eschewed mob protocol and appointed his brother-in-law Paul Castellano as the boss. Castellano handed Dellacroce the consolation prize by allowing him to remain the underboss in charge of ten of the family's twenty-three crews. Observers of organised

> HOWEVER, IT WAS A SLOPPY 'HIT' AND TOO MANY PEOPLE GOT TOO GOOD A LOOK AT GOTTI AND HIS SIDEKICKS.

Above: *The house where John Gotti played the role of quiet family man.*

crime say this was the worst thing the dying Castellano could have done. By allowing a rival to wield such vast power within the empire, he had created two opposing and deadly factions. Paul Castellano had an image of himself as a corporate executive rather than a gun-toting Al Capone. He liked the loyal capo Gotti and displayed his affection for him.

In March 1980, however, Gotti's life took a tragic turn. A devoted family man, he was nevertheless especially fond of his

Above: *Gotti takes a stroll outside his home and shrugs off press questions about his alleged criminal activities.*

Opposite: *The 'Dapper Don' as well dressed as ever enters court to face numerous counts of racketeering and murder. John Gotti faced a long prison term.*

second youngest child Frank, then aged twelve. When this son was killed in a cycling accident Gotti was beside himself with grief. It didn't matter that it was the child's fault, which it was. Frank had ridden straight into the path of the car driven by neighbour John Favara.

Favara began receiving anonymous death threats and began to make plans to move with his family to another part of the state, away from John Gotti who cocked his finger at him in a gun symbol every time he drove past his house. Four months later – while Gotti and his wife Victoria were in Florida on holiday – furniture

salesman Favara vanished forever. He had parked his van in a parking lot near his home when witnesses claimed that they saw a burly figure emerge from the shadows and club him over the head. Favara, fifty-one, was bundled into the back of his van which was then driven away and he was never seen again.

Gotti never got over the death of 'Young Frankie' and he paid a monthly lone vigil to his grave. The front room of his home was turned into a shrine to his dead son, the boy's picture flanked by heavy velvet drapes that fell in folds round the gilded photo frame. However, Gotti continued to prosper as mobsters of the other families were falling like nine-pins to the prosecutions brought by the Feds.

GOTTI ESCAPES JAIL

An FBI wiretap placed inside the Bergin in 1981 (the first of many) gave agents their first glimpse of what made Gotti tick. They were seeking evidence to convict Gotti and his cohorts with running an illegal gambling operation on the premises. The taps paid off and several Bergin underlings were jailed but Gotti escaped.

By this time – July 1981 – other members of his crew were worried by his appalling gambling losses, rumoured to be up to $50,000 a month. More worrying for the crews than his gambling, however, was the new sharp turn the Gambino mob had taken in dealing with drugs. 'Big Paulie' Castellano, the Godfather, had run an organisation that kept away from narcotics, believeing it was a trade fit only for 'the coloureds'. An educated, meticulous man who studied the Wall Street Journal every day from cover to cover, he was furious when the heroin trafficking indictments landed on his doormat one day. Behind his back Gotti, using contacts established by Sammy the Bull in the drug underworld, had been dealing big-time. Gene Gotti was arrested, his old pal Angelo Ruggiero, a lawyer from the Bergin and a director of the Arc Plumbing Company – for twenty years Gotti's 'front' where the books claimed he was a salesman.

A police detective says: 'When we hit those guys back in '82 with indictments for trafficking Big Paulie was beside himself with rage. He screamed at Gotti: "Listen

Johnny, you had better prove you were not involved with this''.' But Gotti was involved and had pushed for drug distribution because he saw the massive profits and the potential power that the narcotics trade could bring to the family.

Castellano himself was indicted and it was the beginning of the end for Gotti under his reign. He let it be known that John Gotti had no future in his organisation. He had let drugs in, carelessly allowed an FBI informer into the ranks, and now he, the boss, was indicted on charges that could put him away for life. Now both men plotted the demise of each other.

The Mafia has a 'Commission' – the mob term for the committee composed of representatives from all five Mafia families that carved up the city.

The Commission met in 1957 at a now historic parley called the Apalachin Conference at which they decided to steer clear of drug dealing. The Mafia hierachy, determined to preserve their image as family men with a concern for the morals of society, decided to leave it to the blacks. The four other clans in New York flagrantly broke the treaty but Big Paulie made his crews stick by it. It enraged him that it was John Gotti's Bergin Crew that flouted his orders. Word was out after the heroin trafficking indictments that there was no place in the hierachy any longer for the upstart capo, John Gotti.

BILOTI NAMED AS SUCCESSOR

It is widely believed that Castellano was planning a hit on Gotti when he was swept along in the drug indictments. Rudolph Giuliani, the new, squeaky clean district attorney, hit him and the four other leaders under the powerful new RICO act which was eventually to lead to the downfall of all the Mafia families save one – the Gambino clan under Gotti himself. Dellacroce, his sponsor and mentor within the family, died from natural causes in December 1985. With him died any further hope Gotti may have had of sticking around in the clan. Thomas Biloti had already been named by Castellano as the successor to the top post – making it clear that Gotti's drug trafficking was the reason for the snub.

On 16 December that same year – according to testimony he has repeatedly

given to federal agents – John Gotti was nowhere near the fashionable Sparks Steak House in Midtown Manhattan. Sparks was Big Paulie's favourite restaurant and he had gone there that day with his chosen successor to discuss family tactics when he was put away on the heroin indictment.

At precisely 5.16pm on that evening Paul Castellano's limousine turned into East 46th Street and purred to a halt at the awnings outside Sparks. Big Paulie was halfway out of the passenger door when the first shots hit him. Thomas Biloti sat behind the steering wheel and the first of five bullets tore into his body and skull. The gunman ran to the corner where a waiting car sped off. Two streets away John Gotti and Salvatore Gravano were toasting each other with expensive champagne in the back of a limousine.

Federal agents say that it was later that night, at an unknown spot in the sprawling city, that Gotti re-swore the omerta and became the Godfather. Reno Franceschini, the New York police expert on the Mafia, said: 'I was in London and as soon as I heard about Paulie getting whacked I said Gotti is the next Godfather.'

Above: *Victoria Gotti enjoys her husband's wealth as she glides round New York with him in a large, armour-plated limousine.*

HE SWITCHED FROM WHITE-COLLAR MONEY LAUNDERING SCHEMES TO THE TRADITIONAL MOB SCHEMES BACKED UP BY VIOLENCE.

It was after the assassination that prosecutors believe that Gotti formally opened the heroin and cocaine pipeline to the Gambino family. He also switched from the white-collar money laundering schemes favoured by Castellano back to more traditional mob schemes backed up by violence.

TRIALS PUT AWAY MOST OF MAFIA HIERACHY

Police say he became Capo di Tutti Capi by dint of staying out of jail rather than by consent. A series of trials in the early Eighties put away most of the Mafia hierachy for life in New York – all except Gotti. His scare tactics, public image, a brilliant lawyer in the shape of Bruce Cutler, ensured that he earned the nickname 'The Teflon Don'.

John Gotti never forgets a double-cross and one of those doomed to find it out the hard way was Willie Boy Johnson. Willy Boy was Wahoo to the FBI, a low-level soldier in Gotti's crew when he was a capo and the one who gave details to the Feds of his boss's moves to begin dealing in heroin and cocaine. Willie Boy had been living under an assumed name in Brooklyn ever since his testimony led to the convictions of several mob figures – not least among them Gotti's brother Gene, who is currently serving a twenty-year sentence for heroin smuggling. On 29 August, 1988, at 6.20am Willie Boy left home to go to work on a construction site. He didn't see the three men stepping out of the stolen car parked opposite, nor their automatic pistols. When the shooting had stopped there were fourteen bullet holes between Willie Boy's head and his toes. The triggerman was Sammy the Bull.

In 1985 Gotti was accused of assaulting a repairman and robbing him of $325 in an arguement over a parking space. The repair-

> 'IT WAS A CLASSIC DOUBLE ACT THAT ENDED IN BETRAYAL AND TREACHERY.'

men learned who Gotti was, checked into a hospital where he said he had developed amnesia and the charges were dropped.

A year later Gotti was accused of running a racketeering enterprise and hit with three charges, including murder. He beat the rap. In 1992 he made it a hat-trick when jurors ruled he did not order the bungled contract-killing of a union official who wasn't paying his dues. But it was the loyal, psychotic lieutenant Salvatore who did most of the dirty work. By his admission he became crazier in the second half of the 1980s and committed so many

Below: Bruce Cotler on the left gives an impassioned speech in defence of his client, John Gotti. Cotler was barred from defending Gotti in the crook's last trial. The lawyer's integrity was under question because of his intimacy with the mobs.

murders he actually forgot many of them. Salvatore was arrested with Gotti.

This time the Feds thought they had a cast iron case. There were dozens of wiretaps and two low level informants willing to testify against them. But they couldn't believe their luck when Sammy, who had only served time in the past for low-level offences like hijacking and theft, offered to become the highest ranking mob informer in criminal history. It turned out that Sammy – who was tipped to be the heir apparent to the Gambino family leadership – had a terrible fear of ending his days in prison. So in a spectacular trial in March and April 1992 he took the stand to testify against John Gotti and his Mafia empire of evil and corruption.

A MARKED MAN FOR EVER

Methodically confessing to all the murders requested by John Gotti, he squirmed under the gaze of the Godfather's steely eyes and knew that he would be a marked man for ever. In return for his testimony Sammy knew he could expect leniency for his own crimes – he has yet to be judged on them – and a life spent looking over his shoulder. On 23 June, 1992, Gotti was sporting his full mob plumage – handmade silk suit and yellow silk tie – for the last time. He was sentenced to life in prison without parole for ordering at least five murders, and on forty-nine counts of racketeering. Going down with him on the one way trip was another underboss, Frank 'Frankie Loc' Locascio, a fifty-nine-year-old henchman also nailed by Sammy's testimony.

Gotti's empire is currently being run by John Jnr, his muscular son. One lawman described him as closer to John Gotti than the stubble on his chin and he's responsible for the day-to-day organisation of the empire. Crime busters predict that the fallout between Sammy and Gotti could lead to a bloody war as the gangsters fight for the right of succession. There is no end, it seems, to Mafia violence despite a keen effort from US law enforcement agencies.

'It would never have happened if they hadn't been friends that became enemies,' said gangland expert George Carmenza. 'It was a classic double act that ended in betrayal and treachery. A fitting end for two guys like that – almost poetic justice.'

JUAN & EVITA
The Corruptible Perons

Proud dictator Juan Peron and his nightclub singer Evita presided over an evil and repressive regime. They brought their country to the verge of bankruptcy as they looted millions from charities and the state to fill their Swiss bank accounts. And they did it all in the name of the Argentinian people they claimed to love.

They were a most unlikely double act, this notorious nightclub singer and the ambitious army colonel but together they shaped the course of South American politics and still enjoy near-mythological status to this day.

Andrew Lloyd Weber's musical 'Evita' was not the only reason that Eva Duarte, mistress of Juan Peron, became a household name. In the southern hemipshere, in the land of the pampas, Peronism has become more than a political movement; it is almost a religious affirmation and to those who supported them; Juan and Evita were the demi-gods who put Argentina on the world stage.

However, it was, mostly, a clever show without real substance, for while the illusion created by this glittering twosome was lapped up by the masses, they used the peoples' ill-judged support to mask their own corruption – a corruption which channelled untold millions from the national coffers into Swiss bank accounts. They also supported the Fascist movements in Europe during wartime, clamped down on the press which opposed them, and even launched an anti-church campaign aimed at those ministers within the Catholic hierachy that they regarded as enemies.

While Peronism may still make the gauchos and the housewives of Buenos Aries misty-eyed for 'the good old days' it was in reality nothing more than a cover for a well-ordered fleecing of the state. It is an indisputable fact that before their rule Argentina was one of the wealthiest nations in the world; afterwards, the nation was ruined and bankrupt.

Before there was an Evita for the crowds in Argentina to cheer there was Colonel Juan Domingo Peron. Born in Lobos in 1895 to poor immigrant stock, he rose through the army ranks thanks to dilligence and ability. Equipped with charm, athleticism and that essential Argentinian characteristic, machismo, he was destined to go far. But he was also a moral and physical coward, a man who shunned reality if he thought confronting it would be unpleasant. He could not endure being unpopular and many of his ludicrous economic policies were pursued so he could enjoy the applause of the mob while he followed them through.

In 1943 Argentina was under the rule of President Ramon Castillo – at least until June that year, when the military decided to stage a coup. It was led by colonels calling themselves the Young Turks, Peron among them. The colonels claimed that the Ramon government was supporting the Allies in the war. This was alien to the Fascist-temperament of the officer corps, many of whom were of Italian extraction and saw

WHILE THE ILLUSION CREATED BY THIS GLITTERING TWOSOME WAS LAPPED UP BY THE MASSES, THEY USED THE PEOPLES' ILL-JUDGED SUPPORT TO MASK THEIR OWN CORRUPTION.

Opposite: *The glittering Eva and her husband Juan Peron managed to keep the adoration of the masses even as they stole from the nation's coffers.*

Below: *The successful politicians who promisd to turn Argentina into a paradise for the workers. But Eva and Jaun fulfilled little of their socialist programme.*

Mussolini in Italy as their kind of leader. At the time of the coup Peron was one of the keenest pro-Fascist officers among the colonels and worked in the Ministry of War, but by the end of October he was promoted when he was granted the critical job of running the Labour Department in the new military junta.

The labour movement in Argentina was split between trades unions and those workers on the ranches and in the slaughterhouses who had no organisation. Peron set out to mould the workers into a single, military-like unit, with the discipline and style of the black shirts he admired at rallies in Nazi Germany and Fascist Italy. Many workers' leaders had suffered cruelly under previous regimes, while the men they represented were mercilessly gunned down in the streets if they dared to strike.

Peron used his considerable charm to become the friend of the unions, the affable big brother who would ease their economic and social woes. Months earlier these same men had been called Communist scum and filth by the military but Peron believed flattery was a better way of attaining what he wanted from them.

What he wanted from them was subservience to the government. He made it, for instance, mandatory for wage negotiations between workers and bosses to go through his office. Kickbacks from the unions and the bosses were discreetly channelled into the seven-figure bank account he held in Switzerland. The more astute union leaders realised what he was up to but he outflanked the old guard. He

ordered free paid holidays, a month's bonus at Christmas for the meat packers and other fringe benefits. While the workers cheered at this short-term philanthropy, the bosses bemoaned the loss of their managerial rights, and the unions felt emasculated. They were both victims of Juan Peron's attempt to create a permanent Argentinian military dictatorship based on the solid support of the masses.

As the dictatorships which the Argentinian military so admired crumbled in Europe, so the movement for freedom and openness in Argentina grew. In August 1945, the military lifted a state of emergency that had existed throughout the war years – causing a half-a-million strong demonstration the following month on the streets of the capital from a populace seeking greater freedom and human rights. It was a frightening display of people-

Below, left: *A young admirer approaches a delighted Eva and Juan in their presidential box at a social event on the River Plate.*

Below, right: *The Perons, while promising a socialist regime, brought expensive glamour into their own lives.*

mistress Eva Duarte. Fierce and brave, she yelled abuse at the soldiers, while reliable sources have it that her colonel fell to his knees and begged for mercy. Eva, the nightclub singer who literally slept her way to the top, rallied support for Peron among the unions that he had helped so much and rioting broke out in the streets. For forty-eight hours, Buenos Aries was paralysed until the military backed down and Peron was released, his stature greater than ever.

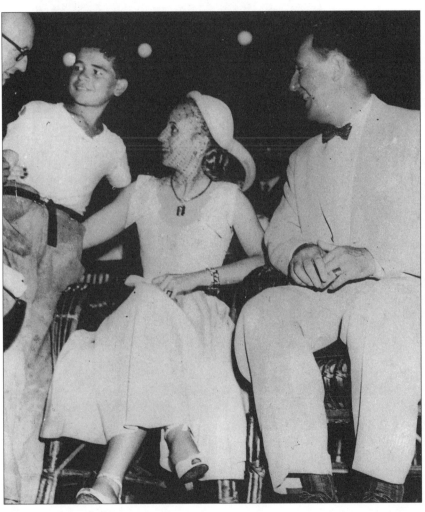

power and sparked a Draconian response from Peron who ordered waves of arrests. But when disputes arose within the ranks of the military themselves (the air force officers standing with the workers while the army were against them), Peron played a gambling rusethat he was doomed to lose. He went on radio urging workers to 'rise up' and follow his path of liberation. It was a valiant but vain plea which ended with his own arrest and imprisonment.

With him when he was arrested in his apartment in the Calle Posadas was his

Opposite, above: *Eva uses the state radio to thank the nation for electing her husband as president. He stands on the left, while the Interior Minister, Angel Borlenghi sits to the right.*

Opposite, below: *Eva loved the glamour of state occasions. The Perons step out at an Independence Ball.*

With the adulation of the workers ringing in his ears, Juan Peron realised that his dreams of a neo-Fascist worker's militia had evaporated; instead he saw in the cheering *descamisados* – the shirtless ones – the roots of a new worker's revolution. So, believing this to be his chance, he resigned from the army and offered himself up as the leader of a new labour party.

His first step towaards domination of the workers was to ruin the unions of the shoemakers and the textile workers, two proud and disciplined welfare groups who

Above: *Eva Peron could rally the crowds, while winning over the army and the church.*

were not convinced by his scheme to bond workers to his state. Within six months they were finished, their leaders driven into poverty and exile. To gain credence for the free elections which were to be held in 1946, Peron also had to win over the Catholic church hierachy, especially because of his relationship with Eva Duarte – 'This woman Duarte' – as the newspaper *La Prensa* called her. Eva, born in 1919 into great poverty, was his real love and several years earlier he had divorced his wife, hoping to marry his 'Evita'. He peruaded the church to recognize his marriage to her in 1945, to view it as reparation for his sin of keeping her as a mistress. The church gave its blessings to the man who would soon be ruler.

'THE PURPOSE WAS NOT TO GIVE POWER TO THE WORKING CLASS, BUT TO ENCOURAGE THE WORKING CLASS TO GIVE POWER TO JUAN PERON.'

Below: *The Perons in Brazil (left) and in London the Worshipful Company of Butchers, pleased with the Argentinian beef trade, welcomed them (right).*

establishing the priorities which are necessary for the operation of any economic system. He taught the community to believe in the instantaneous and total pay-off, so that no one had any order of expectation.' Another study of Argentina, 'The Mothers of the Plaza', by John Simpson and Jana Bennett, says: 'It was all, essentially, a form of charity with Peron. Peron made working-class people feel they had dignity and an importance in the national life of Argentina. The purpose was not to give power to the working class, but to encourage the working class to give power to Juan Peron.'

His brand of socialism bound the workers and the bosses to the state as never before, while he wasted vast quantities of the nation's money by nationalising the run-down railways at super-inflated prices. He became a master of the pay-off, offering kickbacks to critics and bosses, while he remained the darling of workers who had never had it so good. But they never had it so good at the expense of a government that was rapidly paying out more than it was taking in. Peron's largesse in handing out holidays, pensions and bonuses was laying the foundations for Argentina's eight hundred per cent inflation rates of the 1970s and 1980s.

By 1949 his plans were badly adrift; inflation and unrest followed as a government of bribes and torture was exposed. Peron reacted harshly, arresting dissidents, purging churchmen and formulating a law which made it a serious offence to insult

In 1946 he attained his dream in one of the few fair elections ever held in Argentina. He gained the backing of the workers to take over the Casa Rosada, the pink palace of the national leaders, with Eva at his side; the country was his for the taking. Peron came to power with great expectations placed in him. The country was rich, it had been spared the war which had torn apart the Old World, business was booming and there was plenty of money in the bank. What went wrong?

'Indisputably, Peron operated his system extremely badly,' said historian H.S.Ferns in his authoritatve study 'Argentina'. 'Like a spoiled child he wanted everything and he wanted it at once. He revealed himself totally incapable of making choices and

Above: *Eva and Juan pose before their sumptuous country estate, paid for by funds siphoned from Eva's charity organization.*

Right: *Rapt attention on the faces of the leaders as they watch a boxing match.*

the president or any of his public servants. He milked the agricultural aid programme for his own benefit and left the grain farmers and the beef herders increasingly impoverished. Newspapers that criticised him and Evita were closed down – like the honourable and influential *La Prensa*, which was seized and turned into a pro-government trade union sheet.

Evita, during these years, manipulated businessmen and landowners to contribute tinto what has been called the biggest political slush fund in history. The Eva Peron Foundation did indeed build schools, educate children, feed the hungry and shelter the homeless. However, the enormous amount of money that rolled in was administered by people who had to answer to no one but her. Her emissaries travelled to every factory, every workshop, every building site to take the tribute demanded by their new Cleopatra. Those who didn't 'contribute' voluntarily soon found their premises judged unfit by factory inspectors and were closed down.

Experts estimate that Evita stashed away as much as $100 million in hard cash into secret Swiss bank accounts from this fund, flown out twice a month to Geneva in suitcases. Gwyneth Dunwoody, the British MP said: 'With the euphemistically- titled Foundation behind her, Eva Peron handed out Christmas gifts for needy children to

hospitals and schools, while ceaselessly driving home the message that it was because of the Peronistas that these remarkable benefits were available.

'What she omitted to say was that the Foundation, which had initially been billed as a society to be be supported by voluntary contributions, was rapidly taking on the air of a Godfather organisation. She did not hesitate to demand payment from every worker that obtained a rise and from every business that claimed that it needed the government's assistance.

'Every possible source of finance was milked so that this myth of Eva caring for the workers could be promoted. She was not a gentle and gracious woman – she relied on her own regime and army and police power to keep her where she wanted to be. In an organisation with astonishingly few accounts, the amounts of money that were spent were directly connected with what was useful for the Peronista regime. She was no Joan of Arc.'

MORE MONEY LESS LOVE

John Barnes, author of the book 'Eva Peron', says that after her death, investigators of defunct bank accounts traced to her found an estimated $14 million worth of money and jewels that she had literally forgotten she had. No doubt, much of this was stolen from the contributions to the Eva Peron Foundation.

'The love of the people feeds me,' Evita gushed, as large amounts of this unchecked and uncounted money were creamed off into her secret bank accounts. Whole government departments were taken over by her, many of them running twenty-four hours a day, to keep the Foundation supplied with untraceable money. On the government front, Colonel Peron bought off politicians to vote through legislation diverting $5 million worth of public funds into her Foundation. To this day, no one knows exactly how much was stolen from Argentina by the Perons, but it ran into the hundreds of millions of dollars.

She was as vain as she was greedy. Newspapers that did not print mentions of her glittering balls and glittering guests suddenly found that their supplies of newsprint had dried up. Although the workers cheered her and were solidly

behind her, as they were behind her husband, she never gained the acceptance she craved from the upper classes. She knew the whispers surrounding her rise from the streets, the 'favours' she paid to men who helped her singing career.

Her revenge against the snobbish elite knew no bounds – once she paid a fish monger and gave him the necessary permits

Below: *General Peron, Eva and General Dutra of Brazil meet at the opening of a new bridge connecting the two vast countries.*

to sell fish outside the snooty Jockey Club in Buenos Aries for a whole long, hot summer. She saw conspirators everywhere and, when a union boss had the temerity to tell her that she would be better off at home in the kitchen than meddling in politics, she had him arrested and tortured with electric cattle prods. Another man, Victor Belardo, was arrested because he answered correctly the jackpot question on a radio quiz show – and then announced that he would give his money, a large amount, to a charity that

'THE LOVE OF THE PEOPLE FEEDS ME,' EVITA GUSHED, AS LARGE AMOUNTS OF THIS UNCHECKED AND UNCOUNTED MONEY WERE CREAMED OFF INTO HER SECRET BANK ACCOUNTS.

was not affiliated with or overseen by her omnipotent Foundation.

The Perons accumulated further millions from kickbacks they received for import-export permits. Traders literally had to grease their palms with millions of pesos – and do so willingly – in order to trade with the outside world.

Evita became a master of stage-managed rallies, copycat versions of those which the deposed dictators of Europe used to hold so regularly. Weeks before one particular event she invited Argentinian women from

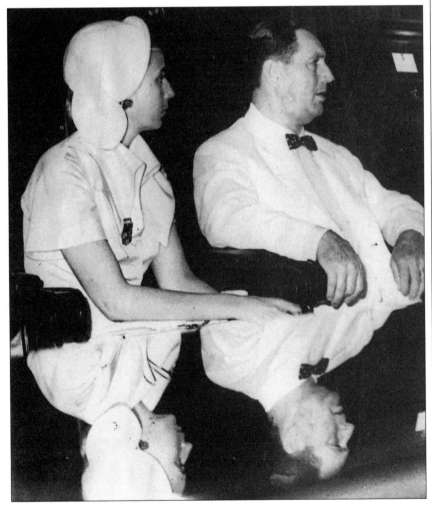

Below: *Eva Peron died a young woman. This photograph was taken shortly after she had undergone surgery.*

all over the country to bring their children to her to receive bicycles and dolls, a symbolic gesture to show that she cared for them, and that as the 'mother of the country' so all the children were her's to love and treat. It was a scene of chaos when they arrived outside the palace, so much so that police had to break up the crowds and at least two mothers went home without their offpsring – the children had been trampled to death by the mob.

In 1951 Peron's grip on polical power was faltering but his live-now-pay-later generosity with the workers still earned them both enormous support. He nearly lost this, however, in the 1951 elections by offering up his wife as the vice-president on his ticket. Much as the people adored Evita, this was still the land of machismo. The thought of Vice President Evita sent a shiver through the ranks of the military, upon whom Peron relied so much, and also troubled the workers deeply. A new slogan appeared on city walls – 'Long Live Peron – As A Widower!' Other graffiti depicted Evita naked, walking like a giant over masses of Lilliputian men. Juan Peron bowed to the pressure of the church and the military and his beloved Evita did not appear on his election ticket.

Shortly before the elections, which Peron was in danger of losing, there was another attempt at a military coup, this time put down by Peron and by the workers who idolised him. It ensured his victory in the October polling, giving him sixty-two per cent of the vote, ten per cent more than he had gained in 1946. And this, despite the falttering economy, the looted millions and the alienation of the ruling class.

But the following year one half of the double act was gone – Evita died from cancer. Juan Peron used her demise to canonise her in the eyes of an adoring people. She was only thirty-three and had recently toured the world, capturing hearts and minds for her country. Nevertheless, her death averted the fall from grace and power that would ultimately have been her lot. By dying, she became to her impoverished admirers a memory of diamonds and furs, not a woman who left her nation stripped of its wealth and teetering on the brink of bankruptcy while her detractors screamed under torture in filthy jails.

Economic conditions deteriorated after the death of Evita. The emperor was beginning to be seen without his clothes by the adoring masses burdened under hyperinflation and suffering increasing harassment from his secret police and torturers. Moreover, the Catholic church, long the traditional dispenser of charity in the country, was beginning to feel aggrieved at having lost its place in society to the Foundation. The universities had been wrecked by semi-literate oafs who were given their posts by corrupt officials in return for kickbacks. Peron's goon-squads burned down the Jockey Club, which had spurned his late wife in the past, and he robbed the magnificent library and art gallery for his own pleasure.

In 1955 it all literally came crashing down when the air force bombed the Casa Rosada – missing him, but killing hundreds of civilians in the process – and armed gangs took to the streets, ransacking shops, businesses and even churches. The army garrison at Cordoba rose against him and there were no workers who believed in his Utopia anymore to save him. He went into exile aboard a Paraguayan gunboat.

A DAZZLING ALADDIN'S CAVE

In much the same way as the mob was allowed to look over the spoils of office of dictator Ferdinand Marcos in the Philippines years later, the poor of Argentina were given a glimpse of how their Evita had really lived when the portals of her stupendous palace were opened to the public after Peron's flight.

'It was a show which would outdazzle Aladdin's cave,' wrote Daily Express correspondent Jack Comben when he gazed at her riches. 'Glass shelves laid tier upon tier in the chandelliered brilliance of Peron's palace displayed gems which are estimated to be worth two million pounds. Diamonds almost as big as pigeons' eggs glittered and flashed. There was a two-inch thick collar encrusted with diamonds.

'I saw at least four hundred dresses – all perfect of their type and all expensive. And experts calculated that Evita owned enough shoes to last her for four hundred years. But all the treasures, the clothes, the pictures, are supposed to be only a fraction of what Peron and his wife acquired during nine years of power. The government believes he sent most of his fortune out of the country to Switzerland. And Peron was once quouted as saying: "The only jewellery I ever gave to my wife was a wedding ring".'

These event, had they occured in any other part of the world other than South America, would have been ended then. In 1973, however, after almost twenty years exile in Spain, Peron returned to power in Argentina with his third wife. Nostalgic,

perhaps, for the good old days that never really existed, the people embraced the man who threw his lot in with the workers,. They forgot all his sins, the massive amounts of money and assets that he looted from them in the past.

He died in 1974, the reins of power passing to Isabelita Peron, whom he had married in 1961. She excelled both her husband and his previous wife in the corruption stakes. Arrested in 1976, after she was deposed as president, she was charged with stealing $1 million intended for charity, convicted of embezzelling cash from a charity and for using government buildings for her own ends and was jailed. She was released in 1981 after serving two-thirds of her prison sentences.

Despite all this, the name Peron can still elicit nostalgia in Argentina – a land where 'strong' evokes a response than 'just'.

Above: *An Italian admirer sent this stone statue of Eva to the people of Argentina. It arouses mixed feeling among the citizens: some adore her memory, others despise her greed.*

LOEB & LEOPOLD
The Perfect Murder

It took two Chicago teenagers to invent a new category of murder – 'thrill-killing'. Loeb and Leopold picked their innocent fourteen-year-old victim at random and brutally murdered him for kicks, all the time convinced that they were some sort of 'supermen', above the law.

The term 'thrill killing' is a relatively new one in the lexicon of crime. From time immemorial, men and women have killed for love, for hate, for money, for revenge, and for dark sexual urges beyond their control. But in 1924 in America, the frontiers of murder were pushed back even further and the phrase 'thrill-killing' was then coined to describe the deeds of an arrogant and evil duo who killed a fourteen-year-old boy merely for the intellectual satisfaction of doing so.

Richard Loeb, seventeen, and Nathan Leopold, eighteen, believed themselves to be so superior to ordinary mortals that they decided to end the life of a schoolboy. They were convinced that detectives would be baffled – no motive, no clues, no suspects – and they would bask in the glory of their secret crime for ever. That they were caught for the simplest of mistakes is testimony to their foolishness – and the end of their theory that applied intelligence was capable of devising the perfect crime.

This loathsome pair grew up together in Chicago and wanted for nothing. Both boys had rich parents who doted on them. Loeb's father Albert was vice-president of the Sears Roebuck chain of department stores. Nathan F. Leopold Snr was a shipping magnate, one of the wealthiest men in Chicago and, like Loeb's father, lavished money on his son.

Strong, athletic, handsome, Loeb – nicknamed 'Babe' by family and friends – was a raffish but clever young man. He was, like his partner-in-crime, a near genius and, at seventeen, the youngest graduate of the University of Michigan. Unlike most other students, he was never short of cash. When he needed more money, the family chauffeur took him from their home in the exclusive Kenwood district of the city to his father's offices, where he would demand $2,000 in cash – and get it. But he soon yearned for something more... something more exciting.

The excitement of murder.

The boy he grew up with was just as clever but less athletically inclined . Leopold had an overactive thyroid gland,

HE WOULD DEMAND $2,000 IN CASH – AND GET IT. BUT HE SOON YEARNED FOR SOMETHING MORE... SOMETHING MORE EXCITING.

was undersized, round shouldered and, when he was fourteen, began to display homosexual leanings. He was, however, a true genius. He could speak ten languages and had an intellect that was well beyond his years – an IQ of two hundred by the time he was eighteen and was the youngest graduate with a Bachelor of Philosophy degree from the University of Chicago. Psychiatrists later said that Leopold was led by Loeb; he looked up to him, admired him, yearned to be strong like him. Historian Irving Stone wrote that he devoured the works of German philosopher Friedrich Nietzsche and longed to be a

Above: *Richard Loeb helps police search for clues in the murder hunt. Despite his helpful attitude, some policemen were not fooled by his manner.*

Opposite: *The teenage 'supermen' who planned the perfect murder, Richard Loeb on the left, and Nathan Leopold sit in court on trial for murder.*

was Leopold who suggested that they should ask for money for the return of the boy – even though the lad they intended to ransom would be already dead. In further letters to each other, they discussed the minutae of the murder. Often the letters were filled with violent, threatening tones as the plotters themselves argued about what they were going to do. But the agreement was reached and the victim chosen; fourteen-year-old Robert 'Bobby' Franks was to die for no reason whatsoever exept as a spawn in a game.

Loeb, a good tennis player, had known Bobby for some time. He had even played tennis with him and classified the boy as a 'friend' – certainly someone who trusted him enough to accompany him and Leopold on a short drive. Bobby was also from a good family and attended a private school in the neighbourhood where his future killers lived.

The date chosen for the murder was 24 May. The first step involved Leopold checking into the downtown Morrison Hotel under the name Morton D. Ballard,

'superman'. When he realised that his stunted form made that impossible, said Stone, 'he longed to be a superwoman, a female slave to some big, handsome, powerful king'. So, when homosexual Loeb sketched out details of his ghastly scheme, it was inevitable that Leopold would be an all-too-willing accomplice.

Loeb's fanatical dream of the perfect crime appealed to Leopold's dark 'superman' urges and he joined in the fantasy. In a letter he wrote to Leopold before they killed, Loeb said: 'The superman is not liable for anything he may do, except for the one crime it is impossible for him to commit – make a mistake.' Another said: 'We are supermen! Nothing can stand in our way.'

The plot was hatched in January 1924 but not carried out until May. Loeb was the brains, Leopold the partner necessary to enable him to execute it. Both polished every detail and added another lurid element to their 'perfect' crime: kidnap. It

listing himself in the register as a salesman from Peoria in Illinois. Next, using the same false name, he rented a car from a downtown agency where the president of the company, Joseph Jacobs, asked for a reference. Leopold was happy to give him the name and number of one Mr Louis Mason – in fact, Loeb. Jacobs made the call and heard a glowing reference as to the would-be renter's fiscal and moral fibre. After leaving a deposit of $50 on the rental of a luxury sedan, Leopald drove the car around for two hours, returned it to Jacobs and informed him he would be around to collect it later in the day.

Back in his hotel suite, he went over the finer points of the murder plan in his head. He checked with a local bank to make sure an acount he had opened in the name of Ballard was active – ready, in fact, to receive the ransom money.

Later that day the twisted 'supermen' drove around to the front gates of the academy at 4pm as the children were filing out for the day. From a local hardware store they had purchased a murder kit consisting

of a home-made garrotte, a chisel, rope and hydrochloric acid. They intended to pour the acid on to the young man's features to obliterate them. Two loaded pistols, taken from the collection belonging to Leopold's father, completed the kit.

Above: *Lawmen sift through evidence relating to the crime. They are studying shoes and socks belonging to the victim and guns belonging to Loeb and Leopold.*

Left: *A detective with a section of the floorboard from the murder car. He is examining bloodstains.*

Opposite: *Richard Loeb (top) and Nathan Leopold shortly after their arrest.*

'THE SUPERMAN IS NOT LIABLE FOR ANYTHING HE MAY DO, EXCEPT FOR THE ONE CRIME IT IS IMPOSSIBLE FOR HIM TO COMMIT — MAKE A MISTAKE.'

Leopold was at the wheel of the car as they spotted Franks coming out. 'Hey Bobby, want a ride?' yelled Loeb, who had concealed in his University of Chicago handgrip, in the back of the car, the heavy-handled chisel that he had wrapped in adhesive tape for a better grip. Bobby, innocent and unsuspecting, bounced over to the car and eagerly got into the empty front seat. As Leopold drove north in heavy commuter traffic, Loeb lashed out viciously with the chisel, driving it down on the boy's head and he went down on to the floor of the limousine. Leopold, glancing in the rear-view mirror, was horrified when he saw the boy's wounds gushing blood and yelled: 'Oh my God! I didn't know it would be like this.'

As Leopold drove on, Loeb calmly stuffed Bobby's mouth with rags and wrapped him in a robe. He slowly bled to death on the floor of the car. Some miles out of town, they parked at a beauty spot overlooking Lake Michigan and calmly had sandwiches while they waited for dark.

As dusk fell they went for a meal in a German restaurant – 'to fortify us for what lay ahead,' Leopold would later say. After that he drove the car with its grim cargo to a culvert at 118th Street on the outskirts of town, near railway tracks spanning reclaimed swampland. Leopold slipped into fisherman's waders and carried Bobby

'HE IS SAFE AND UNHARMED. TELL THE POLICE AND HE WILL BE MURDERED AT ONCE. DON'T THINK THAT WE WON'T DO IT.'

Below: *The victim of an intellectual crime, Bobby Franks. His grieving father and brother can be seen in the picture right.*

through the mud. The boy had been stripped in the car and, once at the flooded culvert, Leopold struggled to shove the naked body into the pipe. Sweating from the exertion, he took off his coat.

It was to prove their undoing.

Gathering up his coat, looking around into the darkness, the two men were convinced that their tracks were covered. But one of little Bobby's feet was left sticking out of the pipe.

They dumped the car near a large apartment building close to Leopold's mansion home and embarked on stage two of the plan. This involved typing a ransom note on a machine Loeb had stolen from his university the previous year. The note read: 'Your boy has been kidnapped.' It went on to demand $10,000 in old, unmarked $20- and $50-bills, to be wrapped in an old cigar box, the box to be further packaged in white paper and sealed with sealing wax. The note was signed with the fictitious name George Johnson.

Three weeks prior to the kidnapping, the killers, each on alternate days, had boarded the 3pm train between Chicago and Michigan City, Indiana. It was their plan for the ransom money to be thrown from the moving train at a specific place, where they would be hiding in wait to collect it.

After posting the letter, the boys drove across the state line to Indiana and picked a solitary spot in a farmer's field where they buried Bobby's clothes. Shortly before

midnight Leopold was ordered by Loeb to telephone the Franks' home, which he did. He told the missing boy's terrified mother: 'He is safe and unharmed. Tell the police and he will be murdered at once. Don't think that we won't do it. You will receive a ransom note with instructions tommorrow.'

There is nothing to suggest that the killers enjoyed anything other than a sound night's sleep after their tiring day playing supermen while brutally murdering a child.

NO PUBLICITY

But, already as they slept, their plot was beginning to fall apart. Jacob Franks, Bobby's father, was, like their own, one of Chicago's richest men, having made a fortune from manufacturing boxes and packing cases. He immediately contacted his lawyer after the call to his wife and secured a pledge that there would be no publicity while they attempted to track down Bobby's abductors.

The next day the killers cleaned bloodstains from the car and drove it to an abandoned building site on the outskirts of the city where they burned the bloodstained robe in which they had wrapped young Bobby. They were methodical. The typewriter was broken up with a sledge-hammer – the keys and carriage hurled into one pond, the bodywork into another.

By midday, however, their chances of extorting money from the distraught father of Bobby were finished. A railway gang doing routine maintenance on the section of line that passed near to the culvert were horrified when they spotted Bobby Franks' foot sticking out of the pipe.

A second ransom note, which Loeb left on the Michigan City train with instructions for it to be handed over to Franks, arrived at roughly the same time as the news that his son was dead. His brother-in-law had identified his pathetic little body so there was no longer any need for secrecy. The silent hunt for a kidnapper became a full-blown manhunt for a murderer.

A SECOND RANSOM NOTE

When the killers read the headlines in the Chicago Tribune, they abandoned their plans to wait by a disused grain elevator near Englewood, on the rail line, for the ransom. The second ransom note was handed over to police. It read: 'Dear Sir, proceed immediately to the back platform of the train. Watch the east side of the track. Have your package ready. Look for the first LARGE RED BRICK factory situated immediately adjoining the tracks on the east. On top of this factory is a large black watertower, with the word CHAMPION written on it. Wait until you have completely passed the south end of the factory count five very rapidly and then IMMEDIATELY throw the package as far to the east as you can. Remember that this is the only chance to recover your son. Yours truly, George Johnston.'

The manhunt was the greatest Chicago had ever seen and, for the likes of gangsters like Al Capone, the source of great discomfort. While police turned over every warehouse and factory in Chicago looking for clues, they interfered so much with the business of organised crime that Capone and a consortium of other hoods offered to contribute cash to find the killers so they could get business back to normal.

Richard Loeb, the supreme hypocrite, joined the outraged citizens who answered police appeals for help in searching premises. He was overheard by one officer to say: 'It is the least any of us can do.' He did, however, betray his real personality to another policeman when he remarked of the dead boy: 'If I was going to pick out a boy to kidnap or murder, that's just the kind of

*Above: **The drainpipe where the boy's body was hidden.***

*Top: **Leopold on the left, and Loeb shortly after their arrest. The boys were stunned to realise the police were smarter than they, the criminals with high IQs.***

cocky little son-of-a-bitch I would pick.' This was part of the thrill for Loeb – seeing 'bumbling coppers' looking for clues in a crime committed by supermen. Pathetic!

In the course of the next few days the supermen realised that things were going badly awry in the smooth course of their masterplan. First, police found the typewriter keys and carcass in the shallow pools, tipped-off by someone who had seen them thrown in. The bloodied chisel was found near the culvert.

And the one clue, the one which would damn them, was found near to the body – the result of Leopold taking off his coat to get on with the grisly business of stuffing the boy's body into the pipe. Out of his pocket had tumbled his glasses – the glasses which belonged to him and which were one of only three pairs sold by a particular Chicago optician. One pair belonged to a woman, who was wearing them when police knocked on her door; the other pair to a wealthy lawyer who was in Europe. And so Nathan Leopold Jnr became the number-one suspect.

'WHAT MOTIVE WOULD I HAVE?'

Police confronting him were met with a flurry of lies. He had been on one of his beloved bird-watching expeditions a week earlier – yes, he must have lost them then. But it had rained hard in the past few days and the glasses were virtually spotless. As he confronted the hard stares of policemen who knew every trick in the book he grew nervous and blurted out: 'What motive would I have for killing him? I didn't need the money – my father is rich. Whenever I need money, all I have to do is ask for it.' He explained that he and Loeb had spent the evening of the murder 'riding around' in his family car and had picked up two girls, girls they knew only as Edna and Mary.

'IF I WAS GOING TO PICK OUT A BOY TO KIDNAP OR MURDER, THAT'S JUST THE KIND OF COCKY LITTLE SON-OF-A-BITCH I WOULD PICK.'

Both boys were taken to separate rooms of the luxurious LaSalle Hotel for further grilling under the orders of Richard Crowe, the district attorney. Although not officially under arrest, Crowe had a hunch that the boys were the ones he wanted. Leopold made a statement to a local newspaper in which he graciously understood the predicament he was in: 'I don't blame police for holding me. I was at the culvert before the glasses were found and it is quite possible I lost them there. I'm sorry this happened because it will worry my family. But I will certainly be glad to do what I can to help the police.'

'BY GOD, I THINK WE'VE GOT THEM!'

The police had no fingerprints to match on the typewriter, but the ransom note was definitely typed on it. Then came the final proof which tied Leopold and his friend Loeb to the murder. Some enterprising journalists had obtained letters which Loeb had written in the past for his legal study group at university on the typewriter. An independent expert confirmed this to Crowe, who punched the air in delight and said: 'By God, I think we've got them!' Leopold named a student friend who had given him the typewriter. The student was quickly found by police and declared innocent. Then Leopold said it was, in fact, yet another friend's machine, then that it was still somewhere in his house. Finally, as he squirmed, Englund, the chauffeur,

came forward to say that the car in which they had ostensibly been joy-riding with the mysterious Mary and Edna had not left the family garage that night.

Faced with the mounting evidence, Leopold was the first to crack, followed shortly afterwards by Loeb. Loeb astonished police with his confession: 'It was a lark, you see, we just wanted to commit the perfect crime. We haven't got anything against the boy. It's just that we thought we could get away with it. I'm sorry for what has happened.'

OBSCENE SEXUAL ACTS

Loeb testified that he was the car driver and that Leopold had killed the boy. He also threw in details of perverse sexual acts which Leopold enjoyed, as if such gossip would soften his own guilty role in the crime which he himself had conceived .

Chicago went wild. The clamour of the mob, upon hearing their confessions, was instant and frenzied and nothing less than their execution would do.

In jail, the thrill-killers who thought themselves supermen were the loneliest felons in the world. No lawyer would take their case – it would be enough to blight even the most distinguished career. It literally took Nathan Leopold Snr to get on his bended knees to famed civil rights lawyer Clarence Darrow to ask him to take the case. 'I knew there was not freedom in store for the boys,' Darrow said later. 'But I wanted to save them at least from the electric chair.' It proved a thankless task.

Darrow was one of the most brilliant lawyers of the time and a relentless pursuer of truth and justice. But he knew that no legal techniques, however smart, would ever result in the boys' freedom. At best he could hope to prove them insane for such a brutal and senseless slaying. He opted for a bench trial, a trial without a jury, before judge John Caverly with the words: 'While the state is trying Loeb and Leopold, I shall be trying capital punishment.'

His decision to defend them was not a popular one. Years later he would write: 'The public seemed to think that we were committing a crime in defending two boys, who probably needed it as much as any two defendants ever on trial for their lives. The most senseless and the most unreasonable criticism was indulged in against the defendants and their attorneys because of the lengthy hearing of the case. The proceedings became front page matter in every hamlet of the country, and were closely followed in all parts of the world. I seldom went to my office in those troublesome days, and rarely read any of the letters that came in stacks. These were usually abusive and brutal to the highest degree.' But Darrow was not daunted.

His was a tireless assault on the taking of human life. While in no way defending or trying to mitigate what they had done in the

Above and centre: *Leopold, in the murder car, describes the crime to a detective. When he believed that he faced execution, he wrote this letter. It shows his intellectual curiosity for it does not express fear but debates the possibility of an afterlife.*

Left: *Loeb as a child playing at cowboys.*

Opposite: *Nathan Leopold grew up in the mansion pictured above. The lower picture shows Richard Loeb's childhood home.*

'THE WORLD IS FULL OF EMINENT LAWYERS WHO WOULD HAVE PAID ME A FORTUNE TO DISTINGUISH THEMSELVES IN THIS CASE.'

Scenes from the trial: a friend, Lorraine Nathan (top right) testified that Loeb was not all bad. The murderers sit each side of defense attorney, Robert Clowe while Leopold's father and brother suffer as they listen to the evidence.

pursuit of fun his eleqouent plea for mercy is liberal, passionate and remains a classic of American bar history: 'I am pleading for the future... I am pleading for a time when hatred and cruelty will not control the hearts of men, when we can learn by reason and judgement and understanding and faith that all life is worth living and that mercy is the highest attribute of man... If I can succeed I have done something for the tens of thousands of other boys, for the countless unfortunates who must tread the same road in blind childhood.'

Darrow's eleqouence succeeded in persuading the judge that the 'incipient paranoia' in both boys had triggered temporary insanity. After a thirty-three-day trial, followed by a three-week period before sentencing, he came back to tell

Loeb and Leopold that they would serve life sentences for the killing of Bobby Franks, followed by ninety-nine-year sentences each for kidnapping.

His fee for the defence of the killers was rumoured to have been $1 million dollars – but years later Darrow stunned the legal world when he revealed what occurred when it came to the settlement of the account. In fact, he received only $30,000 dollars, paid over grudgingly by Nathan Leopold Snr, who displayed arrogance every bit as chilling as his son's. Handing over the cheque, the killer's father said: 'The world is full of eminent lawyers who would have paid me a fortune to distinguish themselves in this case.'

Loeb and Leopold were incarcerated in the Northern Illinois Penitentiary at

'IT WAS A LARK, YOU SEE, WE JUST WANTED TO COMMIT THE PERFECT CRIME. WE HAVEN'T GOT ANYTHING AGAINST THE BOY.'

Left: *A witness points at Nathan Leopold to confirm to the police that he thinks Leopold is the suspect.*

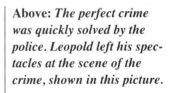

Statesville and, due to their incorrigible, doting fathers, were able to indulge themselves to the full. Although convicted killers, they had an enviable life behind bars, thanks to an ample supply of money.

They shared adjoining cells, complete with books, desks and filing cabinets. They were supplied with bootleg liqour from the guards and allowed to make lengthy telephone calls from one of the prison storerooms. Leopold kept a vegetable garden while Loeb sank further into depravity, stalking the young male prisoners to satisfy his sexual passions while paying off the guards to look the other way. But he went too far.

A GRUESOME FIGHT

In 1936 he set his sights upon James Day, accosting him in the library where he said, 'Be nice to me'. Day refused but Loeb followed him at every opportunity. On 28 January that year, Loeb entered the shower with a cuthroat razor and told Day to submit to him. He refused and there followed a gruesome fight. Day was cut – but he managed to get the razor and slash Loeb fifty-six times, including one stroke right across his jugular vein. Loeb staggered out, bleeding to death, and died hours later clutching Leopold's hand.

Leopold stayed in prison until 1958 when he was finally paroled after thirty-four years in jail. He held a press conference afterwards, proclaiming: 'I am a broken old man. I want a chance to find redemption and to help others.' He travelled to Puerto Rico, where he worked for $10 a week as a technician in a church laboratory and wrote a book called 'Life Plus 99 Years'. Asked at a publicity session for the work whether he ever thought about young Bobby Franks he replied: 'The crime is definitely the central part of my consciousness. Very often it occupies the forefront of my attention and I can think of nothing else.'

On 30 August, 1971 he died of heart failure in Puerto Rico.

Above: *The perfect crime was quickly solved by the police. Leopold left his spectacles at the scene of the crime, shown in this picture.*

PARKER & HULME
Their Secret World

Pauline Parker and Juliet Hulme were anything but normal schoolgirls. These teenage lesbian lovers bashed in the head of Pauline's mother who had tried to separate them. Were they criminally insane or just murderous little minxes?

There is much in 'Partners in Crime' that dwells on the madness generated by two people that would not have have occured had the partnership never been formed. Normal lives and patterns of behaviour vanish as two personalities, each bland and safe on its own, ignite into intrigue and danger when combined.

Such was the madness that descended on two adolescent girls in New Zealand in the 1950s – girls who retreated into their own special world of aloofness, superiority and forbidden sex, a world that held murder.

When Juliet Marion Hulme and Pauline Yvonne Parker were brought before the Crown in Christchurch, New Zealand, in 1954 the case received worldwide attention because of its morbid themes. Like the case of Loeb and Leopold (Chapter xxx), psychologists were at pains to try to explain the fusion of two normal minds into a single entity bent on misery and death. For that is what happened to Juliet Hulme and Pauline Parker when their perfect world was threatened.

In order to prevent separation from one another, they plotted and carried out, the murder of Mrs Honora Mary Parker. Mrs Parker, forty-five, Pauline's mother, was bludgeoned to death by the two, who tried to cover their tracks by claiming she had fallen. But in the end their own inflated ideas of their intelligence and skill failed them badly and the most basic police methods proved that they were the killers.

The full extent of their wickedness and depravity revealed at the trial shocked this colonial outpost as nothing before or since.

It was on 22 June, 1954 that the two hysterical girls, covered in blood, shattered the tranquility of afternoon tea at a sedate Christchurch restaurant when they burst through the doors. 'Mummy's been hurt,' blurted out Pauline. 'She's hurt, covered with blood.' Tearfully they begged the manageress of the restaurant to phone for police while they gulped down sugared tea in an apparent attempt to ease their shock. Some of the customers went with police

and the girls to a beauty spot in a nearby park close to a small bridge over a stream. Lying in a pool of blood, her face unrecognisable, was Mrs Parker. Her head was brutally battered. It was a bad fall.

Initially the girls told police that Mrs Parker had fallen and slipped on a board. 'Her head just kept banging and banging,' blurted out Pauline to police, in a none-too-convincing explanation of why her mother came to have some forty-nine serious head wounds, any one of which would have been enough to render her unconscious. The

Opposite: Juliet Hulme, on the left, and Pauline Parker were so in love that they were prepared to murder anybody who threatened their relationship.

Below: The childish face of Juliet Hulme hid a passionate nature and a wilful nature.

'HER HEAD JUST KEPT BANGING AND BANGING,' BLURTED OUT PAULINE TO POLICE.

officers knew that they were dealing with something far more sinister than an accident and both young girls – Pauline was sixteen and Juliet fifteen years and ten months – were taken into custody for further questioning.

As they were led away a sharp-eyed policeman found near the pathway, a few feet away from the body of Mrs Parker, a

> 'AFTER THE FIRST BLOW WAS STRUCK I KNEW IT WOULD BE NECESSARY FOR US TO KILL HER.'

Above: *The distinguished father of Pauline, Dr H.R.Hulme, Rector of Canterbury University College, Christchurch. He intended to take his daughter away from her friend.*

brick wrapped in an old stocking. It was found to be covered in blood and great clumps of her hair were stuck to it. Clearly, this and not a board or a plank of wood had been the instrument which despatched the unfortunate woman. Later, a pathologist examined the corpse and said there was bruising around the throat consistent with her having been held down as blow after blow rained down on her head.

Once in custody Pauline confessed almost immediately to the murder. She said she had 'made up my mind' a few days before the event to kill her mother during an outing in the park and that Juliet, who was walking with them, was not implicated in the crime. She told detectives: 'She knew nothing about it. As far as I know, she believed what I had told her, although she may have guessed what had happened but I doubt it as we were both so shaken that it probably did not occur to her.'

But while she was being questioned, one of the officers guarding her turned his back to her, and she tried to burn a piece of paper on which she had written: 'I am taking the blame for everything.' This was seen as a message that she intended to smuggle to Juliet – Juliet, who, on learning of the abortive bid to contact her, changed her story immediately and confessed to being a willing accomplice.

IT WAS TERRIBLE BUT INSANE?

'I took the stocking,' said Juliet, 'and hit her too. I was terrified. I wanted to help Pauline. It was terrible – she moved convulsively. We both held her. She was still when we left her. After the first blow was struck I knew it would be necessary for us to kill her.'

There would have been no need for a protracted criminal trial, along with all its publicity, had the pair pleaded Guilty to murder. Instead, they chose to plead Guilty of murder by insanity – something the Crown was not prepared to accept. While in custody they had both seemed perfectly aware of what they had done, had both shown little remorse and had both only wanted to return to their 'perfect world'. Their insistence on a plea of insanity meant that the spotlight would now be directed at their dark world.

In his opening speech the prosecutor Mr Anthony Brown ominously told the jury: 'I feel bound to tell you that the evidence will make it terribly clear that the two young accused conspired together to kill the mother of one of them and horribly carried their plan into effect. It was a plan designed solely so they could carry on being together in the most unwholesome manner.'

Brown went on to explain how something 'unhealthy' had developed

between the two girls; how they had met at school as friends but then their relationship had deepened and broadened into something much more than girlish camaraderie. He remarked that it was a relationship 'more commonly seen between members of the opposite sex, and of a more advanced age', than that seen between two schoolgirls. Unhappy when apart, disturbingly attached to each other when together, Mr Brown painted a portrait of two girls sharing an unnatural love.

Above: *Juliet Hulme photographed at the time she was involved with Pauline but before they turned into killers.*

'WHY, OH WHY, COULD
MOTHER NOT DIE?
DOZENS OF PEOPLE,
THOUSANDS OF PEOPLE,
ARE DYING EVERY DAY.'

Mrs Parker, not surprisingly, was most unhappy about the relationship and was doing her best to break it up when she met her end. She had been in touch with Juliet's father, Dr Hulme, a Rector of Canterbury University College, New Zealand. Earlier that year he had resigned his post with the intention of taking a new position in Cape Town, South Africa. He agreed to take Juliet with him, to get her away from Pauline. The date agreed for his departure was 3 July – and the two girls vowed to kill Mrs Parker before then, her punishment for engineering their separation.

All this was corroborated in a sensational diary kept by Pauline Parker and in notes passed between the two – correspondence which the Crown said was definitely the work of people who were quite aware of what they were doing.

'In it,' said Brown, waving Pauline's leather-bound diary before the jury, 'she reveals that she and Juliet Hulme have engaged in shoplifting, have toyed with blackmail and talked about and played around in matters of sex. There is clear evidence that as long ago as February she was anxious that her mother should die,

Above: *The girls ran to the Victoria Tearooms, crying that Mrs Parker had fallen and was badly hurt.*

'Their first idea was to carry out this crime in such a way so that it appeared that it was an accident which befell Mrs Parker,' said Brown. They persuaded Mrs Parker, having pretended for a couple of weeks prior to her death that they no longer cared about being separated, to take them on a picnic to the country. Juliet Hulme brought along the brick from the garden of her home and the deed was accomplished.

and during the few weeks before 22 June she was planning to kill her mother in the way in which she was eventually to be killed.' It was damning evidence.

On 14 February, he read: 'Why, oh why, could mother not die? Dozens of people, thousands of people, are dying every day. So why not mother and father too?' Later, in April, she wrote: 'Anger against mother boiled up inside me. It is she who is one of the main obstacles in my path. Suddenly a means of ridding myself of the obstacle occurred to me. I am trying to think of some way. I want it to appear either a natural or an accidental death.'

In June it continued: 'We discussed our plans for moidering [sic] mother and made them a little clearer. Peculiarly enought I have no qualms of conscience (or is it just peculiar we are so mad!)' On 22 June, the actual day of the crime, Pauline penned this entry: 'I am writing a little bit of this up in the morning before the death. I felt very excited like the night before Chrismassy last night. I did not have pleasant dreams, though.' She did not elaborate on these.

The reading of the diary caused a stunned shock to the court. The two looked for all the world like normal schoolgirls and yet they had plotted and committed murder. There was even more damning testimony about them which showed that they were sneering, arrogant vixens who enjoyed illicit adult pleasures wrapped up in a fantasy world of their own making. And much of this damaging testimony was delivered by Juliet's mother.

THE STRANGE
DEBORAH AND LANCELOT

Mrs Hulme told the court how the girls were planning to publish a novel (although they hadn't yet written one) and practised writing in strange letters to each other using romantic pseudonyms. Juliet was often called Charles II, Emperor of Borovnia, then she changed to Deborah and then Bialbo. Pauline Parker, at the start of this bizarre correspondence, had called herself Lancelot Trelawney, a Cornish mercenary. Names of medieval drama.

The letters were initially full of romance as they created a fantasy world into which they escaped, but soon the tone changed to something far more sinister. They became violent, sadistic, with maidens raped and knights tortured as the girls' own lust for each other became ever more urgent. Soon they were sleeping together and even indulged in bondage. One said: 'I loved how we enacted how each saint might make love in bed. We have never felt so exhausted... but so satisfied!' It is no suprise that their parents wished to see the girls parted permanently.

Above: *Mrs Hulme broke down frequently during the trial of her daughter for murder. She refused to speak about the case for many years after the event.*

Further details emerged of how they spent their days when they were supposed to be in school. They often slipped away to a country barn where they frolicked in the hayloft as lovers, finishing their day by washing each other in a country stream. They talked of going to America, of becoming rich and famous and buying a house together where they would have eunuchs as servants.

Juliet said she wanted to be 'safe' with Pauline – as a child she was brought up in the East End of London at the time of the London Blitz, something which traumatised her deeply. One of their 'games' involved Pauline cradling her as she made noises like bombs exploding around her. And all the while they played out this weird relationship, all schoolfriends and other playmates were excluded; it was, as described in one of Juliet's missives to Pauline, 'their perfect world', one to which no other was admitted.

Initially, Mrs Hulme, who had emigrated with her husband and Juliet when the child

'I LOVED HOW WE ENACTED HOW EACH SAINT MIGHT MAKE LOVE IN BED. WE HAVE NEVER FELT SO EXHAUSTED... BUT SO SATISFIED!'

was five years old, welcomed her friendship with Pauline because it seemed to bring her out of her shell. 'Had I known where this would lead, I would have killed it stone dead there and then,' she sobbed.

Another entry in Pauline's diary, and one which was instrumental in proving their sanity, was the one which read: 'Prostitution sounds a good idea to make money and what fun we would have in doing it! We are so brilliantly clever, there probably isn't anything we couldn't do.' Was this, said the prosecution, the words of a pair who claimed they did not know what they were doing? Further, when Pauline was called to testify, her own arrogance virtually broke their defence. When asked if she knew that it was wrong to murder she sneered: 'I knew it was wrong to murder and I knew at the time that I was murdering somebody that it was wrong. You would have to be an absolute moron not to know that something was wrong.'

Lawyers for the two girls said there was no question that they were the killers but

'I KNEW AT THE TIME THAT I WAS MURDERING SOMEBODY THAT IT WAS WRONG. YOU WOULD HAVE TO BE AN ABSOLUTE MORON NOT TO KNOW THAT SOMETHING WAS WRONG.'

that they should not hang – a possibility, despite their age because they were being judged as adults – because of the abnormality of their minds. One medical expert, a Dr Medlicott, pointed out that each of the girls had suffered bad physical health as toddlers and that their siblings were also prone to illnesses, suggesting somehow that this contributed to the unbalanced state of their young murderers' minds.

Discussing the bizarre relationship between them the doctor told the court : 'Juliet told me: "I do believe that we are indeed geniuses. I don't wish to place myself above the law – I am apart from it." And when I performed a medical examination upon Miss Parker she turned to me and said: "I hope you break your flaming neck." In my opinion they are aggressive, dangerous, but most certifiably insane.'

It was not an opinion shared by expert Dr Charles Bennett who told the court: 'I find that they probably, very probably, knew what they were doing and knew it was wrong in the eyes of society at large.

Below: *It was on this pathway, near the planking, that the two girls bludgeoned the mother to death.*

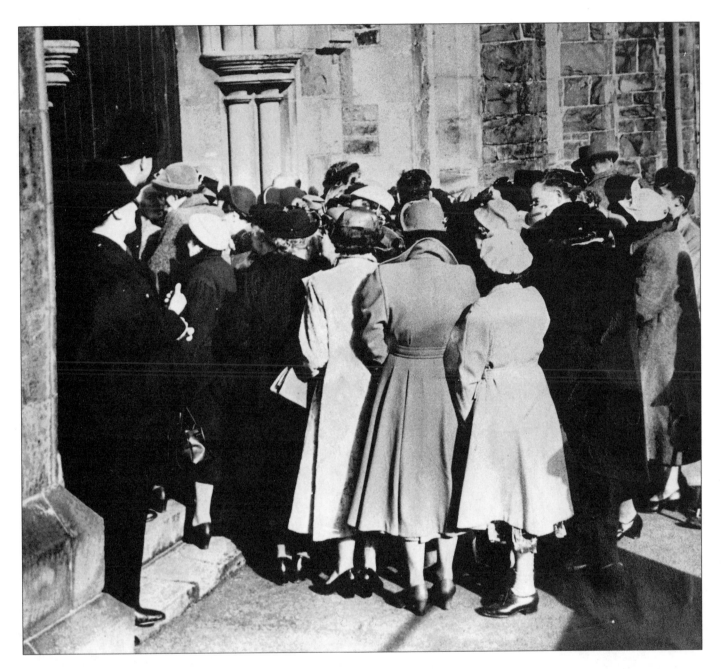

But I doubt very much if they gave any consideration whatsoever to what society thought of them at all.'

In the end, after a careful summing up by the judge, it was left to the jury to decide whether the girls were mad or not. Mr Justice Adams said: 'The important word is the word "knowing". It has to be considered at the very moment of the commission of the crime. Were their minds so confused that they did not know this act was wrong? This is what you, ladies and gentlemen of the jury, have to consider.'

Consider it they did and in just two and a quarter hours returned a verdict of Guilty. There was a fleeting smile flashed between the two girls, these supreme egoists, when they were spared the rope by a merciful judge and ordered to be detained at Her Majesty's Pleasure – which meant indefinitely. But in a move which, to many, seemed to mock justice, they were freed just four years later after intense psychiatric counselling. They remained friends but the spark from that earlier relationship had been extinguished by the separation.

Herbert Rieper – he was with Pauline's mother for twenty-five years although he never married her – never recovered from her death. He never forgave the girl.and when his daughter was freed he said: 'It still doesn't make up for robbing a person of their life. It was evil between them that did it. Pure evil.'

'PROSTITUTION SOUNDS A GOOD IDEA TO MAKE MONEY AND WHAT FUN WE WOULD HAVE IN DOING IT!'

KARL & ILSA KOCH
Beasts Of Buchenwald

Even among the monstrous ranks of the sadistic killers of the Third Reich, Karl and Ilsa Koch stand out. Together they were the masters of the notorious Buchenwald concentration camp where their deeds even revolted their SS colleagues. When Frau Koch made a lampshade, it was from human skin.

The vile racial politics of the Third Reich called for a brutal system of camps across the conquered lands to 'process' the enemies of Adolf Hitler. That these enemies included newborn babies, the crippled and the old, and just about every category of human being in between, was of no consequence to Hitler and the sadists of the SS. Auschwitz, Belsen, Treblinka, Dachau and Buchenwald have gone down in history as the true manifestations of hell on earth, for these were the death factories where some twelve million people, six million of them Jews, were systematically gassed, shot, starved, beaten and worked to death for the purification of the empire that Hitler proclaimed would last a thousand years.

Putting Hitler's warped gospel into practice required men and women so obviously without compassion and decency that it is hard, now, in the post-war years to envision what kind of country or system could ever have produced them. Some camp commanders, like Rudolf Hoess of Auschwitz, were clinically detached from the tortured souls they despatched in the camps' crematoria. Indeed Hoess, at his trial, boasted proudly of the Germanic efficiency that had been brought to bear on the running of the camps.

Karl and Ilsa Koch were a couple whose depravity knew no bounds; whose conduct was so shocking that even their SS masters were revolted. They ruled over Buchenwald concentration camp as supreme arbiters of life and death, reaching previously unplumbed depths of cruelty and evil. These two people personified the

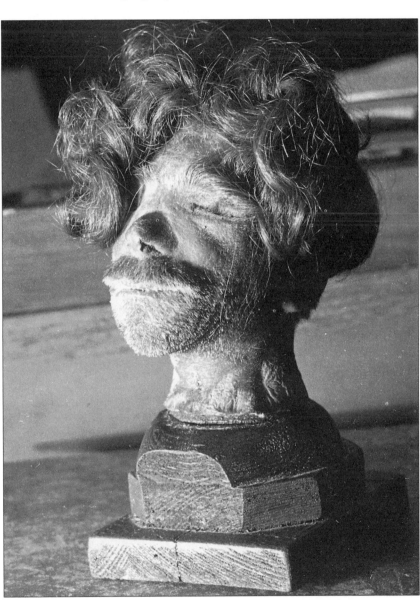

corruption of the Hitlerian ideal: the camp commandant and his wife Ilsa, a woman who spent her evenings making lampshades from the tattooed skins of innocent murdered men.

Ilsa Koch's journey from the rolling hills of Saxony, where she was born in 1906, to the abbatoir of Buchenwald, gives no clue to what turned the former librarian into the woman who sewed human skins together. The daughter of a labourer, she was a

Opposite: *Ilsa Koch was tried after the war for her depraved behaviour towards prisoners in Buchenwald.*

Above: *The shrunken head of a Pole hanged at Buchenwald was evidence of the barbarity of these camps.*

diligent child at school, well loved and well cared for, and popular with village boys. Like so many individuals who descend into evil, it was only when she forged her relationship with ambitious SS man Karl Koch that her latent depravity was released.

When she met Karl in 1936, Hitler had already laid the foundations of the concentration camp network. Karl Koch was employed at the Sachsenhausen facility as a *Standartenfuehrer* (Colonel) and Ilsa became romantically linked with him when she became his secretary. Karl himself was born out of wedlock to his thirty-four-year-

> HE WAS AN ADVOCATE OF THE THUMB SCREW AND THE BRANDING IRON.

Above: *Ilsa Koch talks to the German lawyer assigned to defend her in the trial before the Allied authorities.*

old mother and a fifty-seven-year-old local government official in Darmstadt, central Germany; they married two months after the boy's birth. Karl's father died when the boy was eight. Never a good scholar, Karl left school at fifteen to work as an office boy at a local factory.

A few days after turning seventeen he tried to enlist in the army as the First World War raged across western Europe, but his mother intervened at the recruiting office and he was frogmarched home. In March 1916, when he was nearly nineteen, he managed to enlist as a rifleman and was rewarded with a tour of the trenches in some of the fiercest sectors of the Western Front before being captured in 1918 on a routine patrol in no-man's-land. He ended

the war in a POW camp and like so many other troops finally returned to a defeated, bitter Germany.

He managed to do quite well for himself at first, securing a position as a bank clerk, and in 1924 he married his first wife. However, two years later, after the birth of a son, the bank he worked for collapsed and he was out of work. In 1931, at the same time as his marriage collapsed, he was drawn to the Nazi movement and soon he was in the SS.

His destiny became intertwined with that of Theodor Eicke, head of the Death's Head units which founded the first concentration camps. Eicke had high regard for Koch, writing in 1936, as he set up the camp at Sachsenhausen: 'His achievements are higher than average. He does everything for the National Socialist ideal.' But at Sachsenhausen, among his peers, he quickly gained a reputation for being a sadistic bully. Soon these qualities were to influence and consume the previously gentle Ilsa and to change her personality.

SOME MEDIEVAL TORTURES

The good National Socialist Koch revelled in beating prisoners with a horse-whip that had razor-blade pieces embedded along it's length. He was an advocate of the thumb screw and the branding iron, inflicting these medieval tortures for the slightest infringement of camp rules.

His overlords in the Reich Main Security Office, that oversaw the administration of the burgeoning concentration camp network, singled him out for promotion. In 1939 he was moved to form the camp at Buchenwald, and took with him Ilsa, whom he had married at the end of 1936 in an SS ceremony at midnight in a grove of oak trees. Buchenwald was a 'correction' camp – as were all the original complexes – its purpose was to change in the middle of the war as Hitler's extermination programme was, at last, seriously planned and followed

Like Auschwitz, Buchenwald had a dual role. Those who were sick or too young to work were led to their deaths straight away. Those deemed fit enough to labour for the Reich were put to work under the most appalling conditions in an armaments factory adjacent to the main camp. Here the living dead toiled on starvation rations.

While Koch supervised the grim day to day destruction of those within his charge, his wife Ilsa became as feared as him. She took to walking with a whip across the camp compound, lashing out at any prisoner who displeased her. Sometimes she took her husband's dog with her and squealed with delight when she let it loose upon pregnant women and women carrying heavy loads. It was no wonder that soon she was known to all the inmates as the Bitch of Buchenwald.

Whenever exasperated prisoners felt sure that she was capable of no greater cruelties, Ilsa would dream up new ways to torment and hound them. Then she began to ask male prisoners to remove their shirts. Those without tattoos didn't interest her but when she saw a tattoo, she smiled a smirk that said: 'Those will be mine.'

For since the beginning of the previous year Ilsa Koch had become the lady of the lampshade, using the treated skins of murdered prisoners to make practical home accessories of which she was very proud. She particularly liked the skins of gypsies and Russian prisoners-of-war – men who had swirls of colour across their chests and backs that made very decorative lampshades. Ilsa liked lampshades.

Above: *Josef Mengele who practised bizarre medical experiments on camp inmates. He was known as the 'Angel of Death'.*

Left: *Sad evidence of thousands of lost lives in the camps were the great piles of victims' possessions like these watches.*

IT WAS NO WONDER THAT SOON SHE WAS KNOWN TO ALL THE INMATES AS THE BITCH OF BUCHENWALD.

Albert Grenowski, a Jew who was forced to work in the pathology laboratory at Buchenwald, told Allied judicial authorities after the war, about how those with tattoos were given orders to report to the dispensary. He said: 'After they were examined by her, those who were deemed to have the most artistically interesting specimens were killed by lethal injection. It was important that the skin of the victims was not damaged. There was one sure way to find yourself in a coffin and that was to damage the skin that the Hexe (witch) wanted for her lampshades.

'The bodies were taken to the pathology lab where they were treated with alcohol and the skins were removed with painstaking attention to detail so as not to split them or otherwise mark them.Then they were dried, often oiled afterwards, and taken in small packages to Ilsa Koch so

they could be made into lampshades and gloves. Once we saw her walking around the compound wearing a brightly patterned pair of summer gloves and just sexy underwear – you know, like she had forgotten to put a dress on. I particularly paid attention to the gloves. The last time I had seen their decoration was on the back of a gypsy prisoner in my block.'

Above: *The horrified American Army that liberated Buchenwald placed local German citizens under armed guard and forced them to walk round the camp to witness Nazi atrocities committed in the name of their nation.*

Left: *A woman who survived the Dachau camp places her hand on a man who tortured the inmates. She was testifying at a war crimes trial.*

'THE SKINS WERE REMOVED WITH PAINSTAKING ATTENTION TO DETAIL SO AS NOT TO SPLIT THEM OR OTHERWISE MARK THEM.'

Apparently Ilsa's lust for her lurid pastime became something of a fashion among her fellow tormentors in other concentration camps that had been spawned by the Nazi empire. She took pleasure in corresponding with the wives of other camp commanders and giving them full instructions on how to turn a human hide into a book cover, lampshade, gloves or a fine table covering.

These activities didn't go unnoticed by the authorities and at the end of 1941 the Kochs found themselves before an SS police court in Kassel on charges of 'gross brutality, corruption and dishonour'. For the SS, it was one thing to beat, torture and murder human beings. To be seen to derive pleasure from it, was quite another. In the organisation's loathsome logic, their mission was a crusade, not a means of satisfying sadists. The talk of the lampshades and the whippings had filtered out of the camps through dissatisfied guards and led Ilsa and Karl before Court XXII to answer the charges against them.

This time, the charges were dismissed. The court decided that they were the victims of rumour-mongers and trouble-makers. Koch spent some time at another concentration camp as an 'adviser' to new officers but he was soon back with Ilsa at Buchenwald. But in 1944 there came a second trial in which there would be no escape for the couple.

Commandant Koch was brought before a tribunal on charges that he had killed an SS man who complained about his blatant racketeering. It transpired that much of the loot taken from the victims at Buchenwald, intended for the coffers of the Reichsbank in Berlin to fuel the war effort, had found its way instead into a secret Swiss account that Karl had had the foresight to set up in neutral Switzerland.

Karl had been taking the gold teeth of dead inmates, the pathetic jewels and money they had tried to hide in their clothing, and wedding rings. He intended it to be his nest egg for himself and Ilsa at the end of the war. He was a devoted Nazi but he was even more devoted to the cause of Karl Koch, and realisd Germany was on the losing end of the war. He did not intend to go down with the Third Reich. Racketeering, over and above torture and

KOCH PLEADED FOR A CHANCE TO REDEEM HIMSELF IN A PENAL BATTALLION FIGHTING THE ADVANCING RUSSIAN TROOPS IN EAST PRUSSIA.

Below: *This is the memorial to the dead of Buchenwald, where 250,000 Jews, gypsies, Russians and homosexuals died under Nazi rule. It is built where the camp once stood.*

murder was probably the most heinous crime in the eyes of his SS superiors.

A pastor whom the Nazis wanted kept alive, but imprisoned, was due to give evidence against him at the tribunal. Mysteriously, he was found dead in his cell the day before he was to give his evidence. From his stomach, traces of an almond-smelling compound were removed and mixed in with the food rations for that day for a dozen Soviet prisoners-of-war – a group who, like Jews, suffered dreadfully under the concentration camp system. All the Soviet prisoners died of cyanide poisoning but the deaths spelled the end of the camp's chief tormentor Karl Koch.

EVIDENCE OF CORRUPTION

A further charge of murder of the pastor was laid against him and he was found guilty and sentenced to death. A secret SS tribunal heard how SS magistrate Konrad Morgen was given Himmler's personal authority to travel to Buchenwald to find out the truth about the commandant's thefts. He found plenty of evidence of his corruption, including money stashed under his bed that had been taken from prisoners. Koch pleaded for a chance to redeem himself in a penal battalion fighting the advancing Russian troops in East Prussia but his request was turned down. His reputation for cruelty and evil had even stretched their limits of tolerance and so, on a chilly morning in April 1945, just days before the camp's liberation, Karl Koch was shot in the yard of the very camp he had commanded.

Ilsa, bereft at her husband's death, was equally as guilty as him. Indeed, many of the inmates in the camp felt that Koch was driven to commit his attrocities by the evil influence of his wife. But in the SS eyes she was innocent and acquitted.

However, Ilsa never returned to Buchenwald. She fled westwards in the closing months of the war with the tide of humanity seeking to escape the advancing Russians. By 10 April, 1945, the day that shocked American troops liberated the camp, she was on a farm with relatives outside Ludwigsburg, but her name had not been forgotten by the survivors of the camp. The great American radio broadcaster, Edward R. Murrow, moved his

Below: *Another infamous couple who festered in the camps. Irma Greese, the 'Blonde Beast of Belsen' and her Commandant Josef Kramer after their arrest in 1945. Both were executed for war crimes.*

audience to tears the next day with his report of what those battle-hardened troops had seen there.

'We drove on, reached the main gate. The prisoners crowded up behind the wire. We entered.

'And now let me tell you this in the first person, for I was the least important person there, as you can hear. There surged around me an evil smelling crowd; men and boys reached out to touch me. They were in rags and the remnants of uniforms. Death had already marked many of them, but they were smiling under their eyes. I looked over that mass of men to the green hills where well-fed Germans were ploughing.

'As I walked down to the end of the barracks there was applause from men too weak to get out of bed. It sounded like the hand-clapping of babies. As I walked into the courtyard a man fell dead. Two others, they must have been over sixty, were crawling towards the latrine. I saw it, but I will not describe it. The children clung to my arms and stared. We crossed to the courtyard. Men kept coming up to speak to me, professors from Poland, doctors from Vienna, men from all of Europe. Most of the patients, though, could not move. I

asked the cause of death and a doctor shrugged and said: "Tuberculosis, starvation, fatigue, and then there are those that have no desire to live."

I pray for you to believe what I have said about Buchenwald. I reported what I saw and heard, but only part of it. For most of it I have no words.'

A CAUSE TO FIGHT AGAINST

General Eisenhower ordered that all men of the 80th Division – men from the 80th had liberated Buchenwald – should be made to see it. 'They may not know what they are fighting for,' he remarked, 'but at least now they know what they are fighting against.'

Two names cropped up time and again in the days following liberation as the Americans tried to make some sense of the carnage that was Buchenwald. The names were Karl and Ilsa Koch.

In the days and months following the collapse of the Third Reich, Ilsa buried herself in anonymity, secure in the knowledge that the authorities had far bigger fish in the SS and Gestapo to fry than her. She remained free until 1947 when justice finally caught up with her.

Ilsa was forty and pregnant, by an inmate in the prison where she was held, before facing trial. In Munich she was brought before a US Military Tribunal to answer for her war crimes.

For several weeks a procession of wraith-eyed former inmates came in to testify of her sadism, of her love for the tattooed skins, of her wanton brutality. The blood of over fifty thousand victims of Buchenwald was on her hands, said prosecutors, and the fact that she was now a pregnant woman was no reason to show mercy towards her.

US Brigadier General Emil Kiel read her sentence in staccato tones: 'Ilsa Koch – life imprisonment.'

Ilsa went to jail after reading a statement in which she said she was merely a 'servant' of evil people. She denied manufacturing goods from human skin and said she was framed by enemies of the Reich seeking their own vengeance.

But there was a remarkable break for her in 1951 when an American General earned the scorn of both his nation and the new Federal Republic which had replaced

THE BLOOD OF OVER FIFTY THOUSAND VICTIMS OF BUCHENWALD WAS ON HER HANDS, SAID HER PROSECUTORS.

'I PRAY FOR YOU TO BELIEVE WHAT I HAVE SAID ABOUT BUCHENWALD. I REPORTED WHAT I SAW AND HEARD, BUT ONLY PART OF IT. FOR MOST OF IT I HAVE NO WORDS.'

Hitler's fallen empire. General Lucius D. Clay, in charge of the US occupied zone of Germany, granted Isla Koch her freedom, saying there was 'insufficient evidence' that she had ever ordered anyone to be executed and that no articles of tattooed skin were found linked to her.

There was a worldwide gasp of disbelief when Ilsa was freed, the loudest of all coming from respected Washington lawyer William Dowdell Denson, who had prosecuted her. He spoke for the millions of dead as well as the living when he said: 'This is a gross miscarriage of justice. She was one of the most sadistic in the whole group of Nazi offenders. There was no way to compute the number of people that were willing to testify against her – because she was a depraved woman, because she was the commandant's wife – and because she was just so goddamned mean.

'If there is a cry being heard around the world it is for the souls of the tortured innocents who died in Buchenwald and places like it.'

Freedom, however, was fleeting for her. As soon as Ilsa Koch stepped from the US Military Prison in Munich she was arrested again and put behind the bars of a civilian jail by the German authorities.

Above: *Ilsa Koch enters court. She was pregnant by another inmate in the prison where she was held pending her trial.*

Left: *Gen. Patten's troops assembled this grisly collection of lamps and ornaments made from human skin and organs. Germans were obliged to view this display of barbarity when they were compelled by GIs to inspect the Buchenwald camp at the end of the War.*

ANOTHER TRIAL, ANOTHER SENTENCE

The new republic, mindful for its need to atone for the Holocaust and all of Nazism's terrible crimes, immediately re-arrested Ilsa and placed her on trial again. The Bavarian Justice Ministry scoured the country looking for survivors of Buchenwald, seeking new evidence that would commit her to incarceration for the rest of her days. Two hundred and forty witnesses stood in court and told again their stories of Ilsa's murderous actions and behaviour that defied belief. Second time around, she was tried by her own people in whose name she committed her foul deeds and she was sentenced again to life imprisonment. She was told this time to expect no parole of mercy. Life was life.

Above: *As the liberating American Army advanced towards Buchenwald, the guards started killing inmates but there was a revolt and the prisoners turned on the Nazi minions. This statue commemorates the bravery of these prisoners.*

SHE WAS ONE OF THE MOST SADISTIC IN THE WHOLE GROUP OF NAZI OFFENDERS.

In 1967, writing to her son Uwe, whom she had given birth to shortly after her first sentence, she complained bitterly that she was a scapegoat for the *prominenti* (the important ones), who had got away. There was no remorse from her, only recriminations and bitterness at what had happened.

In that year, on 1 September, at her jail in Aichach, Bavaria, she ate a final meal of schnitzel and potato salad before penning one last note to the son she loved. Then she knotted the bedsheets together, tied them to the lamp strung from the metal cage over her bed, and hanged herself. The Bitch of Buchenwald was dead.

It would be hard for anyone to find redemption for Ilsa and Karl Koch, but her son Uwe tried in 1971. Uwe Kohler – he took his mother's maiden name – made an unsuccessful attempt through the West German courts for the restoration of 'my mother's good name'. Insurance clerk Uwe also approached the New York Times newspaper to tell his story. He said: 'Since a revision of history was practically impossible in the West German courts I thought that the American people, since Americans had sentenced her to life imprisonment, should know her side of the story.'

Uwe was born on 29 October, 1947, the product of the liason between Ilsa and a German soldier inmate in Landsberg prison. The boy was removed almost immediately to a Bavarian foster home – the first of many that he was to grow up in, totally unaware of the identity of his parents or whether they were even alive.

'NO PARDON FOR ILSA KOCH'

At the age of eight he inadvertently saw his birth certificate with his mother's name on it and memorised it. Eleven years later he saw a newspaper with the headline: 'No pardon for Ilsa Koch'. He confirmed that the Koch in the story was his mother after confronting his state-appointed guardian.

At Christmas time in 1966, in a fairy tale setting of deep snow, he visited Landsberg to see his mother for the first time. 'To me she was not the Bitch of Buchenwald,' said Uwe. 'We had a joyous reunion.' He continued to visit her right up until the time she hanged herself the following year.

Uwe said: 'I always avoided talking with her about the war. She always denied her guilt and said she was the victim of libels, lies and perjuries. I didn't discuss it further with her because it was obviously painful for her. I wanted her to have hope that she would get out after two decades in prison. I wanted her to think other thoughts.

THE MADNESS OF THE TIMES

'I really cannot imagine what it was like for her in the War. I am not even convinced she was guiltless. But I feel that she just slithered into the concentration camp system like many others without being able to do much about it. I know that she will not be posthumously rehabilitated, but I do feel that she was not guilty of major crimes. She was caught up in the madness of the times, like so many others...'

Historians and psychiatrists alike have been keen over the years to return to the phenomenon that was Ilsa Koch, the corruption of a member of the 'fairer sex' into the embodiment of everything that is evil on this earth. Analysts decided she was probably a nymphomaniac, a meglomaniac and a sadist to boot.

But historical author Charles Leach said of Ilsa: 'Before Karl Koch and after Karl Koch, she displayed none of the cruelties with which she came be to associated. Her madness, if indeed that was what it was, seems to have been triggered solely by her association with this man. With his death, it seems the spell was broken. Maybe if they had never met, like so many evil partnerships, the murder and the mayhem would never have occurred.'

'MAYBE IF THEY HAD NEVER MET, LIKE SO MANY EVIL PARTNERSHIPS, THE MURDER AND THE MAYHEM WOULD NEVER HAVE OCCURRED.'

Below: *The end at Buchenwald and prisoners mill around in the courtyard after the entry of the American forces. The black flag was raised in mourning for President Roosevelt but it served also for the thousands of innocent people who died in the camp.*

BRADY & HINDLEY
The Moors Murders

Ian Brady and Myra Hindley arouse revulsion and hatred like no other murderers in British history. Together in an evil pact, they systematically tortured and killed more than six children. The real death toll is still unknown, forever locked up in the killers' deranged minds.

He was a twenty-seven-year-old stock clerk who idolised Hitler and sunk into horrible fantasies after drinking bottles of cheap German wine which transported him back in his imagination to the rallies and the marches of the Third Reich. Although the expression had not yet been coined in the Swinging Sixties, she would no doubt have been called a bimbo: a twenty-two-year-old peroxide-blonde typist who nurtured fantasies of eternal love. And, indeed, she did find immortality of a kind with the man with mesmeric eyes and quick temper. Together they have gone down in British criminal history as the most wicked of the wicked, for they are the child-killers, Ian Brady and Myra Hindley.

Even today, in a world hardened by violent crime, their vile acts set them apart as monsters of a very special breed. At 16 Wardle Brook Avenue, on the sprawling Hattersley council estate and on the wild Pennine Moors, children abducted by these two died a gruesome death before being buried in unmarked graves. But death was not all these perverts visited upon their innocent victims who should never have accepted the lifts home they offered.

They were sexually assaulted, they were photographed and, in the case of one victim, her screams were even tape recorded... screams that would later be heard in a criminal court, a shocking testament to evil.

Ian Brady and Myra Hindley are a classic case of partners in crime. Separate and alone, they were ordinary, if stunted, characters who might have lived their lives without ever plunging into the abyss of madness and depravity. Together, they fell prey to what the French call a *folie a deux* – the madness generated between two people. She was the girl he could impress; he was the errant knight for whom she would have sold her soul. In reality, they were bound by perversion and a taste for cruelty. Together they have left an imprint on Britain's national conscience that has not been faded or eroded by the passage of the years.

Brady and Hindley forged their relationship after meeting at work. He was a winkle-pickered youth with a fondness for crime B-movies and Nazi philosophy. An illegitimate child who had never known his father (widely believed to have been a reporter on a Glasgow evening newspaper),

THEY FELL PREY TO WHAT THE FRENCH CALL A FOLIE A DEUX – THE MADNESS GENERATED BETWEEN TWO PEOPLE.

Opposite: *Ian Brady and Myra Hindley frolic for the camera during the thrilling days of their perverse passion.*

he was brought up in the Gorbals slums of the city. His mother, coping with both the stigma of being unmarried and the burden of being poor, put him in the care of a family called Sloan when he was small, during for the formative years of his life.

The kindness they lavished on him was misplaced; he became a cold, sneering, surly youth who shunned kindness as weakness, compassion as foolishness. Brick by brick, he built a wall around

Above: *Police search for clues in the garden of the Hindley-Brady residence.*

himself and convinced himself that he was better than everybody else and that society was against him.

After serving terms in Borstals as a teenager for housebreaking, he was finally given a chance to escape going to the 'big house' – adult prison – by a Glasgow judge who insisted that he live with his real mother. She, by the time he was a teenager, had moved back to Manchester with her new husband, an Irish labourer, but was willing to take a chance, putting her unhappy young son back on the straight and narrow. Here Brady's teenage rebelliousness metamorphosed into something altogether more sinister.

He began buying Nazi books like 'The Kiss of the Whip', which glorified the persecution of the Jews, and to drink heavily. Alternately in and out of work, in trouble with the law for drunkenness, he managed to land a job as a stock clerk at

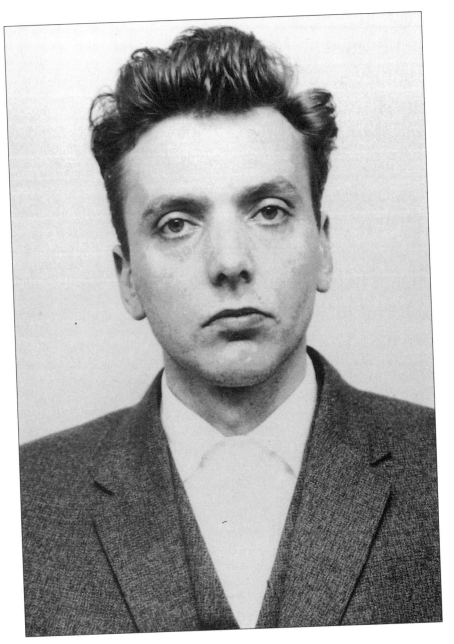

*Above: **Ian Brady's image reveals an ill-tempered and defiant personality.***

*Left: **The entrance to 18, Westmoreland Street, Manchester where Ian Brady used to live.***

Millwards Ltd, a chemical and soap company in Manchester. Here the partnership in evil would be irrevocably forged when Myra Hindley was introduced to him on 16 January, 1961.

Within weeks they had become lovers. Her diaries at the time show the student of crime as a pathetically ordinary, normal, unsophisticated suburban girl who confided to paper her childish hopes and fears: 'Not sure if he likes me. They say he gambles on horses. I love Ian all over and over again!'

Then: 'He has a cold and I would love to mother him.' Other times she is frustrated or cross with him, and determined to end their fledgling love affair.

Yet in the end he became her first lover, on a sofa-bed in the front room of the house she shared with her grandmother. It happened after they had seen one of his favourite films – 'Judgement at Nuremberg', a story of Nazi atrocities.

From these beginnings grew the seed of perversion and corruption. Brady's book collection of pornographic and sado-masochistic material had swelled now and his needs were more than conventional love-making. Soon he was taking lurid pictures of his girlfriend, complete with whips, a hood and even her pet dog. She

over tea, as the buses taking their neighbours to work roared along outside? Or perhaps it happened on one of their weekend excursions to the wild and lonely moors that ring Manchester. But Ian and Myra, the loving couple did cross the line between perversion and murder on Friday, 12 July, when Pauline Reade, aged sixteen, accepted a lift from them on her way to a social-club dance in Gorton.

Then on 23 November, 1963, they crossed it again when little John Kilbride, aged twelve-and-a-half, accepted a lift from them at the marketplace in Ashton-under-Lyne. On Tuesday, 15 June, 1964 Keith Bennett, aged twelve, became their third victim when he took a ride on a busy Manchester road after setting out to buy some sweets. On 26 December, 1964, Leslie Ann Downey, born on 21 August, 1954, died at the age of ten years and four months after she climbed into their car parked at a fairground near Ancoats.

THE HOME OF MURDER

After the disappearances of these children, there were the usual appeals of help, the usual sad pictures of the missing were plastered all over their neighbourhoods and beyond. No clues linked ttheir disappearances to each other, there was no reason to believe an evil pied piper was claiming them one by one. It took the brutal murder of an innocent teenager in the front room of the home Brady shared with his accomplice, to lead the police to uncover the horrific crimes of this couple.

On the morning of 7 October, 1965, David Smith, married to Hindley's sister Maureen, made a frantic 999 telephone call at 6.07am from a coin box on the edge of the housing estate where Hindley and Brady lived. He was a young man with a stammer, who was already known to the police for a string of petty offences, and he blurted out a tale of murder perpetrated, he said, the previous evening in the living room of Brady's house.

Smith said the victim, later identified as seventeen-year-old Edward Evans, had been axed to death by Ian Brady to 'impress' Smith. Brady had often talked of robbery and murders with Smith but Smith had put it down to an overworked imagination fuelled by the wine. This time the

took pictures of him, too, surrounded by mirrors as he admired his body. But the thrill of this soon wore thin. Fuelled by the German wine he habitually drank, he drew her into his evil web of fantasy, when he talked of becoming a gangster and of her becoming his moll while they robbed and pillaged like latter-day Bonnie and Clyde.

They did not have the courage for this, however; it was only Dutch courage inspired by the wine. But they did find the courage to satisfy their expanding sexual perversions, if courage is what is needed for two adult people to lure, humiliate, abuse and then murder little children.

No one knows at what precise moment they slipped over the edge and fantasy became action. Did they decide about it

Above: *Myra Hindley shows a hard, grim vanity in this photograph taken while she was on trial for killing small children.*

HE WAS TAKING LURID PICTURES OF HIS GIRL-FRIEND, COMPLETE WITH WHIPS, A HOOD AND EVEN HER PET DOG.

fantasy became reality before his very eyes. Brady had murdered a boy and Smith was asked to help clean up the blood after witnessing the ghastly scene.

In a calm monotone, he described how the young man had been lured to the house by Hindley, was set upon by the axe-wielding Brady and was finally 'finished off' by a length of electrical flex with

Below, left: *Ian Brady is driven in a police car to the court to answer murder charges.*

Below, right: *Hindley was hysterical at leaving her dog when police bundled her off in their barred van.*

explain why he wouldn't be at work that day – he claimed he had hurt his ankle. In reality, he was planning an excursion to his private cemetery on the moors to make room for one more corpse.

Talbot, upon being greeted by Myra Hindley at the doorway, pushed past her into the house announcing that he was a police officer. Hindley tried to block his entrance to the bedroom but Brady, nonchalantly still lying on the divan, told her: 'Ye'd best give him the key.' Once inside the bedroom Superintendent Talbot discovered the corpse of the young man who died for their thrills.

With Brady in custody, charged with murder, the police re-interviewed Smith who told them that Brady had boasted of killing 'three or four others'. These others were allegedly buried on the bleak, beautiful Saddleworth Moor outside of Manchester. Talbot logged the number-scarefully in his orderly policeman's brain, for he believed he had seen in Brady's arrogant eyes and surly manner the mark of a very dangerous predator indeed.

Brady told police a bland story. He said he had met Edward Evans , the victim, in a

which Brady throttled him. Brady asked Smith to help him in his macabre clean-up afterwards, saying: 'This one's taking a time to go. Feel, Dave, feel the weight of that. That was the messiest yet.' Afterwards, with the glow of a sexual, murderous frenzy bathing them, Ian Brady and Myra Hindley made love as Edward Evans' mutilated body lay upstairs.

A FATAL DELIVERY OF BREAD

Police decided that there was more to Smith's tale than hysteria or mischief. The house in Wardle Brook Avenue was approached and police superintendent Bob Talbot put on the white coat of a local breadman, borrowed his loaves and knocked on the door of number sixteen. Hindley answered it; Brady was inside on a divan writing a letter to his bosses at Millwards. The letter was an excuse to

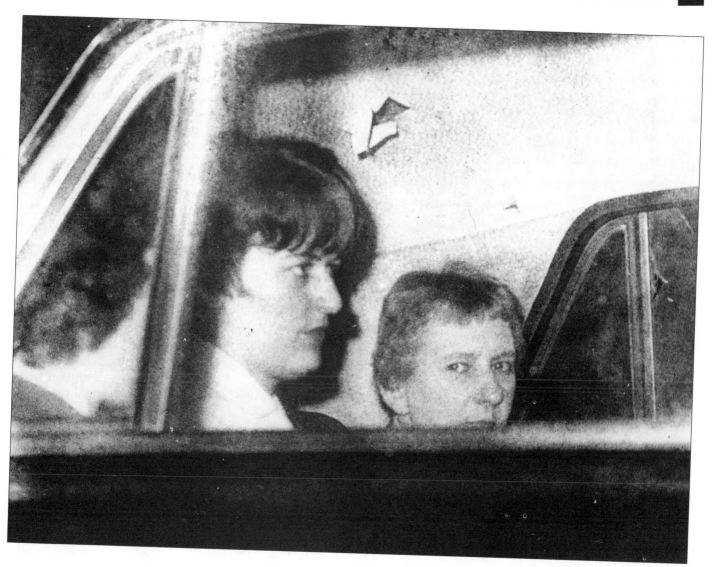

Above: *Myra Hindley's peroxide has faded, but her sneering defiance remains and can be discerned even in this partial view of her.*

Manchester pub, the youngster had come to his house afterwards, they had rowed and, unfortunately, he had killed Evans with a hatchet. Talbot's superior officer, Arthur Benfield, Detective Chief Superintendent for the whole of Cheshire, was down at the police station by noon to investigate the drunken death but he was worried by the boast of 'three or four others'.

A search of the house revealed notebooks with ruled columns in which Brady had written down a series of what appeared to be coded instructions. There was 'meth' for method, 'stn' for station, 'bulls' for bullets, 'gn' for gun. After staring at it long and hard, Benfield realised he was looking at a shopping list for murder weapons. But whose murder?

Days later, as he sifted through the paraphernalia of Brady's bedroom, he came upon a tattered school exercise book filled with scribblings and graffiti. There was a list of names that apparently meant nothing, jotted down by the day-dreaming clerk during moments of boredom. But Benfield read through all the names nonetheless – Christine Foster, Jean Simpson, Robert Uquart, James Richardson, Joan Crawford, Gilbert John, Ian Brady, John Sloan, Jim Idiot, John Birch, Frank Wilson, John Kilbride, Alec Guineas, Jack Polish, J. Thompson. John Kilbride... the name hit Talbot like a hammer blow and suddenly the feeling washed over him that he was on to a monsterous crime, something bigger than he had ever imagined.

The search of the house brought to light the pornographic photographs Brady and Hindley had taken of each other and the sado-masochistic and Nazi book collection. And there were other pictures too, of Hindly and Brady taken on the moors One in particular caught his eye, that of Myra sitting on the ground, looking wistfully at the gorse and peat beneath her, staring at

'THIS ONE'S TAKING A TIME TO GO. FEEL, DAVE, FEEL THE WEIGHT OF THAT. THAT WAS THE MESSIEST YET.'

The police had two lucky breaks. Everyone was eager to help catch the murderers, and vital information from a neighbour's twelve-year-old daughter who accompanied Auntie Myra and Uncle Ian on excursions to the moors to 'help them dig for peat'. The second was from a car hire company that confirmed that they had rented a car to a Myra Hindley on 23 November, 1963, John Kilbride's last day alive. The police used photos removed from the couple's bedroom to locate the burial places of the murdered children. They were helped by the girl who, though she had been taken to the moors by the pair, had survived the trip.

A CASE OF LEFT-LUGGAGE

The body of Lesley Ann Downey was found by the police searchers on 16 October, ten days after the death of Edward Evans. Police thought that they would find the body of John Kilbride but they only found the little tartan skirt belonged to the trusting little girl. Two days later another

Above: *Mr David Lloyd Jones, in front, and Mr Philip Curtis counsel for Brady and Hindley respectively. The defence had an unenviable task.*

Right: *Scenes outside the courtroom as Lesley Anne Downey's uncle lunged at the man who murderd the child. Police restrained him but the public did not.*

nothing in particular except the ground as if... as if she were staring at a grave.

Brady played mind games with the police, claiming the stories he told to Smith were lies to build up an 'image'. He said there were no more bodies and that the name Kilbride in the exercise book was an old chum from Borstal days. Police made door-to-door inquiries in their neighbourhood.

policeman on the team made an even more startling discovery. Hidden in the spine of Myra Hindley's communion prayer book was a left-luggage ticket for two suitcases at Manchester Central Station. Once retrieved, they yielded up more pornographic books, small-arm ammunition, blackjacks, wigs, tapes and photos of moorland views.

And other pictures. Pictures of a little girl with her eyes bulging in terror, naked save for her socks and shoes, bound and gagged. Talbot felt the tears well up in his eyes as he looked into the helpless face of Lesley Ann Downey.

Later, the tapes were played. The first ones was a hotch-potch of Hitler marches and the BBC Goons show, interspersed with a documentary on Hitler's life. Then the second one was played – the tape that numbed the polcemen present, would later make hardened journalists weep and would finally nail Brady and Hindley for the cruel and evil monsters they were. 'Don't... please God help me. Don't undress me will you... I want me mam...'. Interspersed with screams, pleas and futile whimpers, against the barking commands of Hindley and Brady, these were the final words of Lesley Ann as she met her unspeakable end at the hands of the sinister people who gave her a lift at the fair.

Below, left: *Ian Brady takes a last look at the world where he behaved with such depravity.*

Below, right: *Patricia Cairns, second on the right, the lesbian warder who plotted to free her lover, Hindley.*

On 21 October the body of John Kilbride was found in the spot where Myra had been photographed with her beloved dog Puppet. John's underpants had been pulled down to below his thighs, knotted hard in the back to prevent him from moving his legs. He had been sexually assaulted and buried face down. Britain and the world were inflamed with anger at the killers now branded the Moors Murderers. Myra Hindley was now under arrest to face charges of murder along with her lover, Ian Brady.

The trial gripped the public attention as no other had done when the pair came before Chester Assizes on 19 April, 1966. Both pleaded Not Guilty to murder and maintained an arrogance and swagger throughout that earned them the hatred of prosecutors, police, journalists, the judge and the parents of the dead.

In the Evans case, Brady maintained that it was Smith's idea to 'roll a queer' for money and that he had participated in the killing. In Lesley Ann's case, Brady gave the court a totally implausible story that he had taken photos of her after she had been driven to their home by men he didn't know and that he turned her over to them afterwards. In the case of John Kilbride, he denied murder and sexual assault.

It was the tape, however, which dominated the proceedings and for which they will always be damned. Emlyns Williams, in his authoritative chronicle of the crimes and aftermath 'Beyond Belief'

Opposite: *The pair had many snapshots of their excursions with dogs on the moors. Myra, particularly, was fond of animals. However, the police were able, with the help of these 'family' snaps, to locate the burial grounds of murder victims. The photos were grotesque 'souvenirs' of grotesque crimes.*

Right: *Hindley's sister, Maureen with her husband, David Smith. He was seduced by Brady's ideas on dangerous sexual thrills, but the reality disgusted him. Smith reported Brady and Hindley to the police after he witnessed them killing a young man.*

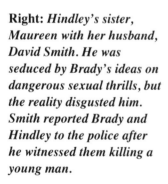

BRADY, WHEN ASKED WHY HE KEPT THE TAPE RECORDING, SAID IT WAS BECAUSE IT WAS 'UNUSUAL'.

wrote: 'This tape was to become the most scaring object ever to lie on the exhibits table below a judge at a murder trial... the tape began. And played for seventeen intolerable minutes. To listen to it was made doubly dreadful by the very nature of the invention which made the experience possible. In the course of murder trials, for centuries dreadful things have had to come to light, not only visually but mumbled by unwilling witnesses. Never before, however, has the modern phenomenon of preserved sound been put to such a grisly use as was the "the Moors tape".' The courtroom listened in shocked horror and disbelief to the pleading of the little girl as she begged for life and her mam, to the backdrop of Christmas carols and the barking commands of Brady for the child to pose in immodest positions.

Brady, when asked why he kept the tape recording, said it was because it was 'unusual'. It was a gross answer.

Hindley, in particular, became the focus of public curiousity. Men like Brady – well, there are many perverts and murderers down the ages, men who have killed to sate their demonic urges. But women were supposed to be the gentler sex, the givers of life, the nurturers of children. How could she have slipped into such an abyss? She gave little indication that she had a 'feminine' heart at her trial. Scrutiny of testimony during examination by the Attorney General Sir Elwyn Jones shows that she had little remorse for what had taken place, even though she pleaded Not Guilty to all charges. The following is an extract from the trial.

Attorney General: Time and again you were driving into this child's ears your orders, 'put it in'.

Hindley: I just wanted her to not make a noise.

Attorney General: Then you say, 'Will you stop it. Stop it'. Did you think there was the most terrible threatening note in the second order to stop it, Miss Hindley?

Hindley: No, it was a desparate tone.

Attorney General: Then one hears the poor little child making a retching noise. This thing was being pushed down her throat, was it not?

Hindley: No.

Attorney General: Who do you say undressed this child?

Hindley: Herself.

Attorney General: Can you therefore explain the child's saying: 'Don't undress me will you?' That was precisely what you were trying to do with the child?

Hindley: No, I was not.

Attorney General: A little further on Brady is saying: 'If you don't keep that hand down I'll slit your neck.' That is why you do not want to be landed with hearing that, is it not?

Hindley: No.

Attorney General: Then when the child was whining you say, 'Sh. Hush. Put that in your mouth again and...'. Then there follow the words 'packed more solid'. Why did you want the mouth to be packed more solid?

Hindley: Why more solid? I don't know.

Attorney General: That was preparatory to suffocating her in due course, was it not?

Hindley: No.

Above: *Police with long poles search near the site where they unearthed the body of Lesley Anne Downey. They were looking for other victims.*

THEY KILLED FOR SICK
AND TWISTED KICKS.
THEY ARE NOT FIT TO
MIX WITH HUMANS.

But no one in the court believed they were innocent. On 6 May, 1966, both were found Guilty of murdering Edward Evans and Lesley Ann Downey, Brady further found Guilty of the murder of John Kilbride with Hindley being an accessory after the fact. Brady was jailed for life on each of the three murder charges, Hindley for life on the Downey and Evans murders with a further seven years for her part as an accesory to the Kilbride slaying.

They were driven off to separate prisons with the screams of the mob outside ringing in their ears, and the lovers were never to see each other again. Hindley appealed her conviction but three appeal judges ruled against her.

The grisly saga of the Moors Murders might have ended then but the disappearances of Pauline Reade and Keith Bennett remained unsolved. Police officers who had worked on the case felt in their bones, that these two monsters had something to do with the disappearances of these two but there were no photographs or tape recordings to link them with the youngsters.

These suspicions continued down the years as Myra Hindley became a model

prisoner, then was involved in a lesbian love-affair that sparked a failed escape plot. She became an Open University graduate, converted to Christianity and established communication with Lord Longford, the prison reformer who is one of very few people who believe that Myra Hindley has been rehabilitated and now deserves to be released.

The correspondence between her and Brady was furious and passionate in the first months of separation, but time cooled the love while Brady slipped deeper into madness before he was finally moved, in November 1985, to a maximum-security hospital. But he was not so mad as to be incapable of thwarting the long-cherished dream that his former lover clung to throughout her long years of captivity.

A LOVER'S FURY

When Brady heard of Myra's attempts to be released, he broke his silence regarding the deaths of Reade and Bennett, prompting police to visit Myra Hindley in her jail cell. On 15 December, 1986, Myra Hindley returned to Saddleworth Moor, her first breath of the moors since the terrible events of more than two decades ago. Her memory, perhaps faded with time, perhaps by the enormity of what she had done, failed to pinpoint any graves, although she was sure she had the right area. But police searched diligently and in June the following year the body of Pauline Reade was discovered. Pathologists analysed that she had been sexually assaulted and her throat slashed from behind.

Her confession to the Reade and Bennett murders has effectively stifled any hope that Myra Hindley will ever be freed and she is said to have resigned herself to death in jail. It is highly unlikely that any prime minister would wish to be known as the premier who sanctioned her parole, even though she will be eligible to apply for release again in 1995.

Brady, meanwhile, continues in his mental degeneration. Now declared clinicaly insane, in the winter of 1987 he mailed a letter to the BBC containing sketchy information about five further murders, including unsuspected Moors victims, a man murdered in Manchester, a woman dumped in a canal and two victims gunned down in Scotland. Police are probing his alleged crimes but at the time of writing it is unclear if more prosecutions will follow.

Other victims of the killings are the families of the murdered children. Mrs Ann West, mother of Lesley Ann, is a vociferous campaigner for Hindley to stay behind bars. On the twenty-fifth anniversary of her child's death she wrote to Home Secretary Kenneth Baker, saying: 'Though a generation has passed since those evil monsters were put behind bars the horror of their crimes remains as fresh as ever. I beg you to turn a deaf ear to those well-meaning, but tragically misguided do-gooders who would now set them free on compassionate grounds. Ignore, at all costs, those who would forgive and forget. For just as there is no parole for we who still grieve, so must there be no parole for them.

'Every night I am haunted anew by the memory of that courtroom. I can still hear the taped screams of Lesley Ann begging for mercy...

'The enormity of those murders has not diminished. They killed for sick and twisted kicks, and showed no compassion. They are not fit to mix with humans. I implore you to make sure they do not.'

Below, left: *The bleak burial grounds of two murdered children.*

Below: *Ian Brady after years in prison. He has grown madder and madder and is in a psychiatric unit.*

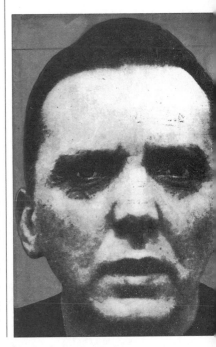

DOWNEY'S BODY FOUND OVER RIDGE

KILBRIDE'S BODY FOUND HERE

THE ROSENBERGS
The A-Bomb Spies

No-one ever thought there was anything special about Julius and Ethel Rosenberg, until they were tried and executed in the electric chair as spies. This ordinary couple were at the heart of a traitorous network which passed the secrets of America's first atomic bomb to the Soviet Union.

J ulius and Ethel Rosenberg were the children of dispossessed Russian Jews who went to the New World determined to make a different and better life. Julius and Ethel were both born in the USA. Of course, as they matured they also nursed their hopes and their dreams. But their dream was not the same dream as that of their family and neighbours; it was one that could only be fulfilled by an alien creed hostile to their homeland, the government of the United States.

For Ethel and Julius Rosenberg were America's 'atomic spies', the suburban couple enmeshed in a plot to sell America's nuclear secrets to their Kremlin enemy. The Rosenbergs were the only Communist agents ever to be executed in peacetime and, while apologists and historical revisionists have argued down the years that the pair were the victims of a ghastly frame-up, experts conclude that the verdicts and sentences passed upon them have stood the test of time.

When the switch was thrown on them in the death chamber at Sing-Sing prison in New York on 19 June, 1953, it was the end of one of the grimmest chapters of international espionage. Many thronged the streets in the hours before they were executed, some protesting their innocence, others merely asking for clemency. The problem

with both Julius and Ethel Rosenberg, for those who believed them innocent, was that they looked so damned ordinary. But that, say the counter-intelligence chiefs who trapped them, was precisely what made them so damn good.

Outwardly, there was nothing to distinguish this married couple from their fellow

*Opposite: **Ethel and Julius Rosenberg who played no small part in the Cold War when they sold A-bomb secrets to the USSR.***

citizens. Ethel, whose maiden name was Greenglass, had graduated from high school on the lower east side of Manhattan – a neigbourhood that embraced most of the races on earth. She left school at sixteen, was employed in various clerical jobs and secretarial posts before becoming an active trade unionist.

Above: *The A-bomb explosion over Japan in 1945.*

Julius, the bespectacled electrical engineer who once underwent religious training in the hope of becoming a rabbi, sprang from similar roots. A graduate of the same high school as his future wife, he studied the Torah for a year before abandoning his religious leanings in favour of a degree in electrical engineering from the City College of New York. He knew Ethel at school as a friend, but when he met her later at a dance, their friendship blossomed into love. In 1939, while the storm clouds of war were gathering over Europe, he married her shortly after his twenty-first birthday.

Below, left: *Given the innocuous name of 'Little Boy' this is an A-bomb, capable of a dreadful, long-term destruction of mankind.*

Below, right: *Dr.Enrico Fermi, the Italian who escaped Fascism in his own country, and worked in the USA. He was the scientist who first produced the chain-reacting fission that led to the A-bomb.*

expelled from the Army when his covert membership of the organisation was discovered by the FBI. America was yet to reach her peak of anti-Communist hysteria under the McCarthy hearings, but to be 'red' was still an alien and utterly distasteful concept to the majority of her citizens. Unemployed and with a family to feed, Julius launched his own business with capital from Ethel's brothers, David and Bernard.

David Greenglass was an integral part of the conspiracy to sell USA secrets to the USSR that Julius and Ethel Rosenberg had willingly joined several years previously. For Greenglass worked during the war at the Los Alamos research centre, the top-secret New Mexico site where Robert Oppenheimer and his scientists worked in a desperate race to build the first atomic bomb before the Axis powers did. This remote site, formerly the home of a boys school, was the centre for the greatest and most destructive scientific achievement of this or any age... and David Greenglass systematically stole its secrets for traitorous sale to the Russians.

Just like the British-born Soviet spies Burgess, Philby and Maclean, who were recruited as agents while at British universities, so Greenglass saw the Soviet Union

A SOCIALIST FAMILY MAN

After a year of odd-jobs Julius became a junior engineer for the Army Signal Corps. In the spring of 1942 he and Ethel, who had been living in cramped conditions with his mother, rented a small apartment in a housing development on the east side of Manhattan. Life was sweet for the Rosenbergs during the war years; he had a desk job which didn't require him to serve abroad, and there were few of the economic privations in America which tested British familes during the War. They had two sons, Michael and Robert and the young Rosenbergs doted on them.

But Julius was already a keeper of secrets. Years earlier he had joined the Communist Party, impressed by what he saw as the 'new order' shaping world events from Moscow. In 1945 he was

as the way of the future. But the FBI later maintained that it was his sister and Julius who had recruited him to the cause. And the Rosenbergs kept him sweet on the idea of world socialism with liberal handouts of money. With the family as his puppet-masters, he agreed to use his work position to deliver the stolen blueprints for the bomb to their Kremlin bosses. When Greenglass eventually came to trial, he turned on his family to save his own neck. By pinning the blame exclusively on the Rosenbergs, claiming their own fanatical Communist leanings were used to intimidate him, he saved himself.

It was the Rosenbergs who were the lynch-pin for the entire spying operation which began to unravel in 1950 with the arrest of thirty-nine-year-old Harry Gold, a bachelor employed as a chemist at a Philadelphia hospital. He was named by the

Above: *Julius Rosenberg is arrested by FBI agents on charges of espionage.*

HE HAD JOINED THE COMMUNIST PARTY, IMPRESSED BY WHAT HE SAW AS THE 'NEW ORDER' SHAPING WORLD EVENTS FROM MOSCOW.

FBI and the US Attorney General as being the accomplice of the disgraced nuclear boffin Klaus Fuchs, who was behind bars in England after pleading guilty to selling nuclear secrets to Moscow.

REVELATIONS OF A BRITISH SPY

Fuchs, a brilliant physicist who had fled his native Germany when Hitler came to power, was part of the British mission that was given access to the highest security levels surrounding the development of the bomb. He received a fourteen-year sentence for his treachery. He admitted that he used Gold as the courier, although it is still unclear to this day whether Fuchs had any contact with the Rosenbergs.

He was indicted on wartime espionage charges that carried the death penalty, even though the War was over. Gold, who had been the contact in America for Fuchs, was a wretched little man who sang like a canary once he was in custody. His confession that David Greenglass, the Los Alamos worker, had fed him atomic bomb secrets throughout the War years, exploded like the bomb itself across the front pages of the nation's newspapers.

The FBI built up a dossier detailing Grennglass' spying activities inside the Los Alamos complex. Greenglass had frequent access to top secret material on the 'lenses' for atomic bombs – the detonators that released the plutonium and uranium to create the single critical mass. On 17 July, under intense pressure from his captors, Greenglass sold out his brother-in-law. His sister's arrest was to follow shortly. Anti-Communist hysteria was rising in America now and Americans were fighting once again, this time against the menace of Communism in Korea.

The Department of Justice press release on the arrest of Rosenberg proclaimed: 'J. Edgar Hoover, the director of the FBI, said that Julius Rosenberg is a most important link in the Soviet espionage apparatus.

'Rosenberg, in early 1945, made available to Greenglass while he was on leave in New York City one-half of an

irregularly cut jelly-box top, the other half of which was given to Greenglass by Gold in Albuquerque, New Mexico, as a means of identifying Gold to Greenglass. Rosenberg aggressively sought ways and means to secretly conspire with the Soviet government to the detriment of his own country. Investigation to date also reveals that Rosenberg made himself available to Soviet espionage agents so he might "do something directly to help Russia".' This was all denied by the Rosenbergs who said they were trapped in a nightmare of which they had no part.

But the FBI had indeed assembled a massive body of evidence which they would later use against the couple at their trial. Another member of the spy ring to be arrested was Morton Sobell, a friend of the Rosenbergs who had studied electrical engineering with Julius. He was charged on a separate indictment of passing to them the details and plans of America's latest radar on its ships and submarines. This too would be used against them when they came to trial in March 1951.

A MISTAKEN IDEALISM

The full weight of the US government's case had shifted from Gold and the other arrested spies to the Rosenbergs. The FBI evidence depicted them as the architects of the spy ring who forged the contacts with the Soviet diplomats and agents. J. Edgar Hoover said that American intelligence predicted that Russia would not have the atomic bomb until the 1960s. But thanks to the secrets passed along by the Rosenbergs, they exploded their first device in 1949, rocketing them into the nuclear age and laying the foundations of the Cold War. This, he said, was the end result of the American spies' 'misty eyed idealism'.

Irving Saypol, the government prosecutor at the trial, left no one in any doubt, when he rose to open the case, that he intended to go for the death penalty. He said: 'We will prove that the Rosenbergs devised and put into operation, with the aid of Soviet agents in this country, an elaborate scheme which allowed them to steal, through David Greenglass, this one weapon which might well hold the key to the survival of this nation and means the peace of the world, the atomic bomb. This

Below: 'Old Sparky' the electric chair that despatched many felons in Sing-Sing, the prison in New York State.

Opposite, above: Enrico Fermi whose brilliant war effort was wasted by the treachery of the Rosenbergs.

Opposite, below: Sing-Sing prison where the traitors, Julius and Ethel Rosenberg, were executed.

love of Communism and the Soviet Union led them into a Soviet espionage ring.'

The fifteen-day trial was a sensation, the more so because of the spectacle of a brother betraying his own sister. But there was a parade of witnesses who testified that the Rosenbergs had sold their souls to the beliefs of the hammer and sickle, not the stars and stripes. Max Elitcher, the first witness, testified that Julius Rosenberg had badgered him, asking him if his job in the Navy Department in Washington gave him access to secrets that he could pass on to the Soviets. Elizabeth Bentley, a Columbia University graduate, told how she was lured into the espionage web through a series of disasterous love affairs with Soviet agents. She testified that the bond was between the Rosenbergs and Moscow was unusually strong.

Undoubtedly, it was the evidence of David Greenglass which sealed their fates. He testified that he worked in Los Alamos and had access to the greatest secrets which he passed to his sister and brother-in-law. 'They preferred Russian socialism to our system of government,' he said. Greenglass said that he began passing on information, initially about the personnel at the closely-guarded complex, later on about the explosives used to trigger the detonator and the detonator mechanisms themselves. He detailed the jelly-box story that had been revealed by the Department of Justice press release at the time of the traitors' arrest. The words 'I come from Julius' displayed on the top of the box flashed by Gold, meant that the coast was clear and that the Rosenbergs required more information for their Russian bosses.

Greenglass passed on data and sketches and in one despatch, for which he received $200, he typed up twelve pages of notes about the mechanism of the bomb. He went on: 'Working in the Rosenberg's living-room Ethel did the typing and Julius, Ethel and my wife Ruth corrected the grammar. Julius told me he communicated with his Russian contacts by leaving microfilm in an alcove at a cinema. He said he had received an alcove table from the Russians as a reward – I saw this table at his apartment. It was used for microfilming.'

A BROTHER'S BETRAYAL

Greenglass said the spying operation was finished with the arrest of Fuchs in 1950. He said that Julius visited him, Greenglass, and said: 'You remember the man who came to see you in Albuquerque? Well, Fuchs was one of his contacts. Doubtless this man will be arrested soon and this might lead to you.' He was referring to Gold and he was correct on both counts. Greenglass said he offered money for him to go away to Mexico and later came back with $4,000 for the purpose. But the plot was already unravelling because, by then, Greenglass was under surveillance .

Ruth Greenglass stepped into the witness box to corroborate everything her husband

'THEY PREFERRED RUSSIAN SOCIALISM TO OUR SYSTEM OF GOVERNMENT.'

Below: *Hiroshima, Japan after the A-Bomb was dropped.*

had said. She produced bank deposit receipts that showed large amounts of cash being placed in their account – sums far larger than her husband's salary at Los Alamos could have provided. She also recalled the last visit Julius made to their apartment, when he said they would have to flee before the arrests began. 'I was worried about my baby,' she said, 'and he at first said we should go to the Soviet Union. When I said that I could not travel with an infant he said: "My doctor says that if you take enough canned milk and boil the water, everything will be all right." He said that they were closing the net, that we could expect arrests soon. But we never intended to go.'

THE MEANING OF TREASON

Harry Gold, the US contact to the now-imprisoned Fuchs, also delivered damning testimony. He said that Anatoli Yakolev, the Soviet Union's vice-consul in New York City, was the paymaster with the money man who controlled him and Rosenberg. He said: 'Yakolev reported that the information I had given him had been sent immediately to the Soviet Union. He said that the information I had received from Greenglass was extremely excellent and very valuable.' Yakolev had left America rather rapidly on a ship bound for Europe in 1946 and was never quizzed on his role in the atom spy ring.

Julius Rosenberg took the stand and answered every specific allegation of treachery with the three words: 'I did not.' He denied giving the Greenglasses any money other than some cash he owed David from the business that he helped finance. But he refused to say whether or not he was a member of the Communist Party – he was – although he admitted that he did have sympathy for the Soviet political system 'as it has done much to improve the lot of the underdog.'

Ethel, too, denied all allegations of espionage. She said she loved the brother who had branded her and her husband as traitors, but could offer no explanation why he had implicated them other than as a ploy to save himself. Observers at the time thought that she didn't help herself by refusing to explain why so often she had pleaded the Fifth Amendment – the right to

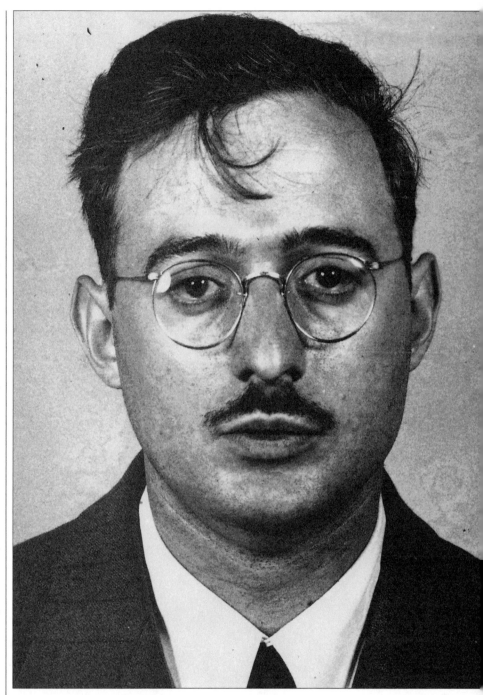

Above: *Julius Rosenberg.*

remain silent – during the grand jury hearings which led to her trial.

Morton Sobell refused to take the stand at the trial of the traitors.

In his summing up the prosecutor was emphatic that the accused were spies. Saypol said: 'This is one of most important cases ever submitted to a jury in this country. We know that these conspirators stole the most important scientific secrets ever known to mankind from this country and delivered them to the Soviet Union. David Greenglass' description of the atomic bomb was typed by Ethel

JULIUS TOLD ME HE COMMUNICATED WITH HIS RUSSIAN CONTACTS BY LEAVING MICROFILM IN AN ALCOVE AT A CINEMA.

Above: 'Save the Rosenbergs'. In Paris, certain groups decried the death sentence on the traitors.

Gold was involved with the Rosenbergs. They were all traitors.

On the morning of Tuesday, 29 March the jurors returned with Guilty verdicts on Julius, Ethel and Sobell. Judge Irving Kaufman told the Rosenbergs: 'The thought that citizens of our country would lend themselves to the destruction of our country by the most destructive weapons known to man is so shocking that I can't find words to describe this loathsome offence.' A week later, on 5 April, 1951, as they appeared for sentencing, he told them: 'I consider your crime worse than murder. Plain deliberate contemplated murder is dwarfed in magnitude by comparison with the crime you have committed. I believe your conduct in putting the atom bomb in the hands of the Russians has already caused the resultant aggression in Korea with casualties exceeding fifty thousand.

A CONTROVERSIAL VERDICT

'It is not in my power, Julius or Ethel Rosenberg, to forgive you. Only the Lord can find mercy for what you have done. You are hereby sentenced to the punishment of death, and it is ordered you shall be executed according to law.'

Morton Sobell got thirty years, of which he would serve sixteen. Later, Greenglass, who stole the secrets, got a remarkably light fifteen years, as did his wife Ruth Greenglass, who collapsed in the dock as the sentence was handed down.

There was to be no reprieve for the Rosenbergs, despite twenty-two appeals and numerous stays of execution. Julius, thirty-five, and Ethel, thirty-seven, died in the electric chair on the night of 19 June, 1953. Ever since then debate has raged about the possibility of their innocence, but top legal experts say their guilt is more than likely. Alexander Bickel, a Yale University law professor, said: 'It was a ghastly and shameful episode, but I believe they were guilty beyond a doubt.' And Roy Cohn, one of the prosecutors, added: 'I feel the guilt was overwhelming. Their apparent "ordinariness" made it possible for them to get away with it for so long.'

Only Cuba, satellite of the now-defunct Soviet Union for which they served, commemorated them as 'assassinated heroes' on a set of postage stamps.

Rosenberg, just so had she, on countless other occasions, sat at that typewriter and struck the keys, blow by blow, against her country in the interests of the Soviets.

'When Fuchs confessed, the Rosenbergs' position in the Soviet espionage hierachy in this country was jeaopardised. The evidence of the guilt of the Rosenbergs is incontrovertible. No defendants ever stood before the bar of American justice less deserving than them and Sobell.' Their defence lawyers tried to pin the guilt on Greenglass, but were unable to dismiss the fact that

WAR CRIMES

POL POT
The Murder Machine

A gentle nation, ancient in its culture, pious in its faith, was cruelly dismembered by a Marxist fanatic. Pol Pot turned Cambodia into a killing field while the world turned its back on this lost nation.

Above: *The grinning face of evil – Pol Pot is a study in tyranny and murder. He turned his gentle land into a vast 'killing field'.*

Imagine a government that comes to power, then declares that money is banned. Not only money, but the forces which provide money – commerce, industry, banking – are also proscribed. The new government decrees that society will become agrarian again, just like it had been in the Middle Ages. Great cities and towns will be de-populated and the people will be moved to the countryside, where they will live and work raising crops and cattle. But families will not be allowed to stay together. The government, in its infinite wisdom, realises that children must not be influenced by outdated and archaic bourgois thoughts passed down by their parents. So they are taken away and brought up as the vanguard of the regime, imbued with and steeped in the philosophy of the new order. No messing about with books until they are in the late teens – there is no need for books anymore, so they are burned – and children from the age of seven will begin working for the state.

For the new agrarian class, there are eighteen-hour days, back-breaking work, followed by 're-education' in Marxist-Leninist thought from their new masters. Anyone who dissents, or who shows signs of 'regression' to the old ways is not allowed to live – nor are intellectuals, teachers and college professors; nor those people who are literate because they might read thoughts which are not Marxist-Leninist, and spread a poisonous philosophy among the re-educated workers in the fields. Priests, with their outmoded theology, politicians of any hue other than that of the ruling party and those who made fortunes under previous governments are no longer needed: they too are eliminated. There is no trade, there are no telephones, there are no churches or temples, here are no bicycles, birthday parties, marriages, anniversaries, love or kindness. At best, there is work for the state – torture, degradation and at worst, death.

This nightmare scenario was not a figment of some science fiction writer's imagination. It became a terrible reality in Cambodia, where leader Pol Pot turned the clock back and pushed civilisation out, hoping to find his own warped vision of a classless society. His 'killing fields' were littered with the corpses of those who did not fit into the new world that his brutal

AS MANY AS THREE MILLION PEOPLE MAY HAVE PERISHED DURING POL POT'S REGIME IN CAMBODIA.

Above: *Leading a column of his faithful followers, Pol Pot treks through the Cambodian jungle.*

subordinates were shaping. As many as three million people may have perished during Pol Pot's regime in Cambodia – the same number of unfortunates killed in the gas chambers of the Auschwitz death factory run by the Nazis in the Second World War. Life under Pol Pot was intolerable and Cambodians were forced to tragically re-christen their South-East Asian country. They gave it the macabre name of the Land of the Walking Dead.

The Cambodian tragedy was a legacy of the Vietnam War that first marked the end of French colonialism before escalating into the conflict against the Americans. Fifty-three thousand Cambodians were slain on the fields of battle. Between 1969 and 1973 American B-52 aircraft carpet-bombed huge tracts of Cambodia, dropping as many tons of high-explosive on the tiny land as had fallen on Germany in the last two years of the Second World War. The Viet Cong fighters in Vietnam used its neighbour's lush jungles as encampments

HE ORDERED THE ABOLITION OF ALL MARKETS, THE DESTRUCTION OF CHURCHES AND THE PERSECUTION OF ALL RELIGIOUS ORDERS.

and staging posts for operations against the Americans, and these hideouts were the targets of the war planes.

Prince Norodom Sihanouk, ruler of Cambodia and heir to its great religious and cultural traditions, renounced his royal title ten years before the onset of the Vietnam War, but remained the head of his country. He tried to guide his country along a path of neutrality, a delicate balancing act for a country surrounded by warring states and conflicting ideologies. He had been crowned King of Cambodia, a French protectorate, in 1941, but abdicated in 1955. However, he returned, after free and fair elections, as head of state.

Between 1966 and 1969, as the Vietnam War escalated in intensity, he upset policy-makers in Washington by ignoring the arms smuggling and the Vietnamese guerilla camps in the jungles of Cambodia. At the same time, he was only mildly critical of the punishing air raids being launched by America. On 18 March, 1970, while he was

in Moscow, his prime minister, General Lon Nol, with the backing of the White House, staged a coup, after which he changed the name of Cambodia back to its ancient title, Khmer. The Khmer Republic was recognised by the United States, which, however, one month later, chose to launch an invasion against the newly-named land. Sihanouk went into exile in Peking... and here the ex-king chose to form an alliance with the devil himself.

Not much is known about Pol Pot, the man with the fat face and sparkling eyes, the man with the face of an avuncular old grandfather and the heart of a murderous tyrant. He was the monster with whom

Sihanouk threw in his lot, swearing with this Communist guerilla chief that they would mould their forces into a single entity with the aim of destroying American forces. Pot, brought up by a peasant family in the Kampong Thom province of the country, had been educated at a Buddhist monastery where, for two years, he lived as a monk. In the 1950s he won a scholarship to study electronics in Paris where, like so many other students of the time, he became involved in left-wing causes. Here he heard about – although it is unclear whether they actually met – another Cambodian student, Khieu Samphan, a political science student whose controversial but exhilarating plans for an 'agrarian revolution' were to inspire the ambitions of the peasant, Pol Pot.

Above: *Government troops surround refugees during the Khmer Rouge fighting.*

Top: *Refugees flee from the city of Phnom Penh.*

POL POT, THE MAN WITH THE FACE OF AN AVUNCU-LAR OLD GRANDFATHER AND THE HEART OF A MURDEROUS TYRANT.

A TERRIBLE REALITY

Samphan's theory was that, in order to progress, Cambodia must regress; it must turn its back on capitalist exploitation, fat-cat bosses created by the former French colonial overlords, reject corrupted bourgeois values and ideals. Samphan's twisted theory decreed that people must live in the fields and that all the trappings of modern life must be annihilated. If Pol Pot himself had remained an obscure figure, this theory may have remained a coffee bar philosopy rattling around the boulevards and parks of Paris. Instead, it became a terrible reality.

Between 1970 and 1975 the Khmer Rouge – the Red Army led by Pol Pot – became a formidable force in Cambodia, controlling huge tracts of the countryside. On 17 April, 1975, Pol Pot's dream of power became a reality when his armies, marching under the red flag, entered the capital, Phnom Penh. Within hours of the coup, Pol Pot called a special meeting of his new cabinet members and told them the country was now called Kampuchea. He outlined the plans for his brave new world which would begin taking shape within days.

He ordered the evacuation of all cities and towns, a process to be overseen by newly-created regional and zonal chiefs. He ordered the abolition of all markets, the destruction of churches and the persecution of all religious orders. Although privileged himself, in having been educated abroad, he harboured a loathing for the educated classes, and so all teachers, professors and even kindergarten teachers were ordered to be executed. The educated peasant, Pol Pot, feared the educated classes.

The first to die were the senior cabinet members and functionaries of Lon Nol's regime, followed by the officer corps of the old army. All were buried in mass graves. Then came the evacuation of the city, towns and villages. Pol Pot's twisted dream was to put the clock back and make his people the dwellers of an agrarian, Marxist society. Pol Pot was aided by his evil deputy, Ieng Sary. Doctors were murdered because they, too, were 'educated'. All religious groups were exterminated because they were 'reactionary'. The term Pol Pot used for his extermination policy was '*Khchat-khchay os roling*' – it translates as 'scatter them out of sight'. The sinister reality meant the death of thousands.

Buddhist temples were desecrated or turned into whorehouses for the troops or even became abbatoirs. Before the terror, there were some sixty thousand monks in Cambodia; after it was over, just three thousand returned to their shattered shrines and their holy places of worship.

Pol Pot also decreed that ethnic minorities did not, in fact, exist. Vietnamese, Thai and Chinese festivals, languages and cultures were ruled illegal, to be practised under punishment of death. His was to be a pure Khmer society. The deliberate and forceful eradication of ethnic groups fell most heavily on the 'Cham' people. Their ancestors had formed the Kingdom of Champa, once a country in what is now Vietnam. The Cham migrated to Cambodia during the eighteenth century to live as fishermen along Cambodia's rivers and the Tonle Sap lake. They were an Islamic people and were, perhaps, the most distinctive ethnic group in modern Cambodia, for they never adandoned or diluted their language, cuisine, costume, hairstyles, burial customs or religion.

The Cham were obvious targets for the young fanatics of the Khmer Rouge who fell upon them like a plague of locusts. The villages were torched, the people marched into the swampy, mosquito-plagued hinterland, fed pork – strictly against their religion – and the religious leaders executed. When villagers resisted whole communities were murdered, their bodies flung into huge pits and covered over with lime. Of two hundred thousand Cham people alive before the new order, barely one hundred thousand survive today. Those who survived the initial terror found that life

Below: *Cambodian defence minister, Keieu Sampen receives a warm hug from Prince Sihanouk (right).*

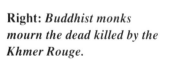

Right: *Buddhist monks mourn the dead killed by the Khmer Rouge.*

BUDDHIST TEMPLES WERE DESECRATED OR TURNED INTO WHOREHOUSES FOR THE TROOPS.

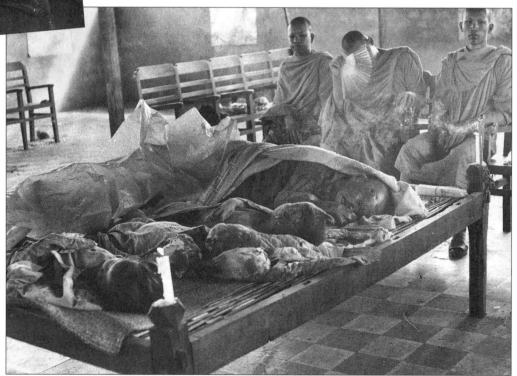

under the new regime was infinitely harder than a quick death – hence the phrase 'Land of the Living Dead', coined by those forced to live under these conditions.

BOURGEOIS CRIMINALS

Pol Pot believed that all adults were tainted by feudal, bourgeois attitudes, with 'sympathies' for foreign regimes which Pol Pot had decreed were alien to the national way of life. Urbanites, in particular, were rooted out and placed in work camps where hundreds of thousands were literally worked to death or murdered if they spoke French – a major crime in Khmer Rouge eyes because it showed a bourgeois attitude, with a link to, and sympathy with, the colonial reign of the past.

In vast encampments, devoid of any comforts save a straw mat to sleep on and a bowl of rice at the end of every day, the tradesmen, dockers, clerks, bankers – many alive only because they managed to hide their professions – and numerous other citizens, toiled in conditions that would have shamed Japanese prison-of-war camps in the Second World War. The camps were organized, much like the concentration camps of the Nazis, to ensure that 'natural selection' took its toll of the aged and the ill, the very young, and pregnant women. Given a poor diet, deprived of strength, hundreds and thousands succumbed to disease, starvation and the clubbings of their brutal overseers. With no medical men to treat them, save for the attention of a few 'traditional' herbalists whom the new government tolerated, the life span of a prisoner in the camps was pathetically low. They were frog-marched out at dawn into malaria-ridden swamps where they worked twelve hours a day, planting rice and clearing jungles in futile attempts to reclaim more farmland. Then they were frog-marched back at night, under gunpoint and often under the blows and bayonet-thrusts of their guards, to a bowl of rice, gruel and a morsel of dried fish. Then, exhausted though they were, they had to endure Marxist indoctrination sessions, when irredeemable bourgeois elements were rooted out to be taken away for punishment while the others chanted, parrot-fashion, the benefits and joys of the new state. There was one day off in every ten, when people could look forward to twelve hours of indoctrination. Wives were separated from

Above: *A weary soldier is welcomed by hysterical refugees fleeing the guerilla onslaught.*

THEY WERE FROG-MARCHED OUT AT DAWN INTO MALARIA-RIDDEN SWAMPS WHERE THEY WORKED TWELVE HOURS A DAY

To re-inforce his battle against enemies real and imagined, Pol Pot set up a system of interrogations, tortures and executions in his prison camps. Much like the Spanish Inquisition of old, Pol Pot and his henchmen knew that all who came through the portals of these grim places were guilty – all they had to do was to confess that guilt. To convince its followers that cruelty was necessary and good for the nation, the regime taught its young bureacrats that torture had a special, political significance.

Taught by the Chinese, the Khmer security officers were enmeshed in a hard and cruel ideology, revealed in documents captured after the overthrow of Pol Pot. These dossiers show that torture attained a high level in his nation. One document, the 'S-21 Interrogator's Manual', later handed over to United Nations' investigators, reads: 'The purpose of doing torture is to get their responses. It's not something we do for the fun of it. Thus, we must make them hurt so they will respond quickly. Another purpose is to break them psychologically and make them lose their will. It's not something that is done out of individual anger or for self-satisfaction. Thus we beat them to make them afraid but absolutely not to kill them. When torturing them it is necessary to examine their state of health first and necessary to examine the whip. Don't greedily want to kill them. Politics is very important whereas torture is secondary. Thus the question of doing politics takes the lead at all times. Even when

their husbands, their children were either put to work at the age of seven or given away to the barren wives of party functionaries, so as to be brought up in the mould of fanatical warriors of the revolution. Pol Pot was a thorough man.

Bonfires were made of the books from universities and schools, as wretched, maltreated citizens were forced to chant as the works of civilisation perished in the flames. There were 'hate-ins', when people were whipped before pictures of members of the old regime. It was a nightmare world, sinister and hopeless, for the Cambodian people were literally isolated from the world. There was no postal service, no diplomatic ties with any country, no telephones and no travel; it was truly a nation lost to the world.

questioning it is always necessary to do constant propaganda.

TORTURE WITHOUT REASON

'At the same time it is necessary to avoid any question of hesitancy or half-heartedness, of not daring to do torture, which makes it impossible to get answers to our questions from our enemies, which slows down and delays our work. In sum, whether doing propaganda or torturing or bringing up questions to ask them or accusing them of something, it is necessary to hold steadfastly to a stance of not being half-hearted or hesitant. We must be absolute. Only thus can we work to good effect. We torture them but forget to give the reason first. Only then do they become totally helpless.' The notorious Chinese water torture, crucifictions and suffocations with a plastic bag were three among numerous torture methods practiced by the evil men of the Khmer Rouge.

The S21 facility, from which the document took its name, was the most infamous institution in the whole of Cambodia. Based in the north-east of the country, at least thirty thousand victims of the regime died there. Only seven prisoners are known to have survived – prisoners kept alive because they had administrative skills necessary to their overlords in the running of the dreadful place.

Torture was only one instrument of fear brandished over the heads of the cowed populace. The frequency with which people were executed was another. Many times, inmates in the new country camps were caught eating the flesh of their dead comrades in their desperation for food. The penalty for this was a horrible death of being buried up to the neck in mud and left to starve and thirst while ants and other creatures gnawed at the victim. Then the heads were cut off and stuck on pikes around the settlement with the words painted on a sign hanging from the neck: 'I am a traitor of the revolution!'

Dith Pran, a Cambodian interpreter for American journalist, Sydney Schanberg, emerged from the years of slaughter as a witness to the horrors of Pol Pot's reign. His own experiences, including his threatened execution, were chronicled in the film 'The Killing Fields', in which the torment of the Cambodian people was, for the first time, starkly revealed to the world. Pran's journey from his civilised childhood to a prison camp, where he pretended to be illiterate in order to survive, was a harrowing tale that reduced audiences to tears of pity. 'Many times,' said Pran, 'I prayed that I was dead rather than having to endure the life that I was forced to live. But some of my family had gotten away to America and it was for them that I carried on living. It was a nightmare time.'

Below: A Khmer Rouge soldier menaces civilians with his gun. The population of Phnom Penh were quickly subdued by the thugs of Pol Pot's army.

STACKS OF SKULLS

Pran was one of the lucky ones who survived the Asian holocaust to be reunited with his family in 1979 in San Francisco. Even now, the mass graves of the unknown, unnamed dead continue to be unearthed in remote corners of the sad country, the skulls stacked against the graves like so many footballs.

It was military muscle and not moral right that, in the end, halted the bloodbath and allowed for some semblance of sanity to return to the blighted land. Britain had, it must be acknowledged, spoken out in 1978 against alleged human rights abuses, after receiving reports, through intermediaries in Thailand, about the reign of terror in Cambodia, but the protest was ignored.

Opposite, top: Peasants feared that they would be forced to join the 'intellectuals' in the labour camps.

Opposite, bellow: Coils of barbed wire marked the Cambodian border with Thailand.

Britain reported to the United Nations Commission on Human Rights, but the hysterical Khmer Rouge representative responded: 'The British Imperialists have no right to speak of the rights of man. The world knows well their barbarous and abject nature. Britain's leaders are living in opulence atop a pile of rotting corpses while the proletariat have only the right to be unemployed, to steal and prostitute.' Regrets were sent from Pol Pot flunkies who said that they were too busy to attend UN enquiries on the allegations to the commission hearings in New York.

In December, 1978, Vietnamese forces, who had been skirmishing for years with the Khmer Rouge over a disputed border region, launched a major offensive with mechanised infantry divisions and full armoured support. The infrastructure of Cambodia had disintegrated so badly by this time, that battlefield reports had to be biked great distances to Khmer Rouge command posts because there were no telephones left in operation.

The Vietnamese, early in 1979, found themselves masters of a blighted land. Pol Pot had fled in his white armoured Mercedes from Phnom Penh, just hours before the Vietnamese troops arrived to liberate the ghostly city. He went scurrying back to his masters in China, glad of the sanctuary, but bitter that they had not come to his aid in resisting the well-armed and determined North Vietnamese onslaught.

*Above: **The fall of Phnom Penh is celebrated by young guerillas of the Khmer Rouge.***

'US SURVIVORS REMEMBER OUR FAMILIES BEING TAKEN AWAY, MANY OF THEM, AND OUR FRIENDS BRUTALLY MURDERED.'

Massive amounts of aid flooded into Cambodia as the world realized the full horror of the Khmer Rouge regime and the devastation of the country. The Khmer Rouge were, like the Nazis, particularly methodical when it came to detailing their crimes; investigators found daily logs of shootings, torture, hundreds of photo albums of those to be executed – including those of wives and children of 'intellectuals' liquidated in the earliest days of the terror – and the detailed loggings of the infamous killing fields. These fields, intended to be the basis of the worker's Utopia, a land without money or want, became, instead, the burial pits of a people crushed under the yoke of a cruel tyranny.

Pol Pot seemed to fade into the background but has emerged in recent years to become a major political force vying for power in this embitttered region. Like all tyrants, he said that mistakes were made by those under him, that he had faced rebellions on all fronts and that those who died were 'enemies of the state'. In 1981, back in Cambodia, he told a meeting of old friends at a secret location near the Thai border that he was 'too trusting. My policies were sound. Over-zealous regional commanders and sub-district personnel may have mis-interpreted orders. To talk about systematic murder is odious. If we had really killed at that rate, we would have had no one left to fight the Vietnamese. I have been seriously mis-interpreted.'

ANGEL OF DEATH

Misinterpretation on the scale of three million dead – almost twenty-five per cent of the population of the nation – seems too small a word to describe what was done in his name and under his orders. But following Hitler's code, that the bigger the lie, the more people will believe it, Pol Pot has, once again, become a power-player in the region and is able to rally forces in the countryside that continue to believe in him, and are still loyal to him. Now he is a major force once again, only waiting to ride into the country, like some avenging angel of death, to finish off what he started before: his great agrarian revolution.

For Dith Pran and other survivors, the prospect of Pol Pot's return to power, the possibility that he will plunge his tortured land into new depths of depravity, fills them with horror. When the United Nations first announced that the Khmer Rouge would be part of the power-sharing peace process in Cambodia, Pran said: 'I am still shocked when I see the Khmer Rouge flag flying on UN territory. How would you feel if you were Jewish and you saw Hitler's flag flying at the United Nations? Some people went on a fast for three days to protest this, but I did not. I have starved for four years and that is enough for any man.'

There is international lobbying for world governments to have the Cambodian massacres recognized as war crimes in the same way as the Hitlerian genocide of the Jews has been recognised. Yang Sam, of the Cambodian Documentation Commission in New York, is the Cambodian equivalent of Simon Wiesenthal, the Nazi death camp survivor who, from his office in Vienna, devotes his life to tracing and collating evidence against Nazi war criminals. Sam, a survivor of the terror, collects information against the butchers of his own land. He said: 'Those most responsible for the Cambodian genocide – the cabinet members of Pol Pot's regime, the central committee of his Communist party, the Khmer Rouge military commanders whose troops committed so much of the killing, those officials who oversaw, directed and ran the nationwide network of torture chambers, prison-execution centres and extermination facilities – continue to remain active in Cambodia and international political life. Based in enclaves along the Thai-Cambodian border, they conduct guerilla war seeking to return to power in Phnom Penh. They have not been held accountable for their crime under international law and that is a tragedy of monumental proportions.

'Us survivors remember our families being taken away, many of them, and our friends brutally murdered. We witnessed members of our families and others die of exhaustion from forced marches and slave labour, and from the brutal conditions of life to which the Cambodian people were subjected by the Khmer Rouge.

'We also saw Pol Pot's soldiers destroy our Buddhist temples, end schooling for our children, suppress our culture and eradicate our ethnic minorities. It is difficult for us to understand why the free and democratic nations of the world do not take action against the guilty. Surely this cries out for justice?' But there is no justice here.

WE WITNESSED MEMBERS OF OUR FAMILIES AND OTHERS DIE OF EXHAUSTION FROM FORCED MARCHES AND SLAVE LABOUR.

Below: *The legacy of the Pol Pot years. The skulls of the anonymous dead serve to remind the world of the man's dreadful regime.*

LAMMERDING
Butchery at Oradour

The Nazis were infamous for their brutal reprisals against partisan fighters. But the villagers of Oradour did not die for their brave resistance. They were slaughtered to avenge the greed of a few German officers.

T he tiny hamlet of Oradour-sur-Glane, a village not too far from Limoges in South-Western France existed for close to one thousand years without any more trouble than a bad harvest or blocked drains. Even the conflagration of World War Two had passed by these simple peasant people. Occasionally, they saw German soldiers passing through, or heard the freight trains in the night taking men and supplies to the front after the Allied invasion at Normandy, but to all intents and purposes, the attack that Adolf Hitler had launched against their countrymen had left them relatively unscathed.

Until, on a hot day in June 1944, the soldiers came.

The troops of the 2nd SS Panzer division 'Das Reich' entered Oradour and, in an afternoon of frenzied butchery, massacred its inhabitants. The men were taken away to a barn and shot, the women locked in the church which was then set ablaze with hand grenades. Every building was dynamited, every animal killed, every child rounded up and sent off to concentration camps. In the madness of that hot June day over six hundred of the citizens of Oradour died at the hands of the Nazi butchers. The question constantly asked by historians is – why? The common explanation, accepted down the years, has been that the villagers were punished by the SS because of increased French resistance activity in the region, following the success of the Allied landings. But another theory has surfaced which deserves consideration – the theory

that the villagers were not, in fact, meant to die. Instead, they were supposed to turn over large quantities of gold that the Germans – mistakenly – believed was hidden in the sleepy hamlet.

Oradour stands today as a ghost town, preserved as it was after the last explosion and last round had been fired on that day, nearly fifty years ago. The burned-out car from which the town doctor was hauled and executed, still lies abandoned on the cobbled streets. In the burned and charred butcher's shop remain his meat scales, in the house opposite is a broken sewing machine – all artifacts testifying to a close-knit community that was literally wiped from the face of the earth.

It was a hot Saturday afternoon, just four days after the Allies had gained their foothold in France with Operation Overlord, that a company from the Das

ON THAT HOT JUNE DAY, OVER SIX HUNDRED CITIZENS OF ORADOUR DIED AT THE HANDS OF THE NAZI BUTCHERS.

Reich division arrived in Oradour. Many were enjoying the serenity of the day – men fished from the banks of the River Glane, others sipped pastis and played *petanque* at the village café.

The SS men, who rode in on half-tracks, in lorries and on motorcycles, were veterans of the Russian front, men who had fought in the 'war without rules' unleashed by their Führer against Slavic 'inferiors'.

Above: *Some of the villagers were lined up against this wall and shot by the SS. Their bodies were then burned.*

Das Reich division were Waffen SS, the fighting SS elite and had conducted their war with ferocity. By all accounts, they did their grim duty in the East, as they were instructed by their Führer, and were responsible for untold massacres of the civilian population.

The division that arrived in Montauban, France, in 1944, was a lot different from the one that went to war against the Soviet Union in Operation Barbarossa. General Heinz Lammerding, its commanding officer, was highly decorated – but he had

RETALIATION AGAINST THE FRENCH FOR ACTS OF SABOTAGE WAS SWIFT, BRUTAL AND ARBITRARY.

fight for the swastika. Not unnaturally, the survivors of the Eastern Front regarded themselves as superior in race, attitude and élan to the many other nations that now constituted Das Reich's ranks.

After the Allied onslaught on Normandy, Das Reich was stirred from its days of rest and relaxation, and ordered to begin the long move northwards to the front. And every inch of the way they were targeted by the *Maquis*, the French resistance. With the liberation of their land in sight, and with Allied air superiority ensuring ample

seen the flower of German youth, in the ranks of his division, fall in their thousands. In March 1944, twelve thousand five hundred of the fifteen thousand men that composed this fighting unit were killed and captured on the Russian front in the actions around Cherkassy. The two thousand five hundred survivors, sent to Montauban to become the nucleus of a new division, found themselves surrounded by men of numerous nationalities who had chosen to

Above: *Scene from the post-War trial of twenty-one German soldiers accused of the murders at Oradour.*

supply drops, the French dogged the German advance northwards. Attacks and sabotage had become so commonplace the Germans were stopping to check every piece of horse manure in their pathway in case it was a bomb, for just such a booby trap had claimed the life of three soldiers.

Retaliation against the French for acts of sabotage was swift, brutal and arbitrary. German soldiers of Das Reich division took part in these loathsome reprisals against innocent civilians and they followed the Führer's orders demanding harsh punishment for anyone who raised arms against his armies. The raids on villages and towns became known as *ratissages*, and it became standard practice for the SS men to fill their pockets with plundered loot on these killing missions. Indeed, Lammerding and two officers under him – Major Otto Dickmann and Helmut Kämpfe – were also not averse to stockpiling some money for after the War. All three, in late night discussions over the General's finest cognac, were convinced that the War was going to end in the total and utter defeat of Hitler. With such an eventuality in sight, the acquisition of a nest-egg seemed the logical thing to do.

Dickmann was based in St Junien, not far from Oradour, and was guardian of a single, special truck in the divisional transportation corps. He said it contained divisional records and the 'order of battle', or make-up of the formations which comprised the unit. He ordered an Austrian Lieutenant, Bruno Walter, to double the guard on this vehicle.

Dickmann was nervous in St Junien on the night of 9 June, not least because he believed that there were no fewer than two thousand armed resistance *marquisards* in the town, waiting for the slightest opportunity to launch an attack against him, his men or his transport.

THE GOLD BOOTY

But there were no divisional records on board the truck, no order of battle plans. It is believed to have contained more than six million pounds worth of gold – at today's prices. This was the booty that would guarantee Dickmann, Lammerding and Kämpfe an easy retirement at the end of the war. They could not send it back to Germany for fear it would be bombed, intercepted or stolen. Besides, the railway network was rapidly disintegrating under Allied air assaults. A third factor – their fear of the disapproval of Heinrich Himmler, chief of the SS, should he learn that they had looted on such a scale – convinced them that they were left with no alternative but to carry their spoils with them into the front line.

The Resistance was aware of the presence of Das Reich division and knew that it

was soon to be on the move again, in preparation to deploy its three hundred heavy tanks and thousands of men against the Allies on the beaches of Normandy. The British had warned the Resistance that it feared the Germans could be in the fighting zone within three days; the French were asked to harass their progress every inch of the way. Dickmann and his superiors knew this – hence the tension felt by those guarding the 'special' truck.

On 9 June, at midnight, Dickmann ordered the truck and a detachment of armed SS men to take the first leg of a journey to move the gold northwards. One plan the trio had devised was to store it in the Loire valley region, while they went up to the front line for the battle. Whatever happened, Dickmann had to get the gold out of the Resistance-infested area as quickly as possible. The night he chose to

Below: *Captain Kahn (inset) ordered the massacre. Photographs of victims (main picture) were used as criminal evidence.*

THE YOUNG AND RECKLESS RESISTANCE MEN, SEEKING VENGEANCE FOR YEARS OF NAZI OPPRESSION, LAUNCHED AN ILL-PREPARED AMBUSH.

Right: *Robert Hebras was one of the few survivors, but he was wounded in the attack.*

Below: *The sad remains of the villagers were mute testament to the Nazi atrocity.*

move was one of chaos and madness for the Germans. Although reprisals were still gruesome and swift, the authority of the Nazi occupiers was rapidly breaking down, as the French sensed that their own liberation was close; they realized that the Allied invasion in Normandy was more than a mere feint or a commando raid, and that the Germans' days were finally numbered. Ambushes, stolen petrol supplies, sabotage – the convoys rolling off that night were plagued by Resistance activity. Dickmann was informed, by his intelligence operatives, that a large group of partisans was operating under the cover of the Forêt de Brigueuil – a densely-wooded area outside of St Junien that covered the road to Bellac, the first stop en route that night for the division. He ordered that the special truck take a different route, one that passed near Oradour. It was a route that was to lead to disaster.

A staff car rolled ahead of the truck, and, in front of that, was a squad of heavily armed soldiers in an armoured half-track. According to plan, they would be in Bellac within thirty minutes, but the local Resistance was to mess up that timing. Planning an ambush on another unit fifteen miles away, the *maquisards* were stunned when they saw the headlights of the half-track glinting at the spot where they had hidden their weapons.

Instantly, plans for the scheduled attack were shelved and the Boche heading towards them became the primary target. The young and reckless Resistance men, seeking vengeance for years of Nazi oppression, launched an ill-prepared ambush. Grenades were hurled at the half-track, killing all of the German soldiers aboard, save one, who scrambled to safety down the road, his clothes smoking from the grenade explosions, but otherwise unharmed. The Germans who survived the grenades were cut down by a withering hail of Sten-gun fire levelled at them from the six partisans under the command of a *maquisard* known only as Raoul.

But the enthusiasm of the attackers far outweighed their military skill. Explosions from the half-track, followed by the car and

truck, spewed shrapnel and burning debris everywhere. That, and return fire, accounted for five of Raoul's men. When the shooting was over and the smoke had cleared, he was the only Frenchman left alive to witness the aftermath, illuminated as it was by the burning wrecks of the staff car and the half-track. The truck had not caught fire. Raoul feared that it might be full of wounded Germans, so he lobbed one more 'Gammon' grenade into the vehicle. When there was no sound from within, he pushed aside the charred and smoking

tarpaulin, expecting to be confronted with a pile of German corpses. Instead there were wooden boxes, each about the size of a shoe box and each tied down with leather straps. Placing his Sten gun to one side, he used a commando knife to slit the securing straps and open up one of the boxes. It contained gold. Raoul had stumbled on to half a ton of gold.

Risking everything, he hastily removed the gold and dug a shallow trench at the roadside near to the bodies of his dead comrades. One by one, he lowered the thirty-odd boxes into the hole, then covered them with earth. Knowing that if his dead comrades were identified, their families would be murdered by the SS, he poured petrol over each corpse, then over the wreckage in the road, before setting it all ablaze. Then Raoul leapt on his bicycle to ride away from the scene.

When General Otto Lammerding learnt that his *ratissage* loot had been stolen, from under his nose, by the French peasantry he fell into a terrible rage. The half-

RAOUL HAD STUMBLED ON TO HALF A TON OF GOLD.

ton of gold that he intended to use as an escape from the madness of war, to start a new and decent life, had fallen into the hands of the French partisans. He was ordering patrols to rake the countryside for his stolen loot, when he recived the second bad news of the day: Major Kampfe, his compatriot in crime, was reported missing and was presumed to have been captured by the Resistance. Kampfe was a close personal friend and his disappearance fuelled Lammerding's rage to new heights.

LOST PENSION FUND

He used Kampfe's disappearance and the attack on the gold convoy – divisional records to anyone who asked – to delay his progress to the front. He did not want to go blundering into a battle while his pension money was in the hands of these filthy peasants. Lammerding requested his superiors let him deal with the perpetrators of the attack on his convoy, and his wish was granted. He consulted Dickmann in a stormy meeting – attested to after the War by an SS telephonist who heard the row – in which he rebuked him for his decision to send the gold with so few soldiers protecting it, yet requested Dickmann's advice on ways of recovering it.

The Germans suspected that the men who had attacked the convoy the previous night came from the town of Oradour-sur-Glane. Not only was it the hamlet nearest the ambush site, but because an SS man who had been captured by the partisans, then managed to escape them, told Dickmann he was 'certain' that Oradour was one of the places where he had been taken as a prisoner.

Below: A monument was erected in Oradour to honour the people whose lives had been so brutally taken from them.

KILLING FOR LOOT

A notorious Nazi called Captain Kahn, who had distinguished himself by his unspeakable brutality in campaigns against partisans and civilians on the Russian front, was chosen to head the *ratissage* against the inhabitants of Oradour. But historians now believe that his troops were not bent on murder when they entered the hamlet – they believe the Germans simply wished to recover the stolen gold. However, when the peasants denied all knowledge of gold, the mindless brutality favoured by Captain Kahn was allowed to find expression in the soldiers' actions. Dickmann and

A LA MEMOIRE DE NOS CHERS MARTYRS

François LAMAUD 72 ans — Jean LAMAUD 47 ans — Marie LAMAUD 47 ans — Marie-Thérèse LAMAUD 4 ans — Marcelle ROBY 6 ans — Maurice ROBY 12 ans — François BRANDY 46 ans — Marthe BRAND 65 ans

Massacrés le 10 Juin 1944

Right: The Nazis were cruel in their reprisals against the French Resistance, but their actions, such as putting a fifteen-year-old boy before a firing squad, only strengthened the French in their guerilla war against the invaders.

Lammerding may have wanted to kill the entire village, but he would have preferred to trace his stolen loot.

Kahn's vengeance on the inhabitants of Oradour was as senseless, and as vicious as any massacre committed by German troops on the eastern front. He and his soldiers entered the town when it was crowded with people. Farmworkers, who had been toiling in the fields all morning, had returned for lunch when the first half-tracks clattered up the cobbled street, following the line of the railway that connected this village with others in the area. Citizens were rounded up into the church and barn, while a squad of soldiers, with fixed bayonets, moved through fields and outbuildings, chasing out villagers who had sought refuge there. One soldier, Heinz Barth, had actually been born a Frenchman, but had chosen the uniform of the SS. Now, he brandished a machine pistol as he told terrified villagers: 'You'll see the blood flow today!'

The people of Oradour watched and listened as the two hundred and fifty-four buildings, that made up their village, were destroyed by grenades and satchel charges of plastic explosive. Roger Godfrin, a fifteen-year-old boy, ran for his life. 'I told my two elder sisters to run and hide with me,' he explained later, 'but they refused. I somehow knew what the Boche were going to do to us that day.'

MASSACRE IN CHURCH

A white flare, fired high into the sky, was a signal to Kahn that all the villagers had been rounded up. The killing began. The old and infirm, who had been unable to march to the church, were shot where they lay in their little houses. Anyone who bolted for freedom was cut down by machine guns, positioned to cover the streets and fields leading away from the central village square.

When more than four hundred and fifty women and children were packed into the church, the Germans set off a huge charge of explosives, releasing billowing clouds of black smoke to asphyxiate the victims in the church. Then, the soldiers hurled hand

Above: *Roger Godfrin, the only child to escape the massacre, gives testimony at the military court trial held after the War.*

HE BRANDISHED A MACHINE PISTOL AS HE TOLD TERRIFIED VILLAGERS: 'YOU'LL SEE THE BLOOD FLOW TODAY!'

---

grenades through the windows; they opened the doors before raking the nave with machine-gun fire. The wooden pews and artifacts caught fire, and the flames consumed most of those trapped in the church, although falling masonry accounted for a number of deaths. Over two hundred men were locked in the barn where they were executed by gunfire. Dickmann, accompanied by two representatives of the hated *Miliciens*, the local militia allied to the Germans, began to question those who had escaped death, demanding they tell him where the gold was hidden. Whenever he met with a denial or ignorance, he shot the person.

In another barn, which had served as execution house to more village men, Jean Darthout was alive, wounded by bullets in his legs. He and three others got away, as did a woman who jumped from a window high above the church altar, although she received five bullet wounds. She hid in a vegetable patch where she was found, close to death, the following day.

THE AFTERMATH

Dickmann, beside himself with rage because the killing and burning had begun before he had had a chance to thoroughly quiz the inhabitants on the whereabouts of the gold, got drunk that afternoon on fine champagne, in the house of a Monsieur Dupic at the farthest end of the village. At seven o'clock that night, as the flames continued to lick at the ruins, Dickmann lurched drunkenly off to his master Lammerding to report that he had failed to find their booty of gold.

Oradour is, today, a ghost town, in ruins, untouched since that dreadful day of destruction. In the little museum that is also a shrine to the dead can be found broken spectacles, love-letters, wine-bottles – the minutae of ordinary peasant life. Many of the victims were burned beyond recognition and are buried in a communal graves in the church and the barns where they were killed. Six hundred and forty-two people died for a hoard of gold about which they knew nothing.

Robin Mackness, a man who once set up the Slumberdown Quilt Company in England, claims he knows what happened to the gold. He wrote a book, 'Oradour –

Above: *The shattered ruins are called the 'Martryd Village' by the French.*

HE SAID THE HISTORIANS WERE WRONG TO ACCEPT THAT ORADOUR DIED AS A MERE ACT OF REVENGE.

Massacre and Aftermath'. It is a book that many leading historians, including a Second World War French Resistance expert, M.R.D. Foot, believe is the true story of the events in Oradour. It details the story of the lost gold for Mackness was involved, quite by chance, in the story of Oradour long after the War was over.

Mackness met Raoul, the French partisan who had buried the gold before fleeing on his bike. In cohorts with business associates in Switzerland, Mackness was smuggling 'black' (illegal) gold across the border from France into Switzerland when he was introduced to Raoul in 1982. The Frenchman told his story, describing the ambush and the reasons why the Germans had selected Oradour as the guilty town. He said the historians were wrong to accept that Oradour died as a mere act of revenge.

Raoul also claimed that he had returned to dig up the hidden gold – stamped with the Nazi *Reichsbank* motif – and that he used some of it to start a business. Now, he wanted to move the remaining loot into a no-questions-asked vault in Switzerland. Mackness says he agreed to help the man, but the mission failed when Mackness was caught by French customs officers. They found twenty thousand pounds worth of the cargo in his car near Lyons in 1982 and he was jailed for twenty-one months.

A SECRET STORY

On his release, Mackness spent years researching Raoul's story and came to the conclusion: 'I don't know exactly what General Lammerding and Major Dickmann said to each other at that meeting on Saturday, 10 June, 1944, but I can guess with some accuracy, because of the story Raoul told me. During my twenty-one months in prison I came to realise that if Raoul's story were true, and there was nothing to finally persuade me that it wasn't, then he and I were probably the only ones alive who knew the secret story behind the events of that day.

'During Dickmann's meeting with his general, he would have learned that Lammerding knew about the ambush from the soldier who had got away. In the event of anything happening to the special unit, it was probable that survivors were given strict orders to report only to those officers most directly concerned – Majors Dickmann and Kampfe or General Lammerding.'

The principal players in the drama are dead and they never told their story while they lived. But it seems certain now, in the light of Mackness' experiences, that the people of Oradour-sur-Glane were killed for their innocence, because they were ignorant of the loot and could not lead a few greedy men to a stolen pile of gold.

HE AND I WERE PROBABLY THE ONLY ONES ALIVE WHO KNEW THE SECRET STORY BEHIND THE EVENTS OF THAT DAY.

Below: *A wooden cross marks a grave in the churchyard at Oradour.*

WILLIAM CALLEY
The My Lai Massacre

The US army sent untrained rookies to battle in foreign jungles. In some of these soldiers, fear turned to madness and, one dreadful day, the boys of Charlie Company became bloodthirsty barbarians in the village of My Lai.

America went to war in Vietnam in an ideological struggle, a clash between the systems of the West and those of Communism. Young American men marched on to die by the thousand in steamy jungles and snake-infested forests, their blood spilled in unprounounceable places by men with unpronounceable names. But theirs, so said their commanders at the front and the pencil pushers back home, was an honourable cause, fought honourably by the heirs of Patton, MacArthur and Eisenhower. They did not stoop to constructing booby traps of bamboo stakes, smeared with excrement, to cause wounds that immediately became infected, nor did they torture POWs, reducing them to automatons pleading guilt to their 'war crimes' as was the fate of so many Americans captured by the enemy. But any claim to unblemished American morality in Vietnam was cancelled on 16 March, 1968, in a tiny village called My Lai, situated in the Quang Ngai province, on the eastern side of the country where Vietnam bordered on the South China Sea.

On that day, the battle-hardened veterans of Charlie Company, of the American Division's 11th Light Infantry Brigade, entered the undefended coastal plain hamlet and murdered, in cold blood, some five hundred villagers – men, women and babies. In alternating bouts of heated frenzy and cool detachment, the troops of Charlie Company butchered the helpless Vietnamese civilians in an orgy of killing that matched the barbarous acts of the SS in Russia or Poland during the Second World War. Old men were thrown into ditches and bayoneted; pregnant women disembowelled; babies seen crawling away in a paddy field were tossed back on to the heap of corpses from which they had escaped, and were either shot or bayoneted.

The collective madness that engulfed Charlie Company has never been fully understood. Only one man, Lt William Calley, was ever punished for the crime – if three days in a prison can be called punishment. He was released after a presidential review of his case. Over and over again, the men who carried out the massacre, the headquarters' staff in the rear and the American people back home have debated those lethal hours of bloodletting. More than any other episode in that tragic war, My Lai became the symbol of madness, a place that revealed how the strain of war can change decent, respectful, worthy young men into blood-stained barbarians. In the elephant grass and paddy fields around My Lai, the American ideals of truth and justice were cruelly forgotten.

The people of Vietnam were peasant farmers caught up in an horrendous technological war. Napalm, phospherous bombs, Agent Orange defoliant – they had seen the

MY LAI BECAME THE SYMBOL OF MADNESS, A PLACE THAT REVEALED HOW THE STRAIN OF WAR CAN CHANGE DECENT, RESPECTFUL, WORTHY YOUNG MEN INTO BLOOD-STAINED BARBARIANS.

Opposite: *William Calley Jnr was to play a ghastly role in his country's war against Vietnam.*

Below: *Captain Medina with his lawyer, Lee Bailey, during a court recess.*

Yankees bring these terrible weapons to the placid villages and many were puzzled by the war. What had they done to incur such wrath from the foreigners?

But My Lai – and every other settlement – in the rural areas of Vietnam were seen by the US commanders as guerilla bases for the 'gooks' – the Viet Cong fighters who, with the support of the peasants, managed to stave off the mightiest nation in the world. Frustration, caused by the difficulties of fighting a hidden, secret peasant army, distilled a certain brutality within the American war leaders; they decided to employ scorched earth tactics, the burning and shelling of villages, as a method of driving the enemy into the open. By the time Charlie Company tramped into My Lai, seventy per cent of the villages in the Quang Ngai area had been razed during the scorched earth policy but anyway, in warfare, mercy is not a ready commodity. 'They were dinks,' said one American infantryman at the time. 'They were gooks, spooks, Charlie. They weren't human beings. We never looked at them as being other human beings. To us they became abstract, things that wanted to kill us, so we killed them first. And that went for the youngest son-of-a-bitch to the oldest. That's what Vietnam did to us.'

A HIGH BODY COUNT

Another soldier, Philip Caputo, a Marine, said that, while orders to kill civilians may not have been written down in black and white, the pressure from the Commanding General in Vietnam, William Westmoreland, on front line units to produce 'kills' was felt heavily by each soldier. Caputo said: 'General Westmoreland's strategy of attrition also had an important effect upon our behaviour. Our mission was not to seize positions or win terrain but simply to kill. Victory was a high body count, defeat a low kill ratio, war a matter of arithmetic. The pressure on unit commanders to produce corpses was intense, and they in turn communicated it to their troops. It is not surprising, therefore, that some men acquired a contempt for human life and a predilection for taking it.'

Charlie Company marched into My Lai with such feelings.

> TO US THEY BECAME ABSTRACT, THINGS THAT WANTED TO KILL US, SO WE KILLED THEM FIRST.

Below: *Captain Medina denied most emphatically that he had ordered a massacre of the people of My Lai.*

The company was initially composed of one hundred and fifty young men who were a typical cross section of the American boys who were sent off to fight in Vietnam. In August 1967, while in their training camp in the USA, they were warned that they may be shipped out to Vietnam at any time. For men like William Laws Calley, now a 2nd Lieutenant with the unit, but who had been a drifter in civilian life, the fun was about to start.

During their training at military installations around America, Charlie Company had gained a reputation as an above-average unit. They excelled in infantry tactics, in jungle warfare simulation exercises and in all-round Army expertise. But there were misgivings among some about the lack of discipline in the squad – and the character of some of the men in it. Michael Bernhardt, one of its number, had trained

force. Their target was a VC battalion that had operated in the region for years, despite massive shelling and the dropping of millions of tons of jungle defoliants intended to lay bare their strongholds. Now technology was abandoned, the human element was sent to quell the guerillas, and it came in the shape of Charlie Company, Alpha Company and Bravo Company.

By the middle of February, a pattern of failure and frustration had established itself among the Americans. Whenever these men fanned out to pre-designated areas, hoping to spring traps on the guerilla positions, they found the enemy had been forewarned and had disappeared. The

as a paratrooper only to find himself teamed up in a unit in Charlie Company. From the moment he joined, he had misgivings about the calibre of his fellow soldiers: 'Some of the men in the company were a little unusual. There were some who were cruel. They weren't the bottom of the barrel – they were men who would have been accepted for military service at any time. I wouldn't expect them to murder or torture anybody...'

BAD OPTIONS

Charlie Company landed in 'Nam', as the troops called it, in the second week of December 1967, and their area of operations was in the Quang Ngai province, a region of innumerable villages where the civilian population had been severely decimated by artillery fire and rapid airborne strikes. The peasants were told to deny their homes to the Viet Cong enemy if they wanted to save their own lives and their land. Sadly, these people were unable to refuse when the Communists chose to use their villages as guerilla bases – the guerillas also threatened loss of life and land. The peasants were trapped between the two opposing sides of the jungle war.

On 26 January, 1968, Charlie Company joined other units to forge a strike force of around five hundred men, destined for search-and-destroy missions in 'Indian Country' – the badlands of Quang Ngai where 'gooks' were said to be operating in

Above: *William Calley escorted from court after the guilty verdict. He faced a life sentence.*

Top left: *Attorney Edward MacGill talks to newsmen outside the court.*

bewildered rookies from America were left with nothing but the sounds of their own hearts beating in terror. And in February they began to suffer casualties – a man had half his left side blown away when he stepped on a booby trap. Ron Weber, Lt Calley's radio operator, took a bullet that shattered his kidney when the men of Charlie Company came under a fusillade of sniper fire by a riverbank. He was the first KIA – killed in action – member of the company and it had a profound effect on the men. Calley, leader of the first platoon of Charlie Company, should never have taken his men out into the exposed position that led to Weber's death. This was the first display of his ineptitude as a leader of men.

Daily Mirror

PINKVILLE

❝All of a sudden the GIs just opened fire on the women and children..I couldn't believe what I was seeing❞

5d. Friday, November 21, 1969 • No. 20,499

THE MASSACRE THAT CHILLED THE WORLD

A HORRIFYING story of a massacre by rampaging American troops stunned the world yesterday.

Hundreds of Vietnamese peasants were said to have been murdered in cold blood.

And a cameraman, 26-year-old Ronald Haeberle, produced grim pictures of slaughter in the tiny hamlet of My-Lai, which the troops called Pinkville—because the area was coloured pink on war maps.

The photographs show scenes of murder and other atrocities, and of soldiers throwing fuel into a blazing hut with the bodies of villagers lying nearby.

Cowering

One photograph shows women and children cowering in a door-way and holding their stomachs. All of them were killed, Haeberle claimed.

He said yesterday that he was appalled by the brutality.

"I never saw GIs act like that before," he said.

The chilling story came as a bitter blow to President Richard Nixon's bid to win fresh support for his war policies.

Haeberle said the GIs believed that the villagers were Vietcong sympathisers.

As the troops moved in, guns at

From RALPH CHAMPION in New York

the ready, a man holding two small children in his arms walked towards them.

Haeberle said: "They saw us and were pleading. The little girl was saying 'No, no.' in English.

"Then, all of a sudden, there was a burst of fire and they were cut down. One machine-gunner did it—he just opened up.

"There was no reaction from the guy doing the shooting. That's the part that really got me—the little girl pleading and they were just cut down."

"That was the beginning of the Massacre of Pinkville," the thirty minutes of killing that left the hamlet destroyed, according to Haeberle.

"A group of people—women, children and babies—were standing around," he said. "The machine-gunner was standing in front of them with his ammo-bearer.

"Then he opened up on all those

people in that big circle, and they were trying to run. I don't know how many got out.

"There was no mercy for some of those who survived the first hail of bullets, said Haeberle.

GIs went to inspect a pile of bodies. They found one man still alive.

"But a soldier leaned over and finished him off," Haeberle claimed.

He said: "There were two small children a very young boy and a smaller boy, perhaps four or five years old.

"A guy with an M16 rifle fired at them and the older boy fell over to protect the smaller boy

Then they fired six more shots. It was done very coldbloodedly.

"The GIs had opened fire on the women and children," he said.

"Besides that, they were shooting at people with grenade launchers. I couldn't believe what I was seeing."

Then Haeberle told of his horror as troops found a group of mothers and children. He said: "A GI grabbed one of the girls and started stripping her. They were keeping the mother away from protecting her daughter—she must have been around

Unarmed

THE SURVIVOR In Vietnam, Do Chuc, 40, who lived through the slaughter, said: "We thought such things were just part of the war."

❝North Vietnam cannot defeat or humiliate the United States. Only Americans can do that❞

President Nixon in a TV and radio report to the nation on Vietnam policy on November 4.

Continued on Back Page

Above: *The British news-papers carried banner headings about the dreadful war crime.*

'I THINK I PROBABLY SAW PEOPLE BEING TORTURED TO DEATH.'

Unfortunately it would not be his last and his weakness was to prove disastrous.

Calley, 5ft 4ins in height, who volunteered for army duty just days before he was drafted, was perhaps typical of the men the army got, rather than the men they wanted. By the time he was wearing fatigues, anti-war sentiments in the USA were being openly expressed, as draft dodgers fled to Canada, peace marchers burned the American flag and people spat on returning servicemen home on leave from the war zone. In such a climate, the army needed everyone they could get to keep the billion pound-per-month war going. In such a climate William Laws Calley, failed diner cook, car wash attendant, insurance clerk and railway ticket collector, became, when he was twenty-two years old, an officer in the United States Army. It is a proud office.

Patrols through the steamy jungle and paddy fields continued and Charlie Company continued to take casualties. They also took some prisoners, but now the one-hour lectures they had received on the Geneva Convention regarding the treatment of prisoners-of-war were entirely forgotten. The sharp end of war had already eroded their morals. They now, as a matter of course, indulged in the brutal, casual beating of suspects. Fred Widmer, who later came to be called 'Mr Homicide' for his acts in My Lai, recalled in the book 'Four Hours In My Lai', by Michael Bilton and Kevin Sim how decency was lost to the men in Charlie Company. He said: 'The first time I saw something really bad was the point at which we stopped taking prisoners. A couple of shots and they were done. As time went by, things were done, ears were cut off, mutilations.'

TESTING THE ENEMY

'One prisoner had his arms tied straight out on a stick... Lit cigarettes were put inside the elastic of the guy's pants and we watched him dance around because they were burning his ass. I think it was a bit of making him talk and a bit of venting our frustration. I don't remember what happened to them. The more it went on the more you didn't trust anyone. You didn't believe anybody because you didn't know who was who, you didn't know who the enemy was.

'As we went on, more and more prisoners would be executed. I would say it was a regular occurrence. I did abuse someone, a *papa san*, a prisoner. I found myself doing the same things that had been going on all along. We cut the beard off him – this was an insult. A *papa san* with a beard is considered as the wise man, and to cut off their beard was a real sign of disrespect to them. You found yourself punching them around, beating them up, trying to get them to talk. I never tortured anyone to death. I think I probably saw people being tortured to death.' It was a sad admission.

The distinction between peasant soldiers and peasant farmers was lost in this dirty war game. In the imagination of the over-burdened, terror-stricken soldiers of Charlie Company, the Vietnamese people were all 'gooks'. They all had to die.

THE MISSION

Charlie Company, reduced to one hundred and five men because of sickness, death and injuries, were informed on 15 March, that they were scheduled for a search-and-destroy operation on the following day. The village of My Lai, so Calley and his men were told, was the HQ for the elusive 48th Battalion of the VC that Charlie Company had been trying to find ever since their arrival in Vietnam. The men were told that the civilian population would be evacuated by the time the unit arrived at 7.30am. Anyone remaining would be gooks – VC – and they could deal with them in the way enemy soldiers are treated.

No written notes about the briefing of this operation exist. But the people who took part in it say that every man was under

> 'THIS WAS A TIME FOR US TO GET EVEN. A TIME FOR US TO SETTLE THE SCORE. A TIME FOR REVENGE.'

Below: *Ronald Haeberle, left, was a photographer. Michael Bernhardt (right) was a serving soldier. Both were to give crucial evidence at the My Lai trial.*

no illusions that the drift of the orders was simple: the destruction of all buildings, the slaughter of livestock and the taking of a few prisoners for interrogation. The rest would be consigned to hell. Sergeant Kenneth Hodges remembers his briefing thus: 'This was a time for us to get even. A time for us to settle the score. A time for revenge – when we can get revenge for our fallen comrades. It was clearly explained that there were to be no prisoners. Someone asked if that included the women and the children, and the order was: everyone in the village. They were not sympathetic to the Americans. It was quite clear that no one was to be spared in that village.'

The next day the men, equipped with phosphorus grenades, extra ammunition pouches, mortars and side arms were chop-pered out on board the green 'Huey' heli-

at the ready. They walked through the paddy fields, moving abreast in lines, and they were shooting. Courts would later be told that women were being cut down by automatic fire before the company had even reached the village.

Once in the village, all sense of American fair play, of decency and humanity, evaporated. The phosphorus grenades were tossed into the straw huts before the villagers were executed at point-blank range with single shots from the men's M.16 rifles. Private Allen Boyce, who, at the subsequent court hearings into the massacre, pleaded the Fifth Amendment on the grounds of self-incrimination, was seen to stab an old man in the chest with a bayonet, then shoot him in the neck. Then he shot another man and threw him down a well. He lobbed a grenade down after him just for good measure.

None of the villagers was armed. From hut to hut Charlie Company moved, grabbing terrified inhabitants by the hair, bellowing 'VC? VC?' at them and then murdering them in cold blood. The shouts

Above: *Survivors of the massacre claimed that they pretended to be dead so that the soldiers would not attack them any further.*

Right: *Ronald Lee Ridenhour witnessed the events. He was so shocked that he informed officials in Washington of the atrocity.*

copters for their appointment with death. The countryside of Vietnam appeared beneath them as a patchwork quilt of greens and browns, with the shadow of their own craft creating eerie silhouettes as they moved across the sky. With them, on the helicopters, were two men who would later be instrumental in confirming events in My Lai – a reporter and a photographer from the Army Information Unit.

THE END OF A VILLAGE

The people of My Lai were following their pattern of traditional village life that morning, as the gunships and troopships approached from the sky and a battery of huge 155mm guns trained their sights upon them. Children played with the pigs in the dirt, the women boiled water on open fires, men drifted off to work in the rice fields. At 7.30 the artillerymen opened fire, sending high explosive and white phosphorus shells into the hamlet. The inhabitants rushed for the crude underground shelters they had hewn for themselves.

Minutes later the barrage lifted and the men from Charlie Company approached the village, weapons fully cocked, grenades

of 'lai dai' – come here – filled the air as the villagers ran away and were mown down from behind. Groups of between twenty-five and forty people, who had huddled in ditches at the side of the road, were hit by bullets fired from the soldiers' automatic weapons.

At one point, Captain Ernest Medina, one of the brigade commanders overseeing operations that day, radioed Lt. Calley to enquire why his men had slowed up in their progress through the village. Calley replied that they had encountered a large group of civilians, some sixty in all. 'Take care of them,' came the reply from Medina. There was no question of asking for clarification of orders; Calley lined them up and from a distance of ten feet shot them dead with a machine gun, aided by two subordinates. Then he grabbed the dead women who had dived on their babies in a frantic gesture at saving their lives, rolled them off and shot the children. Women who made a break for the tree line in the distance were shot at with grenades and machine guns. One man fell when a grenade fired from a rifle penetrated his stomach but did not explode. He was shot through the head moments later.

Another fifty Vietnamese were found in a separate ditch at the far end of the village. Crouching low in the fetid water were old men, old women, young women and babies. Calley screamed at his men to put their M.16s on to full automatic and join him in the execution. Magazine after magazine was pumped into the screaming, writhing mass of humanity. The water in the ditch turned crimson with blood.

Animals fared no better. Pigs and cows were mutilated with bayonets, chickens beheaded. The keening of these animals stayed in some troopers' minds more than the screams of the massacred civilians.

MEN GONE BERSERK

On and on roamed the berserk killing machine that was Charlie Company. Children were despatched with clinical detachment. Widmer, Mr Homicide, killed a boy. 'When I shot him, I was sick to my stomach,' he said. 'Soon as I did it I realised: "My God, what have I done?" ' But there were worse, more heinous acts of depravity than Widmer's. Women were raped and mutilated, corpses beheaded,

some scalped. None of this stomach-churning slaughter affected the appetites of the killers – by mid-morning they had ceased firing and took a lunch break. But the killing was by no means over.

Prisoners who had been taken to a ravine for interrogation were blown away by rifles fired in their mouths. Another hundred civilians were killed in various actions around the village before the company bivouacked for a night when the soft sounds of the jungle were interrupted by the wails of those people who had not been finished off by the death squads. The flames from the burning remains of the villagers' homes lit the night sky.

Dawn revealed the ghastly reality of the previous day's action. Village men who had been working in the fields returned to find their entire families butchered. Weeping, they buried the dead in mass graves, mothers next to fathers, brothers next to sisters, aunts, uncles, cousins. Not one of

Above: *Chief Warrant Officer Hugh Thompson used his helicopter to evacuate wounded women and children from the scene at My Lai.*

'SOON AS I DID IT I REALISED: "MY GOD, WHAT HAVE I DONE?" '

---

these victims had fired a shot in retaliation at these soldiers from a foreign army.

Only one American had been killed by the preparatory artillery barrage.

My Lai had been a victory only for the dark side of war and in the cold light of that day, the US Army began to realise that it had lost forever in Vietnam its status of liberator and defender of freedom. Rumours of a massacre circulated with the speed of a disease among the ranks and soon the brass were being asked awkward questions by the Pentagon. It was only a matter of time before the American nation would know what took place.

Frank Barker, the commanding officer of the task force which mounted the assault on My Lai, and from whom many participants in the massacre say they received their orders to kill civlians, was never able to defend himself – he died three months later in a helicopter crash just as the furore surrounding the slaughter rose to fever pitch. The first the public knew of the mission he led came when a former soldier who was there, and who claimed he had not taken part in the killings, wrote letters describing the My Lai massacre to prominent politicians and government officials in Washington.

WHO GAVE THE ORDERS?

First army, then administration officials began to piece together what had occurred in My Lai. They were given photographs taken by Ron Haeberle, the cameraman included in the mission, who snapped many appalling scenes of the dead. He said, in his statement, that he thought the order to kill women and children must have come from higher up: 'Soldiers just do not start killing civilians in the mass they were doing. This was the first time I have seen something like this. I heard later that the General of the Americal Division praised the task force for the operation, but I take it that he was not told that most of the people killed were unarmed women and children.' His testimony was important.

Stanley Resor, Secretary of State for the army, refused at first to believe the

massacre story and the US government assumed that a strategic error had been made, insisting that any civilians who died in My Lai were caught in the cross-fire of a fierce gun battle between Americans and VC troops. However, when Resor received a confidential memo from his staff saying that all indications were of a massacre, he could no longer cover up. Investigators travelled all over Vietnam, South-East Asia and America interviewing the members of the disbanded Charlie Company. They testified with some honesty to their participation in the events of that day.

On 5 June, Calley was recalled to the USA and identified as the man who had thrown the baby back into the ditch. He was formally served notice that he was a

Below: *William Calley saluted in proper officer tradition after his trial ended in Fort Benning, Georgia.*

FINAL ★★★

DAILY NEWS

NEW YORK'S PICTURE NEWSPAPER ®

10¢

Vol. 52. No. 240   Copr. 1971 New York News Inc.   New York, N.Y. 10017, Thursday, April 1, 1971★   WEATHER: Partly cloudy and cool.

CALLEY GETS LIFE TERM

Lt. William L. Calley Jr. salutes as he leaves courthouse at Fort Benning after sentencing.—Stories on page 3

potential suspect in the mass murder enquiry. As it turned out, he became the scapegoat for *all* the men who murdered innocent people that day.

Several officers above him were charged with dereliction of duty and other soldiers charged with murder as the investigation-rumbled on. Five were eventually court-martialled, but only Lt Calley was convicted. There was no contrition from him in the dock; he spoke of his duty to kill the Communists, and how he had been a good soldier. It was, perhaps, this refusal to admit that his acts qualified as war crimes that made Calley the symbolic representa-tive of every man who, that day in My Lai, fired a round at an innocent human being.

While some American citizens sported 'Free Calley' stickers on their car bumpers, and anti-war protestors blamed the gener-als, and not individuals, for what happened, Calley was eventually Found Guilty of a 'speciman' twenty-two murders on 29 March, 1971 and sentenced to hard labour for life. Less than three days later, he was released from prison on the specific instructions of President Nixon and was allowed appeal. He never went back behind bars again, but spent the next three years under house arrest at his spacious apart-ment in Fort Benning, Georgia, surrounded by the comforts of home, his tropical fish, his dog and other assorted pets.

On 9 November, 1974 he was paroled a free man but was still a victim of war.

The war is long over, the names of the fifty-three thousand Americans who died there etched into the polished granite war memorial in Washington. For Calley, and for the others who were there that day, it is a war that is never over.

NIGHTMARE OF GUILT

Varnado Simpson is typical of the men who went into My Lai that day. Now forty-four, he has attempted suicide three times, seen his son die from a stray bullet – an act that, he believes, was from God as punishment for the massacre – and he gets through each day with endless bottles of pills. 'Yes, I killed. I cut people's ears off. I scalped. Cutting their throats, scalping. Yes, I did that. About twenty-five in all, I guess.

'I have nightmares, I constantly have nightmares of the children. I can go some-

where and see a face that reminds me of the people that I killed. How can you forgive? I can never forgive myself. I don't let anyone get close to me. The loving feeling was killed by My Lai.'

Calley is now a paunched, balding busi-nessman who works at his father-in-law's jewellery store in Columbus, Ohio. He is not on pills, does not need a psychiatrist, has never expressed remorse.

My Lai is never far from his thoughts, but he never, ever speaks of that village. Several years ago he wrote an autobiogra-phy in which he attempted justification for the madness that engulfed him and the men under him. He wrote: 'We weren't in My Lai to kill human beings, we were there to kill an ideology that is carried by – I don't know. Pawns. Blobs. Pieces of flesh. And I wasn't in My Lai to destroy intelligent men. I was there to destroy an intangible idea. To destroy Communism. I looked at Communism the way a southerner looks at a negro, supposedly. It's evil. It's bad.'

It is too late for Calley to learn from My Lai but perhaps not too late for mankind.

Above: *'Take care of them' was the chilling command from Captain Edwin Medina as Calley and his men moved through My Lai.*

How can you forgive? I can never forgive myself. I don't let anyone get close to me.

STALIN
Crime at Katyn Wood

In the secret heart of the forest, the proud officers of the Polish army were brutally executed. Even their murderers were so shamed by the killings that they denied the facts. But the dreadful truth of Katyn Wood has not remained hidden.

Adolf Hitler, leader of the German Nazi party, sent his emissary Joachim von Ribbentrop to Moscow in August 1939. He wanted a pact with Josef Stalin, bloodthirsty leader of the Soviet peoples. Yet Stalin represented the Slavic races that Hitler had threatened time and time again, in his manic outpourings, to destroy for ever. And Hitler, in Stalin's eyes, was a fascist running dog who persecuted without mercy the Communists. The former champagne salesman, von Ribbentrop, emerged after several days of diplomatic niceties with his Soviet counterpart, foreign minister Vyacheslav Molotov, to proclaim to a stunned world that a new non-aggression pact had been signed between the two former adversaries. This was *Realpolitik* at its most cynical – the conclusion of distasteful business for the mutual benefit of mutual enemies.

The West viewed the Molotov-Ribbentrop Pact as the precursor to an aggressive war of conquest in Western Europe. With the Soviets promising no action if Germany made 'territorial claims' upon her neighbours, strategists saw that Hitler had effectively silenced his biggest, and a potentially lethal, foe without a shot being fired in anger.

But what the West did not know – and would not find out until a month later, when the armies of Hitler launched their attack on Poland that was to start the Second World War – was that 'the pact' contained a secret clause that divided Poland between Hitler and Stalin. Between them, the two great dictators, who despised each other and the systems each represented, had forged a compact to ensure that this independent nation should cease to exist.

Betwixt the two, Poland became a vassal state. Polish Jews were soon earmarked for destruction by the Nazis, while under the Soviets, the intelligentsia and anti-Communist elements were rooted out for 'special treatment' by the NKVD, the forerunner of the KGB, but that concentrated less on espionage and more on mass murder and political suppression.

One other segment of Polish national life was hated by both sides – the officer corps of the army who were proud, disciplined, fiercely independent men.

It was precisely because they were troublesome to both dictators, that one of the most heinous crimes in wartime history went unsolved for over forty years. In 1940, four thousand Polish officers, from

Opposite: *Josef Stalin, the man of steel. He has more blood on his hands than any other man this century.*

Below: *Polish women weep over their loved ones after the bodies were disinterred.*

Bottom: *German investigators and Russian peasants exhume the vast mass grave.*

generals to lieutenants, were bound, shot in the back of the head and buried in massive lime pits, surrounded by thick fir trees that made up the forest of Katyn, near Smolensk in western Russia. All the victims had their hands tied to nooses around their necks which tightened when they struggled; all bore the same single-entry head wound testifying to methodical execution by shooting.

For close on five decades the crime at Katyn Wood was not acknowledged or admitted by the perpetrators. The Germans claimed the Russians did it; the Russians that the Germans were the perpetrators. It was not until the demise of the Soviet Union and the release of KGB files that the

Opposite, top: Molotov, seated, signs a non-aggression pact with Germany.

Opposite, below: The Russian admission of responsibility for the massacre at Katyn Wood made headlines all over the world.

Below: The villages of Poland were burnt and abandoned as columns of German troops marched through the conquered land.

truth was out – that the Poles were executed because they were the 'class enemy' of the Soviet people. On 13 April, 1990 Mikhail Gorbachev acknowledged his nation's culpability... forty–seven years after the day that Germany claimed her soldiers in the east had stumbled across the mass graves in the forest.

The events in the clearings of the Katyn Forest during those days of April 1940 make for grim reading. Even now the scars left by the liquidation of these proud warriors remain deep. This is the story of Stalin's massacre of the army allied to Britain – the nation for whom Britain went to war in the first place.

The tale, from being part of the first national army to stand up to Hitler to that degrading execution in the vast mass grave of the Katyn Forest, was a short one for these Polish officers.

IN THESE CAMPS WAS THE BEST OF THE BEST OF POLISH NATIONAL LIFE; EDUCATED, CULTURED, PASSIONATE MEN.

MOLOTOV INFORMED THE POLISH AMBASSADOR: 'THE POLISH STATE CEASES TO EXIST.'

First, Hitler's Stuka dive-bombers and armoured columns brought terror to the civilian population as Operation Case White – the conquest of Poland – began on 1 September. Hitler used a transparently lame excuse for sending his troops across the border; namely, that German soldiers in a frontier post had been killed by marauding Poles. Sixteen days later, with their cities in flames and their armies all but routed, the desperate Poles then had to endure an attack from their eastern neighbour, Russia. Again, it was a flimsy excuse that brought the Red Army pouring over the frontier. In reality, it was the fulfillment of the secret clause in the contemptible Molotov-Ribbentrop Pact.

Stalin camouflaged his military intervention by claiming his soldiers were being sent merely to protect the rights of Byelorussians and Ukrainians, living in Polish territory near the border with the Soviet Union. At 3am on 17 December, hours after Soviet troops, backed up by the death squads of the NKVD, were pouring across the border, Waclaw Grzybowski, the Polish ambassador to Moscow, was summoned to the foreign ministry where he was confronted by Molotov who, shedding all diplomatic niceties, informed him: 'The Polish state ceases to exist. We are aiding you to extricate your people from an unfortunate war in which they have been dragged by unwise leaders and to enable them to live a peaceful life.'

By 5 October, the day the last Polish units ceased fighting, Germany had two-thirds and the Soviet Union one third of Polish territory. Germany took close to six hundred thousand prisoners-of-war; the Red Army captured another two hundred and thirty thousand men. In the wake of the fighting troops came the SS battalions, on the German side, and the NKVD secret police units of Stalin. Both groups were remarkably similar in their initial actions. Round-ups began of intellectuals, university professors, nobles, known radicals, truculent churchmen; anyone who was deemed to pose the smallest threat.

Hitler had used the state as his instrument of repression and murder since he achieved power in 1933, but he was a mere apprentice in the art of massacre compared to Stalin. On his hands was the blood of *tens of millions* of people, murdered across

May, five weeks later. In the previous week the prisoners were rounded up in their camps at Kozelsk, Starobelsk and Ostashkov and taken in batches to railheads to board cattlewagons for unknown destinations. However, the four thousand four hundred Poles from Kozelsk camp were bound for the forest at Katyn.

HOPE OF REPATRIATION

Since their capture, these men had existed on meagre rations and were given few facilities to communicate with their families. During the days that they were herded into trains, they were given a better diet, kindling hope among them that they were

the vast steppes, shot in the cellars of the NKVD prisons, worked to death in the great Gulag archipelago that stretched over the frozen Siberian wastes. Stalin, in his Kremlin office, decreed that the vanquished Poles in the territory he now ruled would, indeed, receive no treatment that had not already been meted out in large measure to his own suffering masses. None could accuse the Man of Steel of inconsistency in his harshness.

Early in November, after a secret edict from Stalin, NKVD units began separating and moving out from a vast string of POW camps the fifteen thousand Polish officers whom they had captured. They were taken to camps set up in old monasteries that had perished under Bolshevism, all of them within Russian territory. In these camps was the best of the best of Polish national life; educated, cultured, passionate men, many of them reservists who had simply abandoned their comfortable lives to put on a uniform and fight for the land they loved.

Only a handful would ever see it again.

The NKVD were preparing for *mokrara rabota* – the agency's slang for bloodletting. For months the NKVD superiors at the prison camps, that held the Poles, had been sending reports back to their Lubyanka masters, suggesting that some of the Polish officers might be transported to Moscow, where they could be assimilated and indoctrinated into the Soviet system. But Josef Stalin had already made up his mind about their fate.

The liquidations at the Katyn Forest began on 3 April and did not end until 13

4 TODAY Saturday April 14 1990 ★★

RUSSIA BLAMES STALIN FOR WIPING OUT 15,000 POLES

50 YEARS ON, KATYN REVEALS THE TERRIBLE SECRET OF ITS 4,254 GRAVES

by OLGA CRAIG

THEY had been told they were going home. Instead, the train taking thousands of Polish prisoners of war across Russia was halted in a remote forest.

The 4,254 officers were ordered out and shot. Their bodies were buried in a mass grave.

The 1941 Katyn massacre was one of the worst outrages of World War Two, but the truth about it stayed an evil secret for 50 years.

It was not until yesterday that the Russians finally admitted Stalin ordered his secret police to slaughter the men and another 10,600 Polish officers whose bodies have never been found.

In an about-turn which stunned the world, Moscow Radio reported the discovery of new archive documents laying the blame firmly at the door of the NKVD, forerunners of the KGB.

Deserted

After the Poles, captured in the Nazi-Soviet partition of their country in 1939, failed to return home, Stalin insisted they had all deserted.

When the mass grave filled with 4,000 bodies was accidently found during forest clearance in 1943, he blamed the horrific mass slaughter on the Nazi invaders.

The Katyn area had changed hands during the war, controlled first by the Russians, then by the Germans.

Letters

But the Russians held the land in April 1940. The officers at Kozelsk camp were told they were being sent home.

They rushed off letters to loved ones saying they were coming back "via Katyn."

When the train jolted to a halt just outside the western town of Smo-

lensk the officers were still in a celebration mood.

Then the doors were wrenched open and they tumbled blinking into the sunshine.

One by one the bewildered men were dragged into a long line overlooking deep newly-dug trenches.

Side by side they stood, trying to make sense of it all.

An order was shouted and a battery of shots was fired. Four thousand Polish officers were shot in the back of the neck by Russian soldiers.

The remains of another 10,600 officers who were held in camps at Starobelsk and Ostashkov have never been found.

Now their families are demanding that the sites of their massacres are revealed too.

They say apologies, compensation and punishment must follow.

The Katyn Family, a Polish organisation for

relatives of victims, said it wanted criminal proceedings brought against anyone still alive who was involved.

The Katyn bodies, stacked in layers, were found by the Nazis in April 1943 and immediately used for propaganda against the Allies.

The Soviets always insisted the officers were killed in 1941 by the Nazis after they invaded the Soviet Union.

Historians

After the war, Poland's Communist governments continued to echo the Soviet explanation.

But most Poles and Western historians had long concluded that the massacre of "class enemies" was committed by the Soviet secret police on Josef Stalin's order in late April 1940.

As Soviet leader Mikhail Gorbachev's glasnost policies took hold, Soviet and Polish historians joined forces to review Katyn and other

historical "blank spots."

The Polish side confirmed Soviet responsibility last year, but a promised joint report never appeared.

The Soviets' formal admission of guilt has been timed to coincide with a three-day state visit to

Moscow by Polish President Wojciech Jaruzelski.

Radio Moscow's report, based on an official statement by Soviet news agency Tass, made no attempt to play down the outrage.

It said: "The Soviet side expresses its deep regret over the tragedy and deems it one of the most horrifying Stalinist crimes."

Justice

Accepting responsibility for the atrocity has been one of the conditions for improvement in relations between Poland and the Soviet Union.

Solidarity leader Lech Walesa last night called the Soviet admission "an act of moral justice which has been awaited for a long time."

He said: "It's good that criminals admit their crimes."

Foreign Secretary Douglas Hurd said yesterday: "We must remember the heavy weight of history there in Russia, the terrible things Stalin did, and the terrible things which were done to Russia during the last war.

"Gradually bits and pieces are coming out, a gingerly, as the Katyn story shows.

"But it must be right that it should come out and that they should admit the truth."

But the admission has come 50 years too late for some of the surviving families.

"I regret terribly that my mother could not live until this day," said Wanda Zadroza, whose father was murdered in the forest.

She added: *"But whatever happens now, it is good that the truth will be finally written in our history books."*

HORROR: Gruesome scene when the grave was found in 1943

TRUTH: The text of the official statement released in Moscow

IN April - May 1940 394 of the 15,000 or so Polish officers kept in the three camps were transferred to the Gryazovetsk camp. The larger part, however, were turned over to the NKVD administrations in the Smolensk, Voroshilovgrad and Kalinin regions and never mentioned in NKVD statistical accounts since.

The discovered archival material puts direct responsibility for the atrocities in the Katyn Forest on Beria, Merkulov and their henchmen. The Soviet side, expressing profound regret over the Katyn tragedy, declares that this tragedy is one of the gravest crimes of Stalinism.

Crusade of anguish

A BRITISH officer led the fight for truth.

Sir Frederick Bennett has shared the anguish of widows of the slaughtered Poles. He has seen the letters, now creased and stained with tears, the men wrote to say they were coming home.

Last night the retired major said: "I can't use the word delighted to describe how I feel. Somehow it wouldn't

seem appropriate, but you've no idea how relieved I am."

Former MP Sir Frederick 71, founded the Katyn Association with top Tory Airey Neave, later killed by an IRA car bomb. Sir Frederick had been approached by Poles he befriended as they fought side by side during the war.

"The letters are tragic," he said. "One soldier jubilantly tells his wife he is being sent

home by train – via Katyn."

The Russian admission has boosted Sir Frederick's fight for compensation for the 15 Katyn widows still alive in Britain.

Next Saturday he will unveil a plaque honouring the dead at the Katyn monument in Gunnersbury Cemetery, West London. It says bluntly: "Murdered by Soviet secret police under Stalin's orders."

indeed being repatriated to a new life. Each man received three dried herrings, half-a-pound of bread and some sugar. For some lucky few there was even an issue of Russian cigarettes to treasure.

The NKVD wanted the officers lulled into a state of well-being. Had there been any inkling of what lay in store for them,

Above right: *Red Cross and other officials are shown the grave site by a German officer.*

Above: *German Red Cross workers search for anything to help identify the corpses.*

Right: *Jewellery and military insignia found on one Polish corpse.*

'I AM NOW COMING TO THE CONCLUSION THAT THIS JOURNEY DOES NOT BODE WELL.'

there would have been bloody mutinies from the brave prisoners in the camps.

But once at the railheads, away from the camps and their comrades, the treatment changed immediately. New NKVD men were waiting to board them on the trains, men armed with clubs and dogs and with the vicious, four-sided bayonets issued to the NKVD. Many prisoners were severely,

gratuitously beaten as they clambered aboard the trains. Waclaw Kruk, a lieutenant, was one of the officers never to return from Katyn.

A diary was later found near his body in which he wrote down his feelings – feelings that must have been those of all the Poles as they moved out of the camps into the unknown. 'Yesterday a convoy of senior officers left: three generals, twenty to twenty-five colonels and the same number of majors. We were in the best of spirits because of the manner of their departure. Today, my turn came. But at the station we were loaded into prison cars under strict guard. Now we are waiting to depart. Optimistic as I was before, I am now coming to the conclusion that this journey does not bode well.' His diary was found in 1943, near a body tagged 'number 424'.

Another corpse, that of Major Adam Solski, also had a journal near it. Experts who examined it concur that the condemned man wrote the final words less than twenty minutes before he was murdered. It makes sad reading. 'Few minutes before five in the morning: reveille in the prison train. Preparing to get off. We are to go somewhere by car. What next? Five o'clock: ever since dawn the day has run an exceptional course. Departure in prison van with tiny cell-like compartments; horrible. Driven somewhere in the woods, somewhere like a holiday place. Here a detailed search. I was relieved of my watch, which showed 6.30am, asked for my wedding ring. Roubles, belt and pocket knife taken away.'

Journey's end for the soldiers was the Katyn Forest, sloping towards the Dnieper River and not far from the town of Smolensk. Here, gigantic pits had been dug in the sandy soil, within the leafy groves of fir trees and silver birch. Not far from the pits was a building known innocently as The Little Castle of the Dnieper; in reality it was a summer house, a dacha, of the local NKVD and now served as the headquarters of the killing squads who were-about to despatch the cream of the Polish army to their deaths.

A SINISTER JOURNEY

The prisoners were taken from the rail cars in what were known as the *chorny voron* – the police buses, which had been a grim feature of Soviet life for years. A glimpse of one of them, in a Soviet street, was enough to send shivers up the back of any innocent observer. These buses were divided into separate steel compartments, each little bigger than a kennel, in which the Polish officers were kept until their turn for execution arrived.

Only one man, a Polish professor, Stanislaw Swianiewicz, saw the killing of his comrades and lived to tell the tale. He was on board one of the trains, but was locked into a compartment by himself, only to be transported to Moscow to face charges of espionage. But he witnessed the scene as his fellow officers were led to their deaths. In the authoritative book 'Katyn' by Allen Paul, the professor was quoted: 'wondered what kind of operation it was. Clearly, my companions were being taken to a place in the vicinity, probably only a few miles away. It was a fine spring day and I wondered why they were not told to march there, as was the usual procedure at camps. The presence of a high-ranking NKVD officer, at what was apparently the simple transferal of several hundred prisoners from one camp to another, could be explained if we were actually going to be handed over to the Germans. But, in such a

case, why these extraordinary precautions? Why the fixed bayonets of the escort? I could think of no reasonable explanation. But then, on that brilliant spring day, it never even occurred to me that the operation might entail the execution of my companions.' Such an act was unthinkable.

Execution at the pits was to be cold, methodical, production-line work. Machine guns or grenades could not be used; people would run, there would be survivors, there

WHY THESE EXTRAORDINARY PRECAUTIONS? WHY THE FIXED BAYONETS OF THE ESCORT? I COULD THINK OF NO REASONABLE EXPLANATION.

Above: *A German officer holds up the decomposing jacket of a murdered Polish officer.*

would be an immediate panic among those prisoners awaiting transport from the train to the execution place. Instead the NKVD agents used 7.65mm Walther German-police issue pistols, considered by handgun experts to be the best pistols of their type in the world. NKVD squads would be waiting with fresh guns to replace those that overheated in the ceaseless slaughter, others with mounds of ammunition.

Once taken, one by one from the buses, the individual prisoners were bound in a particularly gruesome manner – a manner perfected over the years by the murderers from the NKVD. The victim's hands were first tied behind his back, then a second cord was tied over his head at neck level

> AS THE LAST OF THE SAND WAS BULLDOZED OVER THE GRAVES, THE BUTCHERS PLANTED TINY BIRCH SAPLINGS ON TOP.

Below: *Joachim von Ribbentrop announces details of the cynical pact with the Soviet Union to carve up Poland.*

with the victim's greatcoat pulled up over it, like a shroud. From the neck the cord was passed down the prisoner's back, looped around the bound hands and tied again at the neck, forcing the arms painfully upwards towards his shoulder blades. Any attempt to lower his arms put pressure on the neck; repeated pressure would result in strangulation.

One by one these brave, noble men were led to the edge of the pits. Many bodies bore the brutal stab-marks of the four-squared NKVD bayonets – proof that, agonizing though their bonds were, they had attempted to struggle for their lives. Each one was despatched with what the Germans called the *Nackenschuss* – a shot through the nape of the neck which caused instant death and limited blood loss. This method had been perfected in countless

> I SENSED A PROPAGANDA EXERCISE. I HATED THE GERMANS. I DID NOT WANT TO BELIEVE THEM.

cellars and execution dens of the NKVD over many years of Stalinist terror.

They fell into the pits and were stacked like cordwood, one on one, in layers of twelve before lime was sprinkled over them and tons of sand bulldozed back over them. But the tons of sand helped to press the corpses down and literally 'mummify' them as the body fluids and blood was squeezed out. The lime failed to work, so when the advancing Germans discovered the graves of Katyn, the thousands of corpses were well preserved.

On and on went the killing. The NKVD butchers fuelled their spirits with massive quantities of vodka consumed in the nearby dacha. Twelve hours a day for six weeks, nothing but the sound of gunshots echoed from those lonely groves until, finally, four thousand one hundred and forty-three victims were dead. As the last of the sand was bulldozed over the graves, the butchers planted tiny birch saplings on top.

The remaining eleven thousand Polish officers, held in other camps were liquidated at killing sites deeper in Russia. Their graves have never been exhumed but there has since been an admission from the now-defunct Soviet Union that all these Polish officers had been annihilated on Stalin's personal orders.

But Katyn was, and remains, the most significant massacre site. It was a known site, yet for decades it was surrounded by lies and duplicity. It justified a deep-rooted hatred of the Soviet state felt by all the people of Poland.

FRIENDS TURN ON EACH OTHER

It was only a matter of time before those arch-enemies, Hitler and Stalin, were to turn on each other. Hitler had written in *Mein Kampf* that *Lebensraum* – living space – in the east was his single greatest goal. On 22 June, 1941 he set out to achieve that with Operation Barbarossa, the attack on the Soviet Union.

Fifteen hundred miles away from Stalingrad, in the dacha where the NKVD executioners planned the killing of the Polish officers, the soldiers in Lt Col Friedrich Ahrens' signal regiment were having a relatively quiet war.

Ahrens and his men had a strange foreboding about Katyn Wood, the site of the dacha. They heard rumours from the local people about NKVD executions taking place there, and hidden graves. Then, in February 1943, when the German 6th Army was routed at Stalingrad, a wolf unearthed bones in one of the mass grave sites. Ivan Krivozertsev, a local peasant, approached Ahrens and formally informed him of the dark secrets of the forest. NKVD secrecy and planning had not been hidden from the sharp eyes of the peasants.

Below: *British prisoners-of-war were taken to the site. The Germans wanted to convince the Allies that the massacre was a Russian act.*

The Germans prepared to tell the world of the slaughter of the Polish officers, and Dr Gerhard Buhtz, a professor of forensic medicine from a leading German university, was put in charge of the exhumation and examination of the grave pits, which were opened in early March. For ten weeks the stink of rotten flesh and Egyptian tobacco – the Germans smoked it to mask the smell of the dead – mingled with the scents of moss and pine sap as the murdered men were disinterred and laid out. Some prisoners-of-war, American Lt Col John Van Vliet among them, were taken by the Germans to witness the massacre site. He recalled: 'I sensed a propaganda exercise. I hated the Germans. I did not want to believe them. But after seeing the bodies there, piled up like cordwood, I changed my mind. I told the Allies, after the War, that I thought the Soviets were responsible.'

On 13 April, 1943, at 3.10pm Berlin time, the German radio network officially announced the finding of the graves where

Above: *Skulls revealed that execution had been carried out with high-calibre weapons used at point-blank range.*

the Polish officers had been 'bestially murdered by the Bolsheviks'. The world was stunned into silence, choosing to believe that the report was fabricated by the Nazis. But the Polish government-in-exile, in London, had long harboured suspicions that the Russians had copious amounts of Polish blood on their hands.

On 15 April the Soviets counter-attacked, claiming: 'In launching this monsterous invention the German-Fascist scoundrels did not hesitate at the most unscrupulous and base lies, in their attempts to cover up crimes which, as has now become evident, were perpetrated by themselves. The Hitlerite murders will not escape a just and bloody retribution for their bloody crimes.' Three separate commissions were invited to visit Katyn by the Germans. The first was entirely German, the second composed of scientists and forensic experts from Switzerland, Belgium, Hungary and Bulgaria, and the third was entirely Polish. The evidence was mightily in favour of the German viewpoint. Although the ammunition was German, records from the manufacturing plants showed it to be batches sold, before the war, to Lithuania only to be siezed later by NKVD police units.

The Soviets claimed that the men were killed by the advancing Germans in 1941 – although not one document with a date later than 6 May, 1940 was ever found on a single corpse. The bayonet thrusts on the bodies were of the four-cornered NKVD type. The fact that there were no insects found in the graves indicated cold weather-burial, not summer as the Soviets claimed – and besides, all the murdered soldiers wore heavy winter clothing.

But their military fight against Hitler had, for the Allied commanders, at that time, a higher priority than a search for justice and truth. Churchill remarked in a cabinet meeting: 'We must not take sides in the Russo-Polish quarrel.' He assured Stalin in a secret communique that he would do his personal best to silence Free Polish newspapers in London over the affair, while he told Wadyslaw Sikorski, the prime minister in exile: 'If they are dead, nothing you can do will bring them back.' President Roosevelt in the White House preferred to believe the Soviet leader's explanation that the murders were committed by the Nazis.

Right: A priest prays at the graveside for the Polish officers, who were denied the blessing of the last rites at their death.

Below: Row upon row of corpses, all tied in the same fashion, were pulled from the mass burial pit.

When the Soviets finally overran the Katyn territory in their great push westwards, they took the opportunity to cover up the massacre of the Polish officers. The ponderously-named 'Special Commission for Ascertaining and Investigating the Circumstances of the Shooting of Polish Officer Prisoners by the German Invaders in the Katyn Forest' went into overdrive to persuade the world that the murders were the work of the Gestapo and *Einsatzgruppen*. The Soviets stuck to their story that the officers had been murdered a year later than was actually the case – and

as stories of German atrocities throughout the War began to emerge from all over Europe, there were plenty of people willing to believe the Soviets.

By the time the triumphant Red Army rolled into Berlin in May 1945, the myth that the Germans were responsible for Katyn was firmly planted around the world and in the satellite Eastern European nations over which, in Churchill's words, the Kremlin had drawn an 'Iron Curtain'. In Warsaw, the monument to the dead at Katyn blamed the Nazi invaders; at Katyn itself the inscription read: 'To the victims of Fascism. Polish officers shot by the Nazis in 1941.' The Soviets were operating under the maxim that Hitler once used – tell a lie big enough for long enough and it will metamorphose into truth. They denied any reference to the atrocity if it cast suspicion on their forces. Ewa Solska, the daughter of Major Solski whose diary was found on him, wrote 'killed at Katyn' in the box on her university application form which asked for information about her father. She was expelled for giving this information.

Even at Nuremberg, the great post-war trial for the crimes of Nazism, the Soviets were able to bluff the tribunals that Katyn was a Nazi crime. They could not bluff the Polish people, nor the many people around the world who were slowly caming to realise the enormity of Stalin's crimes.

It wasn't until 1990, at a ceremony inside the Kremlin, that Gorbachev, in keeping with the spirit of his Glasnost reforms, handed President Jaruzelski of Poland a box containing NKVD documents and other files, showing that the officers had indeed been murdered by the NKVD. These revealed that the executioners themselves had been 'liquidated' under Stalin's orders, then buried at an unknown grave site somewhere in Russia. Only four hundred prisoners-of-war from the entire Polish officer corps survived, to be taken to Moscow and other Russian cities, where they proved to be willing Communists. Gorbachev labelled the massacre 'one of the gravest crimes of Stalinism'.

Was it all a big mistake on Stalin's part? Some historians believe that his orders may have been 'misinterpreted' by underlings. Stanislaw Mikolajczyk, the successor to Sikorski in London for the Polish government-in-exile, has his view and claims a Soviet bureaucrat secretly gave him the following interpretation of what happened:

A MISSINTERPERATED ORDER

'Early in 1940 the Red Army sent a staff officer to find what Stalin planned to do with the Polish officers. A planned swap in which the officers would be turned over to the Germans in return for thirty thousand Ukrainians had just fallen through. The Ukrainians were Polish Army conscripts captured by Germany the previous September, and were interned in two camps in eastern Poland. The Germans, at first agreed to the exchange but backed out at the last possible moment, telling the Soviets to take the Ukrainians and keep the Poles. Then came rumours in Moscow that the Ukrainian conscripts and the Polish officers would be organised into special units of the Red Army. Senior commanders were aware of such talk but had nothing specific to go on. The staff officer was sent to get Stalin's clarification. The staff officer saw Stalin and briefly explained the problem. Stalin listened patiently. When the staff officer finished, Stalin supplied him with a written order. Such orders were common, often requested by subordinates as a matter of self-protection. In this case, said the informant, Josef Stalin took a sheet of his personal

Above: *The soil in Katyn Wood served to preserve the bodies. This was of considerable help when investigators came to identify bodies and buried papers.*

STALIN TOOK A SHEET OF HIS PERSONAL STATIONERY AND WROTE ONLY ONE WORD ON IT: 'LIQUIDATE'.

stationery and wrote only one dreadful word on it: 'Liquidate'.

The staff officer returned the one-word order to his superiors, but they were uncertain what it meant. Did Stalin mean to liquidate the camps or to liquidate the men? He might have meant that the men should be released, sent to other prisons, or to work in the Gulag system. He might also have meant that the men should be shot, or otherwise eliminated. No one knew for sure what the order meant, but no one wanted to risk Stalin's ire by asking him to clarify it. To delay a decision was also risky and could invite retribution. The army took the safe way out and turned the whole matter over to the NKVD. For the NKVD, there was no ambiguity in Stalin's order. It could only mean one thing: that the Poles were to be executed immediately. That is, of course, exactly what happened.'

Many thought Stalin, the Man of Steel would never have had it any other way.

ADOLF HITLER
The Holocaust

Germany was humiliated by defeat after the Great War. Despair gripped the nation. But one man promised to return their pride. All they had to do was build gas chambers and kill, kill, kill. So began the most shocking mass murder in the history of the world.

They met at a place called Wannsee, a charming suburb of Berlin with ornate houses and tree-lined streets that looked out over the lake which gave the area its name. It was 20 January, 1942 and the Reich had reached the zenith of its military victories. The swastika flew over the Russian steppes, over the Balkans and Greece, France, the Low Countries, North Africa, Poland, Norway and Denmark. The wars of conquest had ended in total triumph for Hitler's armies so it was now time to put into effect phase two of his doctrine of Nazism. It was time to implement 'The final solution of the Jewish question in Europe'.

No one who followed the rise of Adolf Hitler and his Nazi party was surprised that he had a diabolical plan to eradicate the Jews. Hitler began his campaign of state terror against the Jews soon after he came to power. He passed the infamous Nuremberg Laws which stripped them of property, valuables, human rights and political power. Then he organized the terror, which culminated in the *Kristallnacht* – 'Night of Broken Glass' – in 1938. This involved the destruction of synagogues and Jewish property throughout Germany during a frenzied night of state-sponsored terror. But Hitler wanted 'a final solution to the Jewish problem' and this was to become a euphemism for mass murder.

That is why at Wannsee, in 1942, SS and Gestapo chiefs, led by Reinhard 'Hangman' Heydrich, gathered at a villa, once owned by a Jewish merchant, to plot the logistics for the collection, transportation and extermination of millions of men, women and children who had no place in the new world order. The men in black and grey uniforms drew up blueprints for the greatest state-sponsored murder in history.

Since the Nazi seizure of power Hitler had experimented with mass-killing techniques at euthanasia laboratories where the mentally ill were killed in gas-vans or by lethal injection. When his armies overran Poland and parts of Russia he walled his Jewish enemies up in medieval-style ghettoes where he allowed starvation and disease to kill the people locked within. In Russia his *Einsatzgruppen* – action squad – SS commandos shot hundreds upon thousands of Jews and other 'undesirables'. But

Opposite: Adolf Hitler salutes to his followers. Rudolf Hess stands before him.

Below: An SA stormtrooper ensures that shoppers follow the order on the sign: 'Do not buy from Jews'.

HOESS TOOK A SCIENTIFIC DELIGHT IN SOLVING THE PROBLEMS OF MASS MURDER.

NAMES LIKE TREBLINKA, SOBIBOR, BUCHENWALD, DACHAU AND AUSCHWITZ HAVE NOW BECOME HOUSEHOLD WORDS FOR EVIL.

HITLERDEUTSCHLAND – EIN ZUCHTHAUS

200000 POLITISCHE GEFANGENE IN KONZENTRATIONS-LAGERN, GEFÄNGNISSEN UND ZUCHTHÄUSERN

Right: *Survivors stand in bitter mourning for their lost families at the memorial erected to the victims of the Holocaust.*

it was not enough. These methods were cumbersome, slow and inefficient. Hitler was determined to bring some Henry Ford principles into the process of mass murder – a production line of death camps that would dispatch the unfortunates at the greatest speed possible.

Herman Goering, Luftwaffe chief whose first task for the Nazis was setting up the dreaded Gestapo, had Heydrich's orders in a letter, written six months before the Wannsee conference. It read: 'I hereby charge you with making all necessary preparation with regard to organizational and financial matters for bringing about a complete solution of the Jewish problem in the German sphere of influence in Europe.'

Heinrich Himmler, head of the SS; Heydrich, head of the SD, the security arm of the same organisation; Adolf Eichmann, and Ernst Kaltenbrunner, Heydrich's successor after his master was assassinated in Prague in May 1942, can be said to be the architects of the final solution. They built the concentration camp network which spanned all conquered Europe.

Names like Treblinka, Sobibor, Buchenwald, Dachau and Auschwitz – Auschwitz, particularly, the most infamous human abbatoir of them all – have now become household words for evil. In these death factories Jews from all over Europe made a one-way trip to hell. And not only Jews – Gypsies, Poles, Slavs, Russian prisoners-of-war, intellectuals, revolutionaries, homosexuals and artists who did not fit into the racial or political mould were despatched. A new breed of men and

Below: *Former inmates of the death camps show the identity numbers tattooed on their arms by the Nazis.*

Below, right: *A synagogue in ruins after the attacks against Jews during Crystal Night, 9 November, 1938.*

Hoess took a scientific delight in solving the problems of mass murder. Auschwitz, like the other camps, had used mass shootings and hangings to eradicate the inmates, but this was precisely the inefficiency that Hitler and the SS wanted to do away with. Later in 1942 a gas made from prussic acid, that was used to kill rats and mice in German factories, was deployed for the first time against Russian POWs. The Russians were led into a long, sealed room, the walls of which were lined with showers. But the shower faucets were false and the plugholes sealed. And then they heard the rattle of hard crystals dropped on to a wire grating above their heads, before the room filled with a gas, called Zyklon-B, that was released from the crystals. They were all dead within twenty minutes.

At the far south end of the Birkenau camp two massive gas chambers and adjacent crematoriums were built by the inmates themselves. Trains arriving at a railhead were greeted by one Dr Josef Mengele – about whom more will be said later – the SS doctor who became supreme arbiter of life and death within the electrified fences of Auschwitz. With a flick of his riding crop he dictated the fate of the inmates. Those who were to work for the Reich on starvation rations, under the blows of whips and cudgels, marched one way while their elderly parents, sisters brothers, and toddlers walked the other.

women, inconceivable in their cruelty, depraved beyond belief, were recruited to administer these extermination centres.

Such a man was Rudolf Hoess, commandant of Auschwitz where the final solution was to reach remarkable heights of cruel efficiency. Hoess, at his peak, oversaw a complex where men and women lived in filth, were worked like dogs and finally executed when they were no longer of any use to the Reich. Auschwitz, and its annexe camp of Birkenau, where the gas chambers and crematorium were situated, were two miles from the main town of the same name in southern Poland. Every day, in the camps, twelve thousand people died in the gas chambers before being burned in the massive crematorium.

Loudspeakers told the latter group that they were heading off for showers and delousing before they were to be re-united with their families in barracks. In fact, they were taken to a long wooden hut where they were told to strip and place all valuables in a locker. Then their heads were shaved and the hair collected in giant sacks by other prisoners. Then they were marched in to the giant shower-rooms. But these showers did not flow with water and the naked humiliated prisoners were actually in giant death chambers

BODILY REMAINS

Afterwards, men working for the *Sonderkommando* or special commando squads set up by their SS overlords, entered to disentangle the corpses and remove the gold fillings from their teeth. The bodies were then pushed into the ovens, the ashes raked out and spread over nearby woodland or dumped in the River Vistula.

Cruel and inhuman as the killing machine was, death was often the one thing the living prayed for. The camp culture spawned a sadistic, warped race of guards who took morbid pleasure in the mistreatment of their charges. Irma Greese, the 'Blonde Angel of Hell' from Belsen, delighted in flaying women's breasts with a knotted whip. Karl Babor, the camp doctor

Below, left: Inmates were used to clear away the bodies of their fellow prisoners and feed them into the crematoriums of the death camps.

Below: Hitler with his mistress, Eva Braun, relaxes in his mountain retreat at Berchtesgaden.

of the Gross-Rosen camp, amused himself by burning new-born babies on an open fire. And at Auschwitz there was the infamous Dr Mengele, whose smiling face was always there to greet the new arrivals as they arived in stinking cattle wagons.

Mengele was a doctor of medicine who betrayed his Hippocratic oath each and every day, while convincing himself that his scientific research in the camp was carried out on mere 'subhumans'.

His greetings at the train ramp for the Auschwitz arrivals had a dual purpose; he

sorted out those who could work for the Reich before their deaths, and he sought blue-eyed twins so he could perform experiments aimed at cloning the Nordic supermen which Hitler had decreed were to be the new chosen race. And all the while he salved the shreds of his wicked conscience by claiming that *he* was saving life for the future! Yet all experts concur that on his personal orders alone some four hundred thousand Jews were executed. Prisoners, infected with lice, TB, typhus, typhoid and grotesque medieval-style infections – infections bred by the poor diet and insanitary conditions which prevailed in the camps – existed in a twilight zone of brutality that could only be eased by death. When they were no longer able to function in the armaments plants and quarries adjacent to the camps they were eliminated. The gold teeth from the corpses were sent to the Reichsbank in Berlin, their hair was

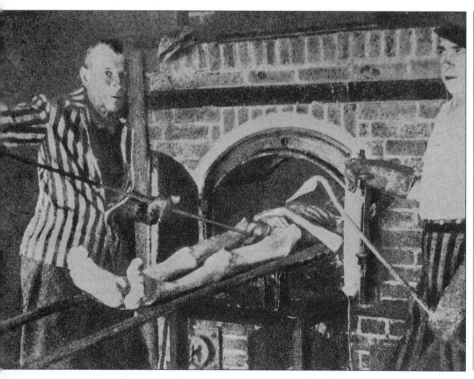

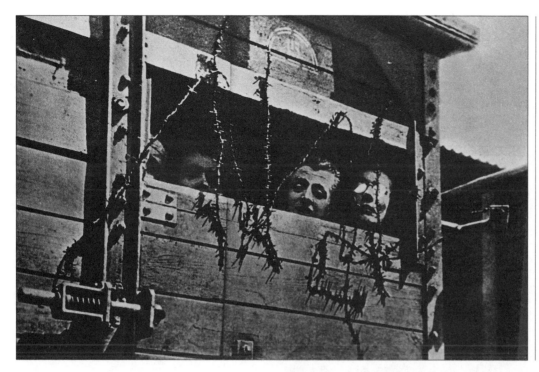

Left: *Those destined for the concentration camps were packed into cattle trucks for the journey.*

Below: *Grim photographs are both proof of, and constant reminders of, the barbaric slaughter of millions of innocent Europeans in the Nazi camps.*

used to stuff mattresses for troops on the Russian front and the fat from their bodies was processed into soap. Such was the efficiency that Adolf Hitler demanded and got from his loyal servants of evil.

Adolf Eichmann, like Mengele, was a classic product of the twisted logic of Nazism. He saw no evil in what he was doing, believed that he was a 'good soldier' who was only obeying orders. Day after day, as Germany was losing the war on all fronts, this son of an accountant re-routed armaments trains headed for the troops with supplies and rations, and cancelled returning hospital trains, so he could use the rolling stock to clear out the ghettoes of Eastern Europe and thus feed the furnaces at the extermination camps. But he was not flamboyant, more a grey bureaucrat and his cruelty only became public after the collapse of the Reich in May 1945.

During the height of the Holocaust one thousand trains a week were criss-crossing Europe with people destined for the camps. In the middle of 1943 fully a third of all camp inmates assigned to work details died each week. Survival became a matter of co-operating with the SS – by getting a job in a camp clinic, becoming a block captain, seizing any chance to please the SS – anything that might bring a chance of survival. The overwhelming horror of these places was belied by the cynical slogan

Himmler placed above the entrance gates of the camps – *Arbeit Macht Frei* – Work Brings Freedom. It was a bitter lie.

Not the campswere not the only disgrace. As brave German soldiers fought valiantly at places like Stalingrad and Kharkhov, the *Einsatzgruppen* squads were forever besmirching Germany's name with their mass executions. Herman Graebe, a German civilian engineer working on road-building in the Ukraine, witnessed just such

HIMMLER PLACED ABOVE THE ENTRANCE GATES OF THE CAMPS – *ARBEIT MACHT FREI* – WORK BRINGS FREEDOM.

Above: *Allied soldiers guard captured Nazi leaders during the massive war crimes trial held in Nurnberg after the defeat of Nazi Germany*

Right: *Adolf Eichmann was finally captured in the Sixties. He pleaded his cause before a weary Judge Moishe Landau (far right).*

Opposite, far right: *Herman Goering in prison, awaiting sentence, during the war crimes trial.*

'WITHOUT SCREAMING OR WEEPING THESE PEOPLE UNDRESSED, STOOD AROUND IN FAMILY GROUPS, KISSED EACH OTHER, SAID FAREWELLS, AND WAITED FOR THE SIGN FROM THE SS MAN WHO STOOD BESIDE THE PIT.

a scene. He wrote: 'Without screaming or weeping these people undressed, stood around in family groups, kissed each other, said farewells, and waited for the sign from the SS man who stood beside the pit with a whip in his hand. During the fifteen minutes I stood near, I heard no complaint

or plea for mercy. I watched a family... An old woman with snow-white hair was holding a child of about one in her arms, singing to it and tickling it. The child was cooing with delight. The parents were looking on with tears in their eyes. The father was holding the hand of a boy about

ten years old and speaking to him softly; the boy was fighting back tears. The father pointed to the sky, stroked his head and seemed to explain something to him.

'At that moment the SS man at the pit started shouting something to his comrade. The comrade counted off about twenty people and instructed them to go behind the earth mound. Among them was the family I have just mentioned. I well remember a slim girl with black hair who, as she passed me, pointed to herself and said: 'Twenty-three'. I walked around the mound and stood in front of a tremendous grave. People were closely wedged together and lying on top of each other so that only their heads were visible. Nearly all had blood running over their shoulders from their heads. Some were lifting their heads and moving their arms to show that they were still alive. The pit was nearly two-thirds full and I estimated that it contained about one thousand people. I looked at the man who did the shooting. He was an SS man who sat at the edge of the narrow end of the pit, his feet dangling into it. He had a tommy-gun on his knees and was smoking a cigarette. The people, completely naked, went down some steps which were cut in the clay wall of the pit and clambered over the heads of the people lying there, to the place to which the SS man directed them. Some caressed those who were still alive and spoke to them in low voices.'

Above: *A rogues' gallery of Nazis. From the left, Propaganda minister, Goebbels; SS Chief, Himmler; Deputy Hess and Hitler, all together at a pre-War rally.*

A DIGNITY IN DEATH

Towards the end of the war the Nazis increased their frantic efforts to wipe out the estimated nine million Jews within the conquered lands. One of Eichmann's greatest coups in the desperate days of 1944, as the Russians were advancing rapidly throughout Eastern Europe, was to get the Hungarians to hand over half of their population of eight hundred thousand Jews. They were all gassed at Auschwitz – an achievement which Eichmann said gave him 'intense satisfaction'.

Most Jews and other Nazi victims went nobly and quietly to their deaths. They had a dignity which mocked the brutality of their tormentors, yet the Nazis liked to crow that the Jews had continually shown their weakness in life's struggle because they did not fight, but meekly submitted to

the sword. But in reality, there was nowhere for these tortured people to go if they had escaped, no prospect of victory over well-trained and well-fed guards.

The Nazis did not have it entirely their own way. At Sachsenhausen many guards were killed in an armed breakout and, in 1944, the Jewish Underground in Auschwitz placed explosives in one of the ovens and blew it to smithereens. The most impressive display of defiance came when Hitler ordered the destruction of the Warsaw Ghetto in 1944. Here, the Jews of Poland were housed, but they refused to be taken to the trains and, with smuggled weaponry, killed SS men.

It took half-a-division of SS men with full anti-tank and armour facilities to rout the defenders in four months of bitter fighting. It cost the Jews fifty-six thousand lives and kept valuable German soldiers away from the fight on the front. Such were the twisted values of Nazism – the defenceless Jew always considered more of an enemy than guns, tanks and armed soldiers.

While they may have salved their own consciences about what took place in the death camps, with the excuse that they were 'only obeying orders', the guilty men

In the west, it was the Americans and the British who liberated the Nazi charnel houses of Belsen and Buchenwald.

Josef Kramer, the commandant of Belsen, was puzzled by the fury of the ordinary British squaddies who liberated his fiefdom; could not understand why they were so belligerent towards him. At his

'I DIDN'T FEEL ANYTHING TOWARDS THE PRISONERS. I RECEIVED ORDERS TO KILL THEM AND THAT'S WHAT I DID. SURELY YOU CANNOT EXPECT A SOLDIER IN WARTIME TO DISOBEY AN ORDER?'

Left: *His charm and determination gave Adolf Hitler a terrible power over a nation broken by their defeat in the Great War.*

Below: *A unique picture of Jews arriving from a train at the Czech concentration camp of Terezin.*

knew what awaited them. Auschwitz personnel fled the camp just twenty-four hours before Russian troops arrived to liberate the wretches left inside. The air was still heavy with the sickly-sweet stench of burned human flesh and the crematorium, the one that was still working, had corpses awaiting burning. In a warehouse barracks that the Nazis dubbed 'Canada' because of its vast size, the Russians found a mountain of human hair, gold teeth, underwear, clothing and jewellery – the last destined for the Reichsbank. Hoess had planned to demolish Auschwitz but he left it too late. But Franz Stangl, commandant of Treblinka, managed to destroy his camp. The only testimonies to its existence are the tracks of the railway line, and the deep green hue of the grass over the rich, fertile ground that, in places, is twelve feet thick with human bonemeal.

from Swiss banks the names of wealthy Jewish clients, now used the same good offices of secrecy for their own flight.

REFUGE FOR THE WICKED

South America, where military regimes had long expressed solidarity and sympathy with the Nazi cause, was a favourite destination. Eichmann headed for Argentina; Mengele for Brazil; Joseph Schwammberger, commandant of the concentration camp at Przemysl, to Argentina; Alois Brunner, designer of the mobile gaswagons and the brains behind the deportation of forty-six thousand Greek Jews to Auschwitz, made it to Damascus where he still lives under Arab protection.

Justice for those left behind was swift; many camp guards were executed within days of liberation. The Nuremberg trials despatched many more, including Kramer and Greese. But it was left to people like Simon Wiesenthal, who lost eighty members of his family in the Holocaust, to become the conscience of the world – to ensure that mankind never forgot what revolting crimes had taken place.

Wiesenthal is an old man now, his shoulders slightly hunched and his hair grey, but his eyes have lost none of their fire. He survived the death camps and has pledged his life to tracking down Nazi war criminals and bringing them to justice. His determination and diligence led to the capture of Eichmann in Argentina and the deportation from South America of Lyons Gestapo chief Klaus Barbie.

Weisenthal's small office in central Vienna is called the Documentation Centre and it is a museum to the memory of the slain. Wiesenthal calculates that as many as fourteen million were claimed by the Nazis in their war of racial purification. From 22 March, 1933, when Dachau, twelve miles from Munich, opened as the Reich's first concentration camp, until the Allies liberated the entire network, Hitler had managed to dispose of over a third of Europe's Jews. Wiesenthal inflates his figures because of the special 'actions' undertaken in Russia, the enormity of which has still to be fully understood.

Even now Weisenthal is still hunting, still ceaselessly bringing to justice those who perpetrated mankind's biggest mass

trial after the war for his crimes at the Natzweiler, Auschwitz and Belsen camps, he told those judging him: 'I didn't feel anything towards the prisoners. I received orders to kill them and that's what I did. Surely you cannot expect a soldier in wartime to disobey an order?'

But Kramer and all the others – Babor of Gross-Rosen, Mengele of Auschwitz, Heinrich 'Gestapo' Mueller, Adolf Eichmann, Franz Stangl of Treblinka – all tried to escape. They knew that their blind obedience to orders would never stand up in a courtroom whose loyalty was not to Adolf Hitler. Using the services of the ODESSA – the Organization of Former Members of the SS – they drew on secret Swiss bank accounts to pay for new identities and lives in distant lands. Much of the money came from the victims whose butchery they had overseen in the camps. It was a final bitter twist of irony that the SS who had tried, without success, to wheedle

Above: *The power-mad, ruthless Herman Goering started the Gestapo to enforce the more ruthless aspects of Nazi rule.*

Opposite, top: *The Nazis sought to whip up antisemitic feelings with crude caricatures meant to persaude citizens that the Jews were untrustworthy.*

Opposite, below: *Gold was extracted from the teeth of concentration camp victims. The gold was boxed and delivered to the Reichsbank.*

murder. He cannot stop, not while revision-ist historians and neo-Nazi sympathisers, now on the rise in Europe and Russia, are busy denying that the Holocaust with its death camps ever happened.

Wiesenthal would die a happy man if he could get Alois Brunner, the committed Nazi, who, in 1965, said to reporters from a German newspaper: 'I'm glad! I'm proud of what I did. If I could have fed more Yids into the flame I would. I don't regret a thing – we were only destroying vermin.'

Simon Wiesenthal finds some solace in the report he will give to the Lord when it is his time to depart. this life

'We will all be called before the Lord for judgement,' he said, 'and we will be asked to give an account of ourselves. One man will say: "I became a tailor". Another will say: "I became a doctor". Yet another will say: "I became a jeweller".

'And I will be able to say: "I did not forget you…".'

SADDAM HUSSEIN
Genocide of the Kurds

The proud warrior tribes refused to bend before a dictator. So he took his vicious revenge. He sprayed them with terrible chemicals, which brought painful and dreadful death to thousands of Kurdish men, women and children.

Long before the high-tech war visited on his country by the Allied forces during Operation Desert Storm, Iraqi despot Saddam Hussein had waged another, dirtier kind of war within his own borders. His enemy was the fiercely proud Kurdish tribe, the hot-blooded warrior race that, for centuries, has longed for an independent Kurdistan that would span the border between Iraqi and Turkey.

Hussein assembled one of the greatest war machines ever seen, before it was dismantled during the Gulf War. In manpower alone, he had the fifth largest army in the world, plus a formidable array of conventional and chemical weaponry. He needed to ensure that he was the master of the Middle East, but part of his arsenal was developed for a plan every bit as sinister as that hatched by the Nazis. He wanted to wipe out the Kurdish people once and for all. In 1988, before his power was stunted, if not altogether broken by the West, Saddam unleashed his appalling chemical weapons against innocent Kurds, as part of his blueprint for their destruction, killing over four thousand people. Against his arch-enemy Iran, whom he fought for eight futile years, he used mustard gas.

His chemical weapons programme was one of the most advanced in the world. America and the former USSR had long ago curbed production of chemical weapons, which are forbidden under United Nations rulings and the Geneva Convention. The world did not want to repeat the horrors of the First World War where chemical weapons had been used. But Saddam, who does not yet have nuclear power, realised that massive stockpiles of lethal gas would give him a huge military advantage over his enemies.

The technology has not changed a great deal in the years since the Great War – the poison is still delivered by shell and bomb – but the chemical content has. Saddam developed hydrogen cyanide, a particularly lethal gas which causes death within two seconds when inhaled. He also developed new versions of the nerve gases Tabun and Sarun, pioneered by the Nazis during the Second World War, though never used by them. A very small quantity of either of these gases, will, when it falls on skin, cause a human being to go into convulsions, followed very quickly by death.

THE MEANS OF DESTRUCTION

The technology needed for his gas programme was provided by the Western

Above: Refugees wend their way to Piranshar in Iran to escape the persecution of Saddam Hussein in Iraq.

nations that would one day be arrayed against him. As long as Saddam Hussein was keeping the forces of Islamic fundamentalism on the opposite bank of the Euphrates River, the West was happy to give him the means for mass destruction. Western companies salved their consciences by saying that much of the hardware necessary for the production of chemical warfare was for fertilizer factories

HUSSEIN ASSEMBLED ONE OF THE GREATEST WAR MACHINES EVER SEEN, BEFORE IT WAS DISMANTLED DURING THE GULF WAR.

Opposite: *Saddam Hussein, the butcher of Baghdad. He is feared because of his ruthless quest for power in the Middle East.*

within Iraq, although any scientist knows that it is but a small step from producing fertilizers to poison gas. Some were merely duped. The Phillips Petroleum Company of Bartlesville, Ohio, was one of the American companies whose security system failed it. Phillips, through a Belgian unit, had sold the Iraqis five hundred tons of a complex chemical called thiodiglycol, believing it was for use as a fertilizer. Combined with hydrochloric acid, it makes mustard gas. An understanding of what had been made from their shipment to Saddam hit company executives, when in 1988, they read news reports of Iranian soldiers on a remote battlefield coughing up their lungs, and of corpses covered with horrifying chemical burns.

Germany, Holland and Britain also sold chemical weapon technology and raw materials to Iraq, enabling Saddam to build up stockpiles which sent shivers through his bitterest enemy – Israel. Israel, long before Saddam unleashed his Scud missiles on her cities during the Gulf War, feared a pre-emptive strike with chemical missiles.

When Saddam used his mustard gas on the battlefield, it was in limited quantities and aimed strategically at Iranian command posts and communications centres; rarely was it used against civilians. But in his war against the Kurds he had no such qualms.

The Kurds were, and still are, Saddam Hussein's biggest political problem. They are not impressed by his bellicose speeches, the huge pictures of him that adorn public buildings and stretch over highways; nor do they pay anything other than lip-service to his regime. The Kurds, armed and virtually autonomous in the northern, mountainous region of Iraq were to be taught a tragic, final lesson that they would never be able to forget.

In March 1988, while the war against Iran was still raging, Saddam received reports from his battlefront commanders that Iranian troops, aided by Kurdish guerillas, had seized control of the Kurdish town of Halabja. The town was based near a vital hydro-electric dam. The information that Iranian troops were involved gave Saddam reason to unleash his deadliest poisons on the innocent civilian population. Yet he must have known that there were, in fact, no Iranian troops in the town because they left within hours of taking it.

Above: *A tent city, housing thousands of refugees, has arisen on the Turkish border as people flee the repression of Iraq.*

THE DEADLY CLOUD

The sun was just rising over the mountain peaks when the first shells began to rain down on Halabja. But unlike the high explosives that the citizens had heard falling along the battlefront with Iran, there was only a soft 'plop-plopping' as the shells dropped without detonating. But soon palls of sickly yellow, white and grey gas began to swell and swirl, drifting like fog through the streets, creeping into every nook and cranny. Saddam had uncorked his evil weapons of Tabun, cyanide gas and mustard gas on the townspeople. Chaos and hysteria reigned as panic gripped the

townsfolk. They ran through the streets, their skin peeling from their faces when the mustard-sulphur clouds hit them. If they ran into Tabun fumes, they were dead within seconds. A shocking photograph recorded a poignant death during this morning of carnage. It shows a mother clutching her dead baby in the main street, both killed as they ran in a frantic attempt to seek cover from the deadly clouds.

By the afternoon the donkeys and goats in the fields were all dead, the vegetation wilted. The sickly smell of rotten onion mixed with burned garlic hung over the air. It was as if someone had gone in with a giant fly spray and snuffed out the life of all the citizens. Only those who had been working in remote fields survived. In all, four thousand men, women and children died on that tragic day in Halabja.

Caglayan Cugen, a Turkish doctor who treated survivors who had burns and respiratory problems, said: 'They talked of seeing these blue canisters from which the gas came. There was an odd odour first and then they remember burning in their eyes, blurring the vision as the eyes smart and itch. There followed uncontrollable bouts of sneezing and vomiting. Their breath shortens in the hours following inhalation of the mustard gas as the inflammation

spreads, swelling the internal lining. Many of them had horrible blisters on their necks, chests and thighs, causing huge patches of skin to fall off. Large lesions broke out over their genital areas. They were young and old but they were not soldiers. The youngest I treated was a baby of four months. I could not help but ask what they had done to deserve this.'

Iraq, usually so adept at controlling press coverage within its borders, made the mistake of allowing Western newsmen and foreign relief workers into the area. The pictures of thousands of bodies without any visible wounds whatsoever belied Bagdhad's statement that they had been killed in the cross-fire of shelling between the forces of Iraq and Iran. It was several months before the Iranian leadership admitted to the use of the gas as 'a necessary measure to drive out the Iranian infidels'.

BUT SOON PALLS OF SICKLY YELLOW, WHITE AND GREY GAS BEGAN TO SWELL AND SWIRL, DRIFTING LIKE FOG THROUGH THE STREETS.

Left: *Hussein may not be a good man, but he is a devout one.*

Below: *Iranian soldiers cower in their trenches during the war against Iraq.*

Above: *Mustard gas killed this woman and her baby during a chemical warfare assault against Kurds in the town of Halabja.*

'DESPITE THE FACT THAT SADDAM HUSSEIN COMMITTED MAJOR ACTS OF GENOCIDE, THE FACT IS, IRAQ GOT AWAY WITH IT.'

A UN official who saw the carnage said: 'The bodies were lying in doorways, in streets, around tables set up for lunch and in cellars where people mistakenly sought shelter from the heavier-than-air gas. Many other corpses were found on the roads leading from the town, where residents had failed to outrun the spreading cloud. The victims seemed to have died quickly, as there were few signs of a struggle. The streets were also littered with the bloated carcasses of cows, dogs, cats, sheep and goats.

A TERRIBLE OUTRAGE

'Some thirty of the victims were flown for treatment at hospitals in the West, which confirmed that several poison gas agents were indeed deployed on the innocent civilians. Iranian doctors I spoke with, who treated those refugees who managed to cross over into their country, said their tests had shown that the gases were mustard, cyanide and nerve gas. The injured suffered from the most appalling burns and their lungs were all but destroyed.'

Western diplomats in Iraq were appalled at the outrage. 'Halabja was inexcuseable in every sense of the word,' said one indignant emissary at the time. 'The use of poison gas against enemy troops is bad enough, but to use it against civilians, and especially your own citizens, is quite unbelieveable.'

Steven Rose, a neurobiologist at Britain's Open University, said: 'Despite the fact that Saddam Hussein committed major acts of genocide, the fact is, Iraq got away with it.' There was no pressure to bring this criminal, a man who clearly and openly violated the rules of war, to justice. No less than six separate United Nations missions went to Iraq before and after the Halabja massacre, each time collecting more information on Iraqi chemical assaults. One team was despatched to the town of Halabja and reported: 'This warns us that the use of chemical weapons against the Kurdish people may become more frequent, even commonplace.'

Saddam was well satisfied with this awesome display of his maniacal power. He had cocked a snook at world opinon, defied

Above: *Western newsmen recorded the murder of Kurds in the streets of Halabja.*

Left: *A frantic and terrified people trekked great distances to reach the safety of Turkey.*

the conventions of the West – which he viewed as weak – and had dealt a stunning blow to his Kurdish enemies. He felt so good about it that he decided to do it again.

TWO BLEEDING NATIONS

In August 1988 the guns finally fell silent in his war with Iran. It had bled the two nations white, ravaged their economies, decimated their populations and cemented the politics of hate for generations to come. But the onset of peace for Saddam meant he could turn more manpower – and more chemical weaponry – against his Kurdish foes.

By the end of August Saddam had moved some sixty thousand troops into the Kurdish region, together with battalions of

'IT IS ONE THING TO BE BLOWN TO PIECES, BUT IT IS ANOTHER TO BE KILLED BY A WEAPON YOU CANNOT HEAR AND CANNOT SEE UNTIL IT IS TOO LATE.'

SEFIKA ALI IS NOW TWENTY-FOUR, BUT HER PRETTY FACE IS WRINKLED LIKE THAT OF A MUCH OLDER WOMAN. THIS IS THE RESULT OF CYANIDE GAS BURNS.

Right: *The presence of their despot cannot be forgotten by the Iraqi people. His image looms on billboards across the country.*

helicopter gunships, tanks and artillery; all effective methods of launching the gas blitz he intended. The first village to die under his onslaught was Butia.

Sefika Ali is now twenty-four, but her pretty face is wrinkled like that of a much older woman. This is the result of cyanide gas burns which happened when her village was wiped out in a gas attack launched from the air. She fled to Turkey with her husband and three children. They were the lucky ones. Left behind were an estimated two thousand neighbours, who suffered the same death as the victims of Halabja. She said: 'I was cooking breakfast for my family when I heard the sound of aircraft. I heard bombs whistling and the next thing I knew was that there was something wrong with my eyes. I started to vomit almost immediately. I knew what was happening. We had heard what had happened at Halabja. My family suffered the same effects. We all drank a lot of milk and then we ran. We ran to get as far away as we could. We know that not many made it out.'

REFUGEES FACING DEATH

In the refugee camps along the Turkish border the hordes of burned, coughing survivors of the latest outrage swelled the hospital tents as medical teams from the West struggled to cope with the aftermath of Saddam's attacks. The refugees were called *Pesh mergas* by the Iraqis – 'Those who face death' – and there were no apologies from Bagdhad for the fate of these victims. It was estimated that along with Butia, two other villages in the Danhuk region of the country were hit, but these suffered few fatalities because the populace were working in far-away fields and strong winds blowing that morning helped disperse the gas away from them.

Kurdish refugees, almost one hundred thousand of them, moved into Turkey, where they were accommodated in insanitary, overcrowded tented camps along the border. Massad Barzani, one of the Kurdish leaders, appealed to the UN to press Iraq not to use any more chemical weapons. He said: 'It is one thing to be blown to pieces, but it is another to be killed by a weapon you cannot hear and cannot see until it is too late. In the name of humanity, the governments of the west must come together to end this nightmare we are suffering. Many women and children who were gassed, but who survived the onslaught were later murdered by Iraqi troops to prevent them from spreading information about what dark deeds were done to them. It is a crime against humanity we are talking about here.'

In September the Reagan administration in America finally woke up to the atrocities, realising that Saddam Hussein was becoming more of a liability than an ally in the region. On 8 September, the State Department said it had obtained proof of the latest outrages and called them abhorrent and unjustifiable. Secretary of State George Shultz met with Iraqi's Minister of State for Foreign Affairs, Saddoun Hammadi, to tell him that the continued use of poison gas would severely affect the future of US - Iraq relations.

Hammadi insisted, despite all the evidence to the contrary, that no civilians had this time been killed by gas. Gwynne Roberts, a British television journalist, had himself collected soil samples from some of the villages he visited in Kurdistan and had them analysed by a laboratory. The laboratory report showed significant traces of mustard gas in the samples.

The anger felt by Shultz and other officials was supported by the American people and there was a popular feeling that maybe America had, after all, been backing the wrong horse in the long struggle between Iran and Iraq. Senator Claiborne Pell, a Democrat from Rhode Island, introduced a bill calling for sanctions against Iraq for what he called its 'anti-Kurdish genocide'. There was a period of an arms embargo after more UN evidence of the chemical atrocities was revealed, but sadly trade soon resumed again.

Below: *The strange dual role played by Saddam Hussein is revealed in this photograph: the militant warrior is also a pious man of God.*

ALFREDO ASTIZ
The Dirty war

The new military government promised to return Argentina to its former glory. Instead, they unleashed a gang of sadists upon the nation – men like Astiz who led a dirty war of murder and torture against his own people.

Between 1976 and 1982 Argentina waged a full-scale war within its own borders. The enemy were classified as those who acted or sympathised with anyone who had a viewpoint other than that espoused by the government. The military junta in power called their reign of terror The Process of National Reorganization. But it was a fancy euphemism for mass murder, whereby people vanished into human slaughterhouses, were tortured there and murdered. Coffee-bar socialists, mothers of radicals, babies of dissidents, long-lost cousins of intellectuals who had once read a Communist pamphlet – these were the victims of this 'Process' known to the rest of the world as the 'Dirty War'. And working within this state terror machine were individuals like Lt Alfredo Astiz.

THE CLEANSING OF SOCIETY

Astiz was a member of the officer corps which took upon itself the burden of 'cleansing' Argentinian society. The military throughout South America has had a long and shameful history of interference in civilian governments but none more so than the Argentinian army. Military rule has dominated Argentina and between 1930 and 1982, the only civilian government to last its full term was that of Juan Peron. For years, after no less than six coups, the men in uniform guided – or rather, misguided – the fortunes of this land rich in minerals, farming and cattle.

When the sophisticated and cosmopolitan citizens of Buenos Aries woke up to the clatter of tank tracks on the cobbled streets of their gracious city on 23 March, 1976 they did not panic; they had, after all, heard and seen it all before.

This time, it was a General Jorge Videla telling the people that massive unemployment, inflation running at eight hundred per cent and a resurgence of left-wing violence had driven the military to grab power. Videla, having seized the radio and

television stations, put it to his people like this: 'Since all constitutional mechanisms have been exhausted, and since the impossibility of recovery through normal processes has been irrefutably demonstrated, the armed forces must put an end to this situation which has burdened the nation. This government will be imbued with a profound national spirit, and will respond only to the most sacred interests of the nation and its inhabitants.'

There was a tone of determination in his voice which made the people of Argentina embrace rather than shrink from military government. Leftist guerillas had, since 1966, been rampant in the countryside, murdering, kidnapping, committing atrocities among the civil population. The country was on an inexorable slide into anarchy as it battled against these guerilla groups, most notably the *Ejercito*

Above: *The Mothers of the Plaza de Mayo defied arrest, torture and even death as they paraded before the junta headquarters in frequent mass demands for the return of their children.*

Opposite: *The raffish, handsome exterior of naval officer, Alfredo Astiz, hid the ugly torturer of the death squads.*

Revolucionarioa del Pueblo – People's Revolutionary Army – and the *Montoneros*. There is a school of thought which says that, had these terrorists not created a climate of fear which brought the army out of its barracks and put the torturers in government, fifteen thousand innocent people might still be alive today. But Videla and his henchmen were welcomed by a tired population who were glad to listen to his ideas on The Process of National Reorganization.

While Videla uttered platitudes and told his own people, and the world at large, that his government would respect human rights, his machinery of terror was being secretly assembled, soon to be unleashed on an unsuspecting population.

The officer corps of the Argentinian armed forces saw themselves as an elite group, imbued with the national spirit as no other body within Argentina. Many proved very happy to oversee the terror required to reorganize their countrymen, but none

Above: *Dagmar Hagelin, a young Swedish woman, disappeared after the junta kidnapped her.*

Opposite, top: *Alfredo Astiz enters the court where he faced charges regarding the disappearance of Dagmar Hagelin.*

Opposite, below: *Ragnar Hagelin stands outside the military court after he was notified of the acquittal of Astiz who was charged with the disappearance of Hagelin's daughter.*

more so than Alfredo Astiz, who was to develop into an infamous torturer, his name forever linked with this shameful period of Argentina's sad history.

THE DEATH SQUADS

Astiz, a handsome naval lieutenant of wealthy parents, drank deeply from the poisoned chalice offered by Videla. He believed the General when he said that the enemies of Argentina were within its own frontiers. With the zeal of a Spanish Inquisition cardinal, Astiz helped enthusiastically in the founding and operation of ESMA, the Navy Mechanics School in Buenos Aries, which was nothing more than a human abbatoir hiding behind the name of an institute of marine engineering.

Thousands of victims of 'The Process' were brought as prisoners to the Navy Mechanics School where they were subjected to the most horrific beatings and torture, then taken out for execution; very few made it back to families and loved ones. It was not only the navy that organized this kind of torture centre; the army, air force and police were also involved, each one vying for glory as they hunted the 'enemy within'. They operated in squads called *patotas* and they each found places to turn into centres of hell, where they dragged the dissidents who, they believed, were destroying the Argentinian way of life and its cultural traditions.

One of the few victims to survive after Astiz and his men had captured her has a horrifying story to tell. Twenty-seven-year-old nursery school teacher Isabel Gamba de Negrotti was pregnant when she was seized at gunpoint by the *patotas* and taken away in a green Ford Falcon car – a make of car that came to be indelibly linked with death – and dumped in the Navy Mechanics School. The young woman described her ordeal: 'They took me to a room after arrival where they kicked me and punched me in the head. Then they undressed me and beat me on the legs, buttocks and shoulders with something made of rubber. This lasted a long time. I fell down several times and they made me stand by supporting myself on a table... While all this was going on they talked to me, insulted me, and asked me about people I didn't know and things I didn't understand.

The junta was going after the children, the students and the trade unionists, the journalists and the teachers – all were swept up in the vortex of terror. Victims were picked up at random and, as these citizens were bundled into the death cars, they would yell out their names and addresses to passers-by who, in turn, would inform families that their relations had joined *los desparecidos* – 'the disappeared'.

Often the military disposed of their victims by pushing bodies, dead or alive, out of helicopters as they flew over rivers. Almost five thousand people are believed to have met their deaths on these 'NN' – 'No-Name' – flights. Others were buried in mass graves on the pampas or in remote corners of country churchyards, buried without name, sacrament or ceremony.

Inside the Navy Mechanics School, Astiz and other torturers preferred even crueller forms of death and practised bizarre forms of torture and sadism against men, women and children.

Many people who came across Astiz compared him to Dr Josef Mengele, the Nazi death camp doctor at Auschwitz. Astiz who was fair-haired and blue-eyed,

'I pleaded with them to leave me alone, otherwise I would lose my baby. I hadn't the strength to speak, the pain was so bad. They started to give me electric shocks on my breasts, the side of my body and under my arms. They kept questioning me. They gave me electric shocks in the vagina and put a pillow over my mouth to stop me screaming. Someone called 'The Colonel' came and said they were going to increase the voltage until I talked, but I didn't know what they wanted me to talk about. They kept throwing water over my body and applying electric shocks all over. Two days later I miscarried.' She survived the ordeal.

Enemies real and imagined were seen everywhere by officers of the junta. Their paranoia is revealed in a telling comment from Fifth Army Corps Commander General Adel Vilas, that he made some months after 'The Process' had started: 'Up to now only the tip of the iceberg has been affected by our war against subversion... it is necessary to destroy the sources which feed, form and indoctrinate the subversive delinquent, and the source is the universities and secondary schools themselves.'

Right: *These men of the Junta faced murder charges. Clockwise: Jorge Videla, Emilio Massera, Orlando Agosti, Omar Graffigna, Basilio Lami Dozo, Jorge Anaya, Leopoldo Galtieri, Roberta Viola and, centre, Armando Lambruschini.*

Opposite: *Alfredo Astiz in his role as naval officer signs his surrender to the British during the Falklands War, and in the lower picture, he goes to court as a suspected criminal to face charges of kidnap and murder.*

was nicknamed 'the blonde angel' and he revelled in his sadistic work. He was keen from the very beginning of 'The Process' to take on the dirty, murderous tasks that many of his naval comrades refused.

Raul Vilarano, the killer who later confessed to the horrible deeds perpetrated by himself and Astiz, said that he and his cohorts did not work to any pattern at the Navy Mechanics School; rather, they roamed at will, at any hour of the day or night, satisfying whatever grotesque lusts came upon them with any victim they happened upon. Dagmar Hagelin happened to be one of those victims.

Dagmar was arrested on 27 January, 1977. She had Swedish nationality even though she was raised in Argentina, and

was a gifted eighteen-year-old classical music student with coffee-table ideas about socialism, but no affiliation with any guerilla groups or other Communist subversives. As she rang the bell at a friend's house two men – a *patota* squad from the Navy Mechanics School – appeared and Dagmar ran, only to be shot down in the street. She was dumped in the boot of a Ford Falcon and driven away. The man who had fired the shot was Astiz.

Unlike other 'no-names' who had disappeared, Dagmar did not come from the poor and powerless. Her father ran a profitable business and was on good terms with the Swedish ambassador but, though he used every influence to trace his daughter, his efforts were to no avail. Dagmar, another innocent among thousands, died in the Navy Mechanics School and her remains have never been found. The Swedish ambassador refused to accept honours from his host country when it came time for him to take up another diplomatic posting – he did not want to give credence to a regime that, he was convinced, murdered young girls.

Jacobo Timerman, a Jewish newspaper editor who was deemed sympathetic to the enemies of the state, was tortured by Astiz but he survived to shame the military men with an account of his suffering in the book 'Prisoner Without a Name, Cell Without a Number'. He wrote: 'When electric shocks are applied, all that a man feels is that they're ripping his flesh apart. And he howls. Afterwards, he doesn't feel the blows. Nor does he feel them the next day, when there's no electricity, but only blows. The man spends days confined in a cell without windows, without light, either seated or lying down. The man spends a month without being allowed to wash himself, transported on the floor of an automobile to various places of interrogation, fed badly, smelling bad. The man is left enclosed in a small cell for forty-eight hours, his eyes blindfolded, his hands tied behind him, hearing no voice, seeing no sign of life, having to perform his bodily

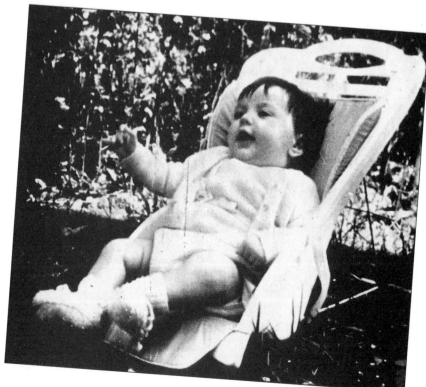

functions upon himself. And there is not much more. Objectively, nothing more.'

Astiz reached new heights of cynicism and cruelty when he posed as Gustavo Nino, a peasant boy who had lost relatives to the *patotas*. He infiltrated the ranks of the women who came to be called 'The Mothers of the Plaza de Mayo,' the head-scarved women who paraded silently in front of the junta's pink palace with the names of missing loved ones on boards hanging from their necks. These women were the true heroines of the Dirty War, defying truncheons and tear-gas to stage their weekly vigil, a vigil that played a powerful role in bringing the world's atten-

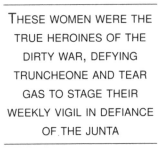

'WHEN ELECTRIC SHOCKS ARE APPLIED, ALL THAT A MAN FEELS IS THAT THEY'RE RIPPING HIS FLESH APART. AND HE HOWLS.'

THESE WOMEN WERE THE TRUE HEROINES OF THE DIRTY WAR, DEFYING TRUNCHEONE AND TEAR GAS TO STAGE THEIR WEEKLY VIGIL IN DEFIANCE OF THE JUNTA

THE MAN SPENDS DAYS CONFINED IN A CELL WITHOUT WINDOWS, WITHOUT LIGHT.

Opposite, top: *A woman weeps at a 'No-Name' cemetery where thousands of Argentinians were dumped in unmarked graves after their murder by the junta.*

Opposite, below: *The baby Clara Anahi Mariani disappeared after her parents were murdered. This baby was either abducted or killed by the junta.*

Left: *The Mothers grew bolder and bolder. They knew they had to attract world attention to their plight if they were to defeat the regime.*

who were waiting with the whips and the electric cattle prods and the flames.

For a time Astiz also worked out of his government's naval bureau in Paris, where he spied on exiled Argentinian human rights groups. After he was rumbled in Paris he headed for South Africa on a naval posting, but was hounded out of the country in 1981 when journalists learned of his unsavoury work at the Mechanics School. His superiors decided to pack him off to the war against Britain in the Falkland Islands in 1982.

THE TORTURER IS FREED

Astiz was captured by Royal Marines and when his name appeared in British newspapers, alarm bells began to ring in the capitals of the world. There were calls for his blood from Stockholm to Paris to the capital of his homeland, where thousands had a righteous claim on his murdering hide. But, under the terms of the Geneva Convention, Astiz was a prisoner-of-war and could not be handed over to foreign powers who suspected him of domestic crimes. He returned home after the war.

In Argentina, the following year, Raul Alfonsin was sworn in as the democratic president, the forty-first in the nation's history. His mandate was not only to steer the country towards democratic reforms, but also to exorcise the evil perpetrated upon his people by the junta. Some of the guilty men were brought to trial – including the suave torturer, Astiz. But he was never punished, never served time in a prison. At his pre-trial hearing his lawyers refused to admit that he had abducted and killed Dagmar – but in a supreme Orwellian twist said that if he had, it did not matter, because he was operating in a 'war time' situation. The military really did believe they were at war with their own people. He is now free in Argentina, a forty-two-year-old man with a wicked past but not a troubled conscience.

A commission was established after the war by the Alfonsin government to probe the terror. It found that the 'final purpose' of the terror was to exterminate the detainees and disfigure the bodies, so they could never be identified. The commission found no common factor to link the victims – they came from every level of

tion to the mass killings taking place in what the West had long regarded as the most 'civilised' of the South American nations. However, when the women's ranks were depleted by arrests, when their homes were raided or set on fire, when more members of their family disappeared, Gustavo Nino was always there to comfort them, never letting on that he had been the one who fed the damning information about their families back to his colleagues,

Above: After the junta fell, Argentinians began to dig up the unmarked graves.

Opposite, top: The military roll their weapons through Buenos Aires.

Opposite, below: Soldiers were seen as heroes before the ignoble Dirty War.

Argentinian society. Almost nine thousand of 'the disappeared' have never been found, despite the fact that more than sixty per cent of those seized were abducted in front of witnesses in public places. Three hundred and forty torture centres were unearthed – centres which, according to the junta, never existed. The commission produced a report fifty thousand pages long but the government failed to bring any of these state murderers to account.

Democracy now rules in Argentina, the dark days of 'The Process' are over. But the men in the olive green uniforms with the dark glasses are still there, lurking, waiting their next chance. Hebe Bonafini hopes they stay hidden. She was one of the founding members of the Mothers of the Plaza de Mayo and lost two sons and a daughter-in-law in the terror. She said: 'The military went to war against people who spoke their own tongue. They never got the right ones anyway, just children, really, no one who was ever a threat. What happened to us must serve as a warning to all people all the time. It can happen anywhere you know, making people disappear. That is the tragedy of it. It can happen to anyone...'.

MAJOR PEIPER
Slaughter in the Snow

Adolf Hitler sneered at the traditions of war and even the most gallant German soldier was corrupted by him, but the heartless massacre of unarmed prisoners-of-war, left to die in the snow, will forever stain the honour of the German army.

By December, 1944, Adolf Hitler had lost his war in Europe but he refused to believe the truth. As the Russians advanced on Germany from the east, determined to vanquish the Germans and punish them for the cruel campaigns of the SS and Gestapo against their people, the Führer concocted one last-gasp scheme aimed at staving off defeat. He underestimated the Russians, and concentrated on the Western Front for he was convinced he could alter the course of the War by smashing the American and British advance. Operating from his 'Wolf's Lair' redoubt in Rastenburg, East Prussia, he was certain that by depriving the advancing armies in Belgium and France of their biggest and most vital supply port – Antwerp – he could slow down the advance, split the armies, starve them into submission, sue for peace and then turn every remaining piece of armour, every aircraft, artillery piece and his men against the Reds.

Any general in the German High Command, who was not a lickspittle or a flunky tried to dissuade Hitler from his scheme. At a time when reserves of men and material should have been preciously conserved, he wanted to waste them on a final, futile mission that everyone else knew would end in failure.

It not only ended in failure, it ended in dishonour as well. A renegade unit of SS troopers forever stained their gallant battle honours with the brutal, cold-blooded slaying of one hundred American troops. They were butchered in the snow, cut down by heavy machine-gun fire under a battle-group commanded by SS Major Joachim Peiper, and their bodies left to be covered by fresh snowfalls. For the Americans, who had seen SS brutality when they had liberated French towns and Nazi labour camps, the massacre made them fight even harder, made them more determined than ever to finish the War and settle the final score with Hitler once and for all. This massacre of one hundred soldiers, in the snow around the Belgian town of Malmedy, was a spur to the American troops in a way that no general's speech or extra training could ever have given them. The Battle of the Bulge in general – and the massacre at Malmedy in particular – served to hasten Fuhrer Adolf Hitler's demise.

THE REICH'S REMAINING HOPE

The German offensive was launched amid great secrecy on 16 December, 1944, in the mountainous, foggy region of the Ardennes Forest in Belgium. General Gerd von Runstedt, acting on Hitler's orders, had gathered together as many serviceable tanks, as much fuel, ammunition and heavy weaponry as he could, and forged them into a force on which every remaining hope of the dying Reich was pinned. There was no lacking the will to win – the Germans remained highly disciplined and supremely ordered – until the very end. But they were exhausted; morale was low.

Opposite: Young American soldiers, including medics, were mown down in the snow. They were unarmed prisoners-of-war.

Below: Adolf Hitler ignored his army officers and launched a futile attack against the Allies in 1944.

It was a great Bulge in the Allied sector – and the fight to regain it became known as the Battle of the Bulge.

Hitler hoped to capitalize on the bad weather that shrouded this region in winter. He knew that the Allied air forces, which now roamed freely over Europe, would be grounded. Counting heavily on speed and surprise, he expected his armoured SS units – SS because he no longer had complete faith in the army, riddled with so many officers involved in the July 1944 plot that almost claimed his life – to be in Antwerp two thousand three hundred tanks, fifty self-propelled assault guns, and, miraculously, half of the three thousand combat aircraft promised by the chief of the Luftwaffe, Hermann Goering.

When the blow fell on the Allied lines it was shattering. Quite simply, complacent intelligence services of both the American and British armies had totally underestimated the reserves and willpower of the

Above: *This Ardennes landscape shows the harsh weather conditions in Europe when the Allies determined to crush the Germans.*

in a week. He put four armoured divisions of the SS Sixth Army under the command of his old pal Josef Dietrich at the spearhead of this important operation codenamed Autumn Mists.

Another specialist task, fiendishly concocted by Hitler who was forever pushing back the frontiers of conduct in war, was given to his master commando, Otto Skorzeny. Skorzeny, who had rescued Hitler's ally Mussolini in a daring glider operation on a mountaintop the previous year, was instructed to equip three thousand troops with American uniforms and put them behind American lines, thus causing confusion and chaos.

By the time the operation was launched von Rundstedt had scraped together a remarkable force from a nation that had lost nearly four million men since the start of the War. There were thirty divisions, t

enemy facing them. The bad weather had, in fact, grounded Allied air operations, and would continue to do so for the next eight days. The sound of the German preparations for the commencement of the attack was drowned out by the relentless roar of V-1 rockets fired on Antwerp and the city of Liege. At 5.30am two thousand German heavy guns opened up with a storm of fire and steel on the Allied lines.

SS troops penetrated six miles of the line within hours at five different points. It was a great Bulge in the Allied sector – and the fight to regain it became known as the Battle of the Bulge. Hitler chose his élite Black Guard to spearhead the operation to spite the army officer corps. Of all the SS units thrown into the cauldron, none was braver or more decorated than the division which bore the Führer's name – the 1st SS Panzer Division *Liebstandarte* – 'Life

Guard' – Adolf Hitler. And commanding one battle group was the man whose name would always be linked to the infamous incident known as the Malmedy Massacre – Colonel Joachim Peiper.

Peiper was the epitome of gallant German manhood that Hitler adored. At twenty-nine, he was handsome, smart, fluent in three languages, supremely courageous and, unlike many fervent officers,

had never joined the Nazi party. He was also possessed of a sparkling sense of humour, another trait uncommon among his officer comrades. By the time his Panzers shattered the American front line in the Ardennes, Peiper was known personally to his Führer. He had served with incredible bravery in the campaigns in Russia and had developed a reputation as a commando who knew when to obey orders and when to break them.

Among his men he was revered as a 'soldier's soldier' who did not go medal-hunting for the sake of it, although his exploits served to reward him with the Knight's Cross, Germany's highest battle-field honour. And he never left a wounded comrade in the field to be captured by the enemy if he could avoid it. Under Dietrich's command he was heading for Antwerp... but he doubted if he would ever reach it.

Peiper rationalized that if he managed at least to reach the heights over the Meuse River he would have done his duty.

Like all SS formations at this stage of the war, with Germany having suffered over three million dead at the front, the once-strict Adolf Hitler division which once had not allowed foreigners to serve, had been forced to water-down its entry qualifications. *Volkdeutsche*, or ethnic Germans in conquered lands, were absorbed to fill the gaps in the ranks, along with other more racially-dubious candidates that would not have been given a second glance during the heady days of victory. Belgians, Rumanians, Dutchmen, Lithuanians – the turncoat youth of Europe were now being led by Joachim Peiper in this last-chance crusade against the allies.

ADVANCE ON ANTWERP

Peiper commanded five thousand men with a formidable array of Tiger, Royal Tiger and Panther tanks, backed up with anti-aircraft units, self-propelled guns and heavy artillery. His job was to punch a hole in the line and race onwards to seize the Meuse bridgeheads – vital strategically if the mass of German armour was to cross the river to advance on Antwerp.

The initial hours went better than expected, the American line shattered, their mighty air armadas grounded. Panic swept

PEIPER WAS REVERED AS A 'SOLDIER'S SOLDIER', WHO DID NOT GO MEDAL HUNTING ... AND NEVER LEFT A WOUNDED COMRADE TO BE CAPTURED BY THE ENEMY.

Below: *Joachim Peiper was a brave soldier who had proved himself on the eastern front. Here, he leans over a jeep near Malmedy, the place where he lost his military honour.*

Above: *Passing through woods infested with enemy snipers, weary troops dragged their equipment on sledges.*

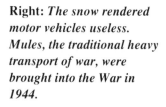

Right: *The snow rendered motor vehicles useless. Mules, the traditional heavy transport of war, were brought into the War in 1944.*

weather broke, at any time, his armour would be smashed on the ground by tank-busting fighters. Supply trains got lost or were held up at choked railway junctions and a fourth problem was the countryside; thick woods, and narrow medieval streets in the villages which were not easily navigated by seventy-ton metal monsters. Soon the advance momentum was lost.

HOPELESS TANGLE OF CONFUSION

In the fog of war – aided in part by the confusion created by Skorzeny's American-dressed commando squads – US units found themselves in a hopeless tangle of confusion and disorder the day following the initial assault. One such unit was the 285th Field Artillery Observation Battalion, a relatively inexperienced cadre of men composed mostly of teenagers who knew the business end of a rifle from its stock, but little else. Heading towards the Belgian town of Ligneuville, at a place called the Baugnez crossroads, the unit was trying desperately to link up with the US 7th Armoured Division which it believed had headed in the direction of Viesalm. But the 285th battalion was lost.

The company halted opposite the Bodarwe Café, where an officer enquired of the surly inhabitants if they were headed the front as the battle-hardened *Liebstandarte* troops proved more than a match for the boys from Nebraska, Omaha and New York. But soon logisitical problems – problems that Peiper knew would make or break the operation – began to pile up. For one thing, he had been told to seize the bridgeheads although the high command knew full well he did not have enough fuel for such a venture. And, if the

in the right direction because many road signs had been switched or simply torn down by Skorzeny's men. But these folk were not the welcoming oppressed villagers that had greeted the Allied advance throughout western Europe. Many of these 'border people' were fiercely pro-German, a traditional alliance that had been forged throughout centuries of shifting frontiers but unchanging causes and aims. The American was met with a mute shrug of the shoulders from the people inside.

As he went out to get his column moving again, the tanks of Kampfgruppe Peiper appeared like black beetles on the horizon. One of the beetles, a half-tracked armoured vehicle barked and a split second later the lead Jeep in the American column vanished in a flash of orange flame and black smoke. Then all the guns of the panzers opened up, one by one, as they crested the ridge and began their clanking crawl towards the scene of chaos and murder before them. The surprised and frightened American soldiers dived for cover in ditches, in a nearby barn, behind haystacks and even in a garden hedge. As soon as the German tanks were upon the shattered column, the cobbled road rang with the metallic clatter of dropped weapons as the Americans raised their hands in surrender and turned themselves over to their S.S. captors.

The Germans rounded the captured men up, frisked them for concealed weapons and pushed the prisoners into a field next to the crossroads. Peiper arrived on the scene, a Schmeisser machine pistol slung over his right shoulder. He ordered several of his men to stand guard on the captured 'Amis' then moved his other men off.

MENACE HUNG HEAVY IN THE AIR

Several of the prisoners began to have doubts for their safety. The guards seemed surly, angry, almost eager for an excuse, perhaps an escape attempt that allowed them to shoot. In the town of Bullingen, which the Germans had just left, they had captured one hundred American prisoners-of-war. Three had broken out, killing an S.S. guard by slitting his throat from ear to ear. Little wonder that a sinister menace hung heavy in that misty, damp air on the afternoon of 17 December, 1944.

'MACHEN ALLE KAPUT,' A VOICE WAS HEARD TO YELL ABOVE THE RACKET OF THE GUNS. 'KILL THEM ALL!'

Above: *The field of slaughter in Malmedy. Those investigating dishonourable behaviour in the German unit marked the bodies of the murdered Americans with numbers.*

The Americans sat and smoked in the snow-covered fields, watching glumly as prodigious amounts of enemy armour snaked and struggled to manoeuvre the tight crossroads along the road to Ligneuville, the route they had intended to take before they were ambushed. Young 2nd Liutenant Virgil Larry felt his throat going dry, as he gazed into the hard-eyes of the young stormtroopers, intoxicated with the flush of their small victory, as they sat atop their mighty panzers. He began to wonder what was going to happen to him and his company. At one point a massive self-propelled 88mm gun stopped in its tracks and traversed its menacing barrel directly at the American prisoners sitting quietly in the snow. But an angry German sergeant ordered it to move on with a curse.

Then Peiper himself showed up again, riding on top of a King Tiger tank. With a smile and a wave he yelled out in perfect English: 'See you in Tipperary boys!' and was gone as the Tiger accelerated with a puff of blue diesel smoke belching from its twin rear exhausts. Finally, two armoured vehicles swung around the tight bend at the crossroads and stopped. Rumanian-born Georg Fleps, private first class, a member of the elite German division that would

Below: *Facing the Allies were German veterans of the Russian Front (top picture) The Americans (lower picture) were not daunted. They knew they were on the road to victory.*

have sneered at him in 1940, unbuttoned his holster, withdrew a Luger pistol and jumped to the ground. Walking like a gunslinger, he moved close to the massed ranks of the defenceless prisoners, raised his weapon and fired. An American dropped. He fired again and another dropped. Then the air was rent with the noise of automatic weapons as the heavy machine guns on the armoured vehicles barked in unison and the Americans were

mown down like corn under the relentless onslaught of a combine harvester. '*Machen alle kaput*,' a voice was heard to yell above the racket of the guns. 'Kill them all!'

Virgil Lary saw his driver drop dead, heard the shouts of an officer telling the men to 'stand fast' before he too was shot through the throat and killed. Homer Ford, a military policeman who survived the shooting, later said: 'Men were lying around moaning and crying. I dived under a body and feigned death. The shooting kept going on and on and I felt the blood of one of my buddies running over me.

'Soon the shooting stopped and I heard the Germans coming over. They would say: "Is he breathing?" and would either shoot or hit them with the butt of their guns. The closest they came to me was about ten feet. After they fired at us, I lay stretched out with my hands out and I could feel my blood oozing. I had been hit. I was lying in the snow, and I got wet and started to

shiver, and I was afraid they would see me shivering, but they didn't. I had my head down and they couldn't see, but they were walking around the whole bunch and then they went over toward the road junction. I heard them shoot their pistols right next to me. I could hear them pull the trigger back and then the click. The men were moaning and taking on something terrible. I also heard the rifle butts hit guys' heads and then a terrible squishing sound.'

Samuel Dobyns, a medical orderly who had been recommended for a gallantry award, was one of the unit's few veterans who had been in Europe since D-Day in June. He was lying under the bodies, feigning death like Ford, when he heard the shooting stop and the single pistol shots which indicated that his comrades were being despatched with bullets in the head.

'I didn't want to die like a rabbit,' he said. 'I saw some woods off to the left and suddenly decided to make a run for it. I hadn't got more than twenty yards when I heard a heavy machine gun open up. I felt the slugs rip into me. I took four bullets, I later learned, and my clothes had been shredded by a further eight slugs. I heard Germans coming towards me, their boots crunching in the snow, and I knew they were going to finish me off. But they must have figured I was already dead. They turned around. I saw three or four Germans shoot wounded men who were crying for help. I thought I was the only one left alive.'

SHALL WE MAKE A RUN FOR IT?

Virgil Lary also survived and testified after the war at the trial of the killers: 'After the first machine guns fired, men fell dead and wounded all around me. The firing lasted for about three minutes, maybe a little longer. A man came by me as I lay feigning death and I heard a pistol shot nearby. Then I heard the sound of a new clip being inserted in a pistol and the individual passed me. I heard someone say to someone else: "Have they killed you yet?" He replied: "No not yet... but if the bastards are going to kill me I wish they would come back and get it over with." A bullet had severed my toes and I was in extreme pain and frozen from head to foot. Here and there I heard more raised voices: "Have they gone?" "What shall we do?"

"Is it safe?" "Shall we make a run for it?" Suddenly about fifteen of us decided to make a break for it. We had moved a few yards when rifles cracked, then a machine gun. I managed to clamber over a fence into a wood and ran along a dirt road until I came to a tumbledown shed. There were bundles of sticks inside and I pulled these all over myself. I waited.'

DRUNK WITH BLOOD

A few wounded men managed to crawl across the road to houses of local farmers as the 'Blustrausch' – 'intoxication of the blood' – continued. But they were mown down before they entered, their bodies mangled by the tracks of the tanks and armoured vehicles of Peiper's rearguard that were now racing to catch up with the forward columns on the road to Ligneuville. Other Americans made it into the Bodarwe Café, but were flushed out by Germans who set it ablaze with flame-throwers. As they ran into the streets with their hands raised high they were mown down by the maddened German soldiers.

Soon silence settled on the field and the SS were gone. All that could be heard as dusk fell were the moans of the wounded and the dying, like the lowing of cattle. It was the most hideous crime ever visited upon American troops in the European theatre of war – one hundred men dead, forty-one alive, many seriously wounded. Soon the Germans in the front line would face the angry retribution of the US forces when they tried to surrender and found their enemy distinctly without mercy.

Word of the massacre sread faster than the bubonic plague through a medieval city. American units in their foxholes that night or billeted in girls' schools and town halls felt a bitterness welling inside them, a determination that turned them from raw troops into that most lethal of battlefield opponents – vengeful soldiers fighting for a cause; in this case, revenge for their murdered comrades. Hal Boyle and Jack Belden of 'Time Magazine' were allowed by the army brass into the crossroads, near the town of Malmedy, to photograph and record what the Germans had done that afternoon. One of the first people they interviewed was Lt Lary who had hobbled painfully from his hiding place. He shook his dismembered toes from his boot, along with the bullet that had severed them, and sobbed: 'We didn't stand a goddamned chance... We just didn't have a chance.' When the story reached the front page of the 'Stars and Stripes', the troops' newspaper, the 328th Infantry Regiment, in the thick of the fighting, received a written order: 'No SS troops or paratroopers will be taken prisoner, but will be shot on sight.'

Peiper's advance, and that of the rest of

Below: *A captured SS trooper was shown more mercy than was given to GIs caught at Malmedy.*

the German attacking force, ground to a halt before the Meuse eight days later. The weather cleared, the Allied air forces pounded the tanks and guns of the Germans into scrap metal and the final attempt by Hitler to hold Europe ended in defeated. Peiper retreated with his men... determined that no comrades should fall into enemy hands for as long as he led and controlled his men.

In the days after the massacre, but before the German surrender, the Judge Advocate's branch of the US army formed a special staff to collect evidence against the murderers at Malmedy. Peiper was captured defending Vienna at the end of the War, when he was an assistant divisional commander. He would pay the price for the crimes of his men at Malmedy, regardless of who had given the orders to open fire. With eight hundred survivors of his unit he was interrogated. Eventually he, the commanding SS General of the operation, Sepp Dietrich and seventy-three others, including

"HAVE THEY GONE?" "WHAT SHALL WE DO?" "IS IT SAFE?" "SHALL WE MAKE A RUN FOR IT?"

BASTOGNE
BASTION
OF
THE BATTERED
BASTARDS
OF THE 101ST

Above: *The relief of Bastogne, the 'Bastion of the Battered Bastards', spelt the end of the German offensive – and the beginning of the Allied hunt for those responsible for the murders of GIs at Malmedy.*

the Romanian gunslinger who had fired the first shots into the unarmed American soldiers, stood trial.

The trial took place in Dachau, a fitting setting for retribution, for it was the site of the first concentration camp founded by the Nazis. The trial opened on 16 May, 1946, with chief prosecutor Lt Colonel Burton Ellis saying: 'The troops of the *Liebstabdarte* Adolf Hitler were told to excel in the killing of prisoners-of-war as in fighting. Others were told to make plenty of *rabbatz*, which in SS parlance means to have plenty of fun killing everything that comes in sight. Each defendant was a cog in a giant slaughter machine.'

Several of the prosecution witnesses were German soldiers themselves, sickened by what had taken place at the crossroads near Malmedy. Four enlisted men testified that Peiper had told them to 'give no quarter' in the battle and 'take no prisoners.' Corporal Ernst Kohler told the tribunal: 'We were told to remember the women and children of Germany killed in Allied air attacks and to take no prisoners, nor to show mercy to Belgian civilians.' Lt Heinz Tomhardt said: 'I told my men not to take prisoners.' So the Americans were killed.

There was gripping evidence at the trial from the survivors, men like Lary and Dobyns, who confronted Georg Fleps, the

man who had first opened fire, and they said: 'This is the man who opened fire into unarmed prisoners-of-war.' As evidence piled on evidence it became clear that Peiper and his men were guilty. Peiper said that he had given no orders for the massacre. Dietrich said that he too had not passed down orders for prisoners to be murdered. But on 16 July, 1946, the dreadful words *Tod durch erhangen* – death by hanging – fell upon the ears of the once-gallant soldier, Joachim Peiper. Dietrich was also given the death sentence as were forty-two other German soldiers.

In the end, none was executed. An Atlanta lawyer, William Meade Everett, who had been appointed defence counsel for the Germans at their trial, uncovered evidence that several German confessions of guilt had been extracted by the Americans using the methods that they had gone to war to abolish – namely torture and beatings. Burning matches were inserted under the fingernails of imprisoned SS troopers; several jaws were broken and men burned with cigarettes. It was shameful conduct, worthy of the Gestapo that they had defeated, not officers and men of the US army. Such charges sorely diminished the integrity of the tribunal and Everett, a lawyer with a keen sense of right and wrong, plunged thousands of dollars of his own money into having the cases re-opened.

On 29 July, 1948, a Senate Army Services Commission in Washington was empanelled to review the cases. By 1951 all the death sentences had been commuted and in 1958 Dietrich and Peiper were the last to be released. Justice had not served the dead of Malmedy well.

Joachim Peiper became the butt of many dishonourable accusations, but it seems clear that he was not tainted with any other acts of atrocity during the course of the War. He refused to talk about the old days, and explained his feelings: 'I am sitting on a powder keg. One day someone will come along with another accusation and the powder keg will explode. I'm a fatalist. The world has branded me and my men the scum of the earth. And no one will be able to clear up the Malmedy mess now. Too many lies have been told about it.'

And certainly, the truth died along with those brave men in the pasture next to the Baugnez Crossroads all those years ago.

JUSTICE HAD NOT SERVED THE DEAD OF MALMEDY WELL.

MISCARRIAGE OF JUSTICE

THE GUILDFORD 4
& BIRMINGHAM 6

These IRA atrocities horrified and enraged Britons who demanded instant and terrible punishment. In the name of justice, the police became as corrupt as the men they hunted. How were the wrong men imprisoned and where are the real killers?

Justice stands blindfolded over the Old Bailey in London, Britain's highest criminal court. She also stands tarnished in many people's eyes after a series of miscarriages of justice that deeply shook the ingrained faith of the British people in the equality and fairness of their country's judicial system. With the overturning on appeal of convictions against supposed IRA terrorists in the case of the Guildford and Birmingham pub bombings, the system that is admired the world over was shown to be deeply flawed.

Ten people, totally innocent, languished in jails for many years, their pleas of innocence not believed, the testimony against them thin at best and fabricated at worst. Victims of a deep-rooted national need to punish anyone for the outrages that left innocent civilians dead, these unfortunates paid the price in the witch-hunt that followed each bombing. Only by learning the lessons from each case can Britain hope to restore the lustre to the lady with the scales on top of Old Bailey.

THE GUILDFORD FOUR

Guildford is a quintessentially English town, a Surrey oasis of green, with quaint pubs and neat houses set in the suburban London sprawl. But in October 1974 five people died in two of those quaint pubs, the Horse and Groom, and the Seven Stars. Massive bombs, one a 'missile' device,

shattered the bars and claimed the lives of the innocent people, wounding thirty-five, some seriously, in the process. Both pubs were often used by army guardsmen from barracks at nearby Pirbright and Aldershot. A month later, on 7 November, a massive explosion at the King's Arms pub in Woolwich – long an army arsenal with

numerous garrisons – claimed two more lives and injured many more. The Irish Republican Army's assault on the British mainland was being stepped up.

Since 1969, when the Provisional IRA leadership was re-formed, with the hardliners winning office. The avowed aim of the organisation was to bomb, shoot, murder the British out of Ulster. The Seventies were to be the inglorious decade of the terrorist in the world and Britain was not spared. However, bombing pubs and so killing people like twenty-one-year-old secretary Jillian Johnston, when she was enjoying a drink with friends, with her whole life stretched before her, did not intimidate the British. Such acts did not alter government policies. The outrages served only to strengthen the national contempt of such barbarians – and created a climate in which hatred would eventually pervert the course of British justice.

In the months before the bombing an IRA active service unit was officially formed in London. It had a long list of potential targets and a supply of bomb

Above: *Victory signs can be glimpsed through the bars of the police van as the Guildford Four are driven away during their re-trial.*

Opposite: *Gerry Conlon is led from the Old Bailey after his release from false imprisonment.*

TEN PEOPLE, TOTALLY INNOCENT, LANGUISHED IN JAILS FOR MANY YEARS, THEIR PLEAS OF INNOCENCE NOT BELIEVED, THE TESTIMONY AGAINST THEM THIN.

Below: *The Guildford Four were naturally jubilant at their release after many years in prison for crimes they did not commit. Their families had also had their lives blighted.*

making materials hidden at various points on the mainland. Shortly after the arrival of this murder team came Belfast-born Gerry Conlon and his girlfriend Eileen McCann. They came to England to seek work in August and were joined later that month by Paul Hill, his sister Elizabeth and his girl-friend Gina Clarke. In London, they would later meet Paddy Armstrong, an Irish drop-out with a drug problem who lived in a squat in Kilburn, North London, he shared with his girlfriend Carole Richardson. In the mania to find culprits for the hideous crimes of the active service unit, Hill, Conlon, Armstrong and Richardson would soon be charged and would go down in criminal history as the Guildford Four.

Conlon was a petty thief, a gambler, a bit of a drunkard by his own admission, who liked to steal solely in order to pay for his pleasures. He was regarded by the IRA in his native Belfast as unsuitable for service because of his thieving. He got the money for the trip to Britain from the Criminal Injuries Compensation Board – the sum of £200 for being stabbed in a Belfast disco in a fight over a girl. Once in Britain he linked up with Hill, his old schoolfriend from Belfast, and the pair eventually lodged together in a Catholic boarding house in Kilburn. Paddy Armstrong had had a drug problem for years. Also from Ireland, he was badly down on his luck, and was living in squalor with Carole, an English girl who had first used drugs when she was only eleven. This misfit team were convicted of being an elite IRA unit.

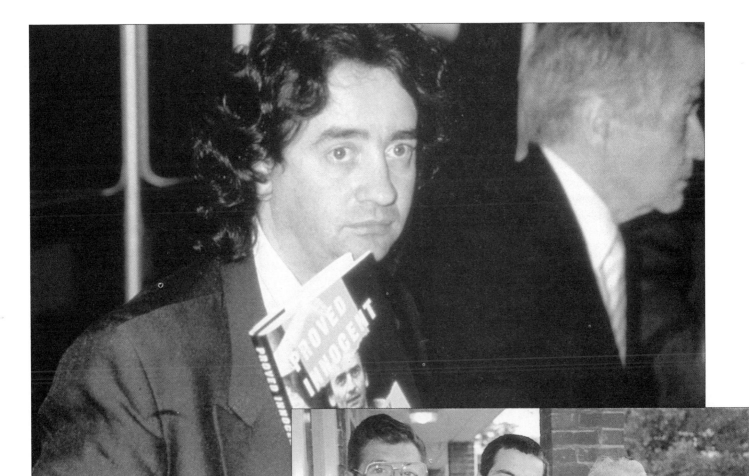

When they were arrested, the Guildford Four were the first people who, under the terms of the recently-imposed Prevention of Terrorism Act, were denied the right to have a lawyer present during interrogation. This Act was aimed at eliminating IRA activities. When the four went to court they were convicted solely on their confessions; there was not one supporting piece of forensic or other physical evidence linking them with the bombings. Consequently, when they retracted their confessions in court the prosecution mocked them and the jury believed they were liars. The Guildford Four said that their confessions has been beaten out of them; that the police officers who interrogated them behaved with all the finesse of wartime Germany's Gestapo, or so the accused claimed.

Conlon was in Belfast when he was arrested. It took fifteen years for a British newspaper to publish this account of his seizure. He said: 'They were slapping me all over the place. My clothes were covered in blood and my family had to bring clean ones for me. At Heathrow things got worse. The station was cold and frightening. There was a reception committee. There must have been around twenty-five policemen all crowding round me, all glaring and shouting things like "you Irish bastard". They made me take off my clothes in front of them all and they made some sarcastic comments. Some were spitting on me.

'They took me down to a cell. All it had in it was a wooden bench. I was like that until twelve o'clock the next day. People kept coming down to look at me like some

Above: *Sean Smyth, Patrick Maguire, Paddy Maguire and Ann Maguire. The Maguire family fought long and hard to prove their relatives were innocent.*

Top: *Gerry Conlon holds his book 'Proven Innocent' which is a document of his experience.*

animal in a zoo. I was interrogated for two days. I couldn't believe police officers, people who are supposed to be serious, intelligent people, could go down to that level. I couldn't believe anyone could go off the handle like they did. Two officers were particularly hard on me. One said he would show me an old RAF trick. He put his hands behind my ears and pulled me up off the chair. It was very painful.

'Another senior man was more aggressive verbally than physically but he slapped

> 'THREATS FROM A SENIOR SURREY CID OFFICER MADE ME SIGN TWO CONFESSIONS. HE TOLD ME AN ACCIDENT COULD BE ARRANGED FOR MY MOTHER AND MY SISTER.'

According to the other three, there was similar treatment for them. In fear, Conlon was named by Hill, who was the first to be arrested in November 1974. The others were named by Conlon. The police were now eager to clear up the bombing. At the trial at the Old Bailey in 1975 there was no mercy; all accused were sentenced to life on the strength of their confessions. Hill and Conlon were convicted separately of the bombing at Woolwich and received life sentences in relation to that crime. They

me in the face, wagged his finger and pulled my nose. He told me, he assured me, that I would make a statement. It seemed they would do anything to convict me. They were under enormous pressure from the Press and the television. Threats from a senior Surrey CID officer made me sign two confessions. He told me an accident could be arranged for my mother and my sister. He told me that if a soldier shot my mother it would be put down to an accident and British soldiers were never convicted in the courts. That's when it became a whole different thing. I knew he could probably do what he said.'

Above: Paddy Hill takes the microphone to proclaim his release. He is one of the Birmingham Six.

Opposite, above: Paddy McIlkenny waves jubilantly as he walks to freedom.

Opposite, below: Gerry Conlon, of the Birmingham Four, arrives at court with Maggie McIlkenny, daughter of Paddy, to listen to her father's appeal.

appealed in 1977 – an appeal that was rejected. Meanwhile the true active service unit of the IRA continued to create mayhem on the British mainland.

It was at the trial of this terror squad in early 1977, the terrorists having been caught after a siege in London's Balcombe Street, that one of the men read out a statement. These terrorists were the core of the active-service unit and they were cornered after shooting up a restaurant in Mayfair. But they escaped and held a couple hostage for six days in a siege with police in an apartment at Balcombe Street, Marylebone before they finally gave themselves up.

In part the statement read: 'We are all four Irish Republicans. We have recognised this court to the extent that we have instructed our lawyers to draw the attention of the court to the fact that four totally innocent people – Carole Richardson, Gerard Conlon, Paul Hill and Patrick Armstrong – are serving massive sentences for three bombings, two in Guildford and one in Woolwich which three of us and another man now imprisoned have admitted that we did. The Director of Public Prosecutions was made aware of these admissions in December 1975 and has chosen to do nothing.' Was this true?

A LIMITED APPEAL

When the Guildford Four went to the appeal court to have the Balcombe Street siege gang's confessions put before a new jury at a fresh trial, the judges heard evidence in person by the self-confessed bombers. However, the court decided, on the evidence that was given, that both the Balcombe Street Siege gang and the Guildford Four were responsible for the

THE COURT DECIDED THAT BOTH THE BALCOMBE STREET SIEGE GANG AND THE GUILDFORD FOUR WERE GUILTY.

bombings. No controversy about forensic evidence of the authenticity of police reports,were raised during this appeal.

Even before this, early in 1975, the Director of Public Prosecutions received two secret Scotland Yard reports that cast serious doubts on the guilty verdicts handed down on the Guildford Four. One document was prepared shortly before and the

Above: *The Birmingham Six greet well-wishers as they leave the court that granted their appeal.*

THESE SECRET REPORTS SUGGESTED THAT ALL THE EVIDENCE POINTED AWAY FROM, NOT TOWARDS, THE GUILDFORD FOUR.

other shortly after the convictions. Essentially, the documents chronicled the IRA terror campaign on the mainland, linking incidents both before and after the four were arrested. This meant that someone else was doing the killing. One of the police reports said that there appeared to be a 'common thread and purpose' between the Guildford attacks and other IRA bombings in Britain. The reports could find no link between the convicted four and the IRA – and no physical evidence to suggest they did it. They were sent down on confessions made under duress.

These secret reports, which suggested that all evidence pointed away from, not towards, the Guildford Four, were adequate testimony to spare the innocents their fifteen years in prison. When these documents were made public, in 1989, Alistair Logan, a solicitor who represented two of the Guildford Four, said: 'The reports clearly show that the police knew the bombings at Guildford were linked to other bombings. I had no idea at the time that the

police had this evidence. It is shocking.' Why did the police hide these documents?

MORE NAMES, MORE REPORTS

The second police report was written after conviction of the four, in December 1975, and it named Joseph Patrick Gilhooley as a senior IRA man involved in mainland terror operations. Gilhooley is suspected as the third man involved in the Guildford pub bombings along with Balcombe Street siege terrorisst Joseph O'Connell, and Brendan Dowd, who was arrested in the north of England early in 1975 for terrorist offences. O'Connell and Dowd always refused to name this accomplice, or two women who helped them plant the bombs. However, there is a suspicion that Gilhooley was involved in the Guildford bombings but there is no evidence to support this.

For the Guildford Four, the years passed, slowly and painfully. They alledged they were beaten up in various jails – the general prison population has never been overly friendly to child molestors or terrorists. Although the families of the men kept up a constant campaign, it seemed as if justice truly was blind to their case.

Even so, the four attracted a significant clique of wealthy and influential people to their cause: former Home Secretaries Roy Jenkins and Merlyn Rees, former Law Lords Devlin and Scarman, and the Archbishop of Westminster Cardinal Basil Hume. These men were concerned exclusively with new evidence that had turned up in the years since the bombing. Richardson and Armstrong had witnesses to say that they were in a pub in the Elephant and Castle in South London on the night of the bombing, while Hill had a witness to testify that he was in the hostel. In April 1989, lawyers for Conlon discovered that a witness vital to their client's case whom they had been unable to trace had been interviewed by Surrey dectectives in 1975 – a crucial part of the investigation that was never submitted at the trial yet would have given Conlon an alibi.

The Home Secretary Douglas Hurd ordered an inquiry to be conducted into the Surrey police handling of the case in 1989. Officers of the Somerset and Avon force gave their disturbing findings to Sir

> THE FOUR ATTRACTED A SIGNIFICANT CLIQUE OF WEALTHY AND INFLUENTIAL PEOPLE TO THEIR CAUSE.

Below: *Smiles of relief and happiness were on the faces of every one of the Six as they drove off to re-start their lives.*

Partrick Mayhew, the Attorney General, who in turn passed them on to Mr Hurd in October. It was bad news for the government; the police probers had found evidence of the initial Scotland Yard reports, the dismissal of the alibi witness so important to Conlon and numerous allegations of brutality towards the suspects. Hurd had no choice but to report before Parliament that the case would be going back before the Court of Appeal.

A CRY FOR FREEDOM

When the four were brought before the judges at the court where they were sentenced, they were informed that the Crown had withdrawn all charges against them and that they were free. On 19 October 1989, they walked out to a crowd whose cheers that echoed from the rooftops around the Old Bailey.

Paul Hill was thirty-four; Richardson, thirty-two; Conlon, thirty-four; and Armstrong, thirty-nine. It was time to rebuild their lives with the compensation money due to them, but who can really put a price on fourteen years in prison? Nothing can give them back the lost time.

THE BIRMINGHAM SIX

For the men wrongly accused of the murder of twenty-one people in the worst IRA carnage on mainland Britain, there were sixteen agonising years in jail, served for offences they didn't commit. The Birmingham Six, unlike the Guildford Four, had Republican sympathies which weighed against them at their trial – and there was forensic evidence (since discredited) that seemed at the time to point to them. Their conviction was further proof that some police tailored evidence while under intense pressure to find those guilty of a crime that stunned the nation.

The Tavern in the Town and Mulberry Bush pubs in Birmingham, in the heart of the city, were obliterated on the night of 21 November 1974, and with them any lingering tolerance that certain sections of society may have harboured for the IRA and their aims. In the appalling carnage that killed twenty-one innocents, a further one hundred and sixty-two were injured, many of them seriously. The scenes of devastation looked like something hit in the London Blitz at its worst. One of the pubs was underground, making the explosion that much more effective. Some of the victims were literally blown to smithereens. In the aftermath of the bomb-

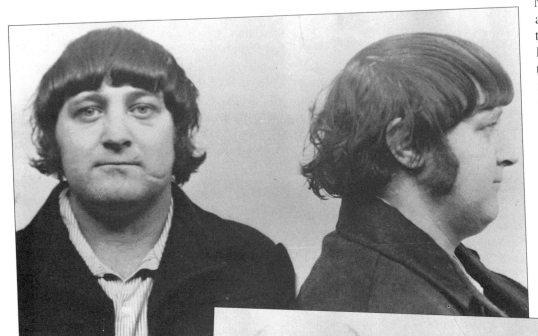

Top: *Families discuss proceedings during the appeal hearing.*

Above and right: *Paddy Hill, above, and John Walker, right, innocent men wrongly convicted.*

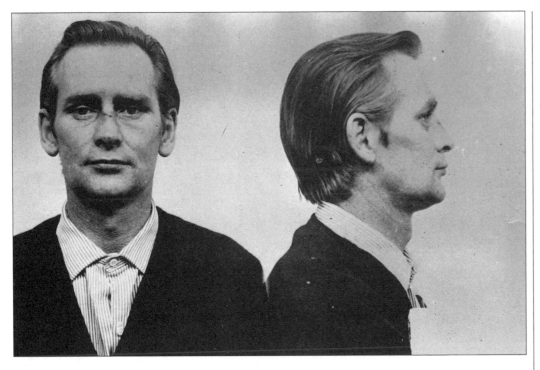

ings, grief was soon followed by angry cries of vengeance. The public demanded that the Birmingham pub massacres were avenged and the guilty men caught and punished for their dreadful crimes of terror and the murder of innocent people.

The West Midlands police force was given responsibility for tracking down the IRA team. The usual trawl of suspects began with heightened surveillance at air and sea ports. Police infiltrated the Irish communities of Birmingham and Liverpool. The law officers were all too aware of the public desire for a swift and total conclusion to the terrorist crimes.

Detectives couldn't believe their luck when they intercepted the party of six men heading for the ferry in Liverpool that was sailing to Ireland the next morning; the men were on their way to the funeral of an IRA bomber and had come from the West Midlands area. The men were named as John Walker, Patrick Hill, Hugh Callaghan, Richard McIlkenny, Gerard Hunter and William Power. Like the Guildford Four, they were interviewed without solicitors present and the interviews were not tape recorded, as is now required by law. There were

confessions from the men – confessions obtained, it was admitted sixteen long years later, by police methods that were entirely unacceptable. The Birmingham Six claimed that the only way to stop the police beating and threatening them was to sign false confessions, the confessions that were used as evidence at their trial.

But for the Birmingham Six there was also forensic evidence against them. Tests carried out on the men showed that at least two of them had minute traces of nitroglyc-

Richard McIlkenny (above) and Hugh Callaghan (below) as they were when they went to prison for a crime neither committed.

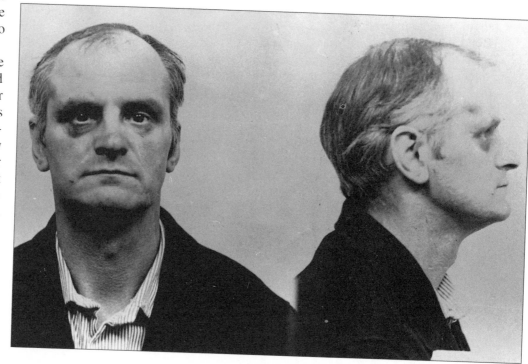

Above: *The aftermath to the bombing in Birmingham.*

erine on their hands. It was enough for them to be convicted at Lancaster Crown Court where Mr Justice Bridge, sentencing them to life prison terms, said: 'You stand convicted on each of twenty-one counts, on the clearest and most overwhelming evidence I have ever heard, of the crime of murder. I am entirely satisfied that the investigations were carried out with scrupulous propriety by all officers.' The men descended to the cells, their pleas of innocence lost on a court that had unwittingly accepted false evidence. It seemed, at the time, to be a fair trial based on scientific proof of guilt.

ANOTHER TRIAL FOR THE LAW

It was in 1985, ten years after they were sentenced, that a Granada 'World in Action' programme began to seriously question the convictions. Chris Mullin, the Labour MP, became one of their unstinting supporters, despite the hatred still directed at the accused by a public unaware of the dishonest police role. Politicians in the Irish Republic began demand a review of the trial and the verdicts, as did the Roman Catholic Archbishop of Birmingham, who several times called into question the validity of their convictions. But after the release of the Guildford Four, the public began to suspect the police role in the Birmingham Six affair, and a final and successful review of their convictions was ordered by the Home Secretary.

Forensic science technology, which played a considerable part in the conviction of the men, also contributed in a major way to their freedom. The six were incriminated initially by a scientific test designed in the 1860s by Johann Peter Griess. Most explosives contain nitrogen and the Griess test detects nitrogen-containing chemicals (nitrites) which can be liberated from explosives when they are treated with alkali solutions. Interpretation in the testing is critical – anything which contains nitrite or something that can be converted to it will produce a positive result. Essentially, a scientist must be extremely cautious when examining test results to ensure that he has detected the right kind of nitrites. At the trial, Home Office scientist Dr Frank Skuse testified that the Griess test given to William Power and Patrick Hill made him 'ninety-nine per cent certain' that they had handled nitroglycerine, the explosive used in the bombs. But it was later learned that common household soap could produce the same chemical result.

Another explosives test was done – the gas chromatography/mass spectrometry test, regarded as more sensitive and more reliable. But the trace used for the test was later found to be too small – it could easily have come from the tobacco residue on a

> 'I AM ENTIRELY SATISFIED THAT THE INVESTIGATIONS WERE CARRIED OUT WITH SCRUPULOUS PROPRIETY BY ALL OFFICERS.'

Below: *Police and rescue workers discuss strategy after the bombing in Birmingham.*

cigarette smoker's hand. In appeal evidence, Home Office scientist Dr Alan Scaplehorn agreed that the test, in regard to the positive nitroglycerine traces found on Hill's hands, was 'not acceptable'.

Advanced machinery in the form of an electrostatic document analysis apparatus supported part of their appeal. Police claimed that material in their notebooks was written as interrogations were taking place. The electrostatic document analysis process proved them wrong. The ESDA machine proved that four different pads and inks were used in nineteen pages covering two interviews – suggesting they were completed at different times.

At the appeal in 1991, Mr Michael Mansfield, their QC, said the discrepancies were part of an 'intricate web of deceit' involving a pattern of altered timings and later insertions. The tests were conducted in 1990 by officers from Devon and Cornwall police who were given the task by the Home Office of investigating the convictions. It was after the results of the

Above: *The Birmingham Six from left to right: top, Patrick Hill, Hugh Callaghan, John Walker; lower row, Richard McIlkenny, Gerry Hunter and Billy Power.*

forensic evidence that the Director of Public Prosecutions decided that he could no longer believe that police reports on interviews with the men were accurate or truthful. In short, there was no longer a case for them to answer.

Older and greyer, robbed of the best years of their lives, the six walked into the street outside Old Bailey on 14 March 1991, their ordeal over, the lost and wasted years a tragic but ever-present memory. Families had been deprived of their husbands and fathers. A deafening cheer went up as they emerged as free men for the first time in sixteen years, their supporters mobbing them as police fought to keep a path clear for them. The six – McIlkenny, fifty-seven; Callaghan, sixty; Hill, forty-five; Hunter, forty-two; Power, forty-four; and Walker, fifty-five – were all naturally bitter.

Patrick Hill said to wild applause outside the court: 'For sixteen years we have been political scapegoats. Police said to us from the start that they knew we had not done it but they told us they did not care. We were selected and they were going to frame us for it to keep everybody happy.' Hugh Callaghan said: 'Justice has been done today. It has taken sixteen years for it to happen. Thank you very much.'

'WE ARE LEFT WITH NOTHING'

For the victims of the bombers – the real bombers, who have never been brought to trial – there was only a hollow emptiness left. Ivy Roberts, whose daughter Maureen was among the dead, said: 'There was some compensation in knowing that the guilty men were in jail, but now we are left with nothing. The families of the dead have had to live with this every day since the bombings. But the victims appear to have been forgotten by others. If they did not plant those bombs somebody else did. Are the police now going to bring them to justice?' Mrs Elizabeth Gray, sixty-eight, is also horrified that the guilty men are still free. Having lost her brother-in-law Charles in the Mulberry Bush explosion, she said: 'At the time we thought they had got the right men but mistakes can be made. There were terrible doubts, I now know, from the beginning. The men's families must have suffered terribly. But whoever did it is free and that sickens me.'

There are now calls for reforms of the judicial system and a Royal Commission was charged, after the success of the appeal, with reviewing the entire process. But it will, in all likelihood, be several years before any reforms can be implemented. In the meantime, the murderers of twenty-one innocent people remain free and the six people who were accused of killing the victims are left to pick up the remains of their shattered lives.

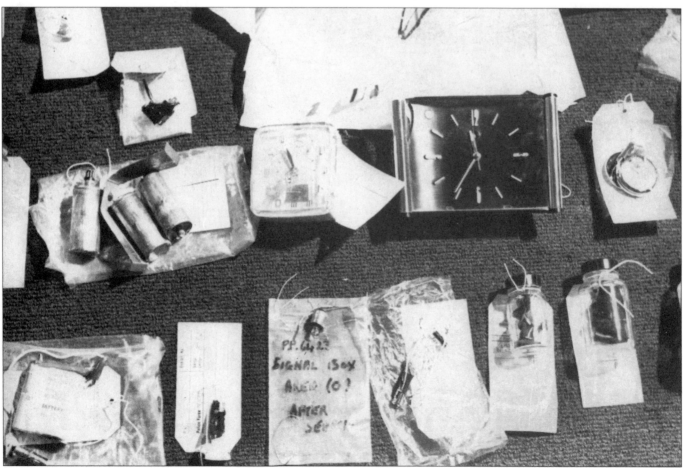

JAMES HANRATTY
The Wrong A6 Murderer

James Hanratty was wanted for burglary but was hanged instead for the brutal A6 Murder. This sad small-time crook who insisted on his innocence was long dead when the real killer, who remains unpunished, confessed.

The mortal remains of James Hanratty have long turned to dust but his ghost will not lie down. The conviction and subsequent execution of twenty-five-year-old Hanratty for the crime known as the A6 Murder has been a subject of controversy ever since he was put to death in Bedford on 4 April 1962. Books by such eminent scholars as Lord Russell of Liverpool have cast doubt upon his guilt; more recently a television programme about the case was broadcast and campaigners seeking to have his innocence restored have pressed Scotland Yard for DNA samples for 'genetic fingerprinting' tests which could conclusively prove or disprove his involvement in the murder of Michael John Gregsten.

Hanratty was born in Wembley, Middlesex, in 1936, the eldest of four sons. He was a slow learner at school, a child who needed special attention, and he never learned much more than basic arithmetic and English. Evacuated during the height of the London Blitz, he ran with street toughs upon his return. In the post-war years he was a young man heading downwards into a life of crime.

From the age of fourteen he was a shoplifter and a car thief, graduating to his first prison sentence for housebreaking when he was eighteen. His father tried many times to get his son to go straight but it was to no avail. In 1957 he was in jail again for burglary, released at the end of the year, and imprisoned again in 1958, this time for three years. When he was freed in 1960, his father gave up his job as a dust-

man in order to start a window cleaning business with his son – a vain attempt to keep the boy out of trouble. It failed, and in the autumn of that year young Hanratty went on the run for a burglary when he knew police had him in their sights as the prime suspect. It was when he was hiding out that his underworld contacts tipped him off that he was also wanted by the police for the horrifying killing of a scientist which the papers had called the A6 Murder.

Michael Gregsten was thirty-six and enjoying a passionate affair with Valerie Storie, a twenty-three-year-old research assistant who worked with him at the Road Research Laboratory near Slough. Gregsten was married but separated from his wife. She had custody of their two small sons, he took the Morris Minor saloon car.

In the early hours of 23 August 1961 Gregsten and his girlfriend shared a few drinks together at a pub in Taplow, on the Thames not far from Slough, and then drove to one of their favourite 'courting

couples' spots at a nearby cornfield. It was while they were sitting in the car that a tap came on the window. Annoyed that their tryst had been interrupted, Gregsten opened it and found himself staring down the barrel of a revolver pointed straight at his face. The mystery man, his face shrouded in shadow, demanded the car keys.

GREGSTEN FOUND HIMSELF STARING DOWN THE BARREL OF A REVOLVER POINTED STRAIGHT AT HIS FACE.

Below: *Obscured beneath a blanket, Hanratty arrives at court to face charges of murder. He was a petty thief but nothing in his past suggested that he was prone to violent crime and attempted murder.*

Opposite: *James Hanratty may have been the victim of a monstrous frame-up.*

Above: James Hanratty as a five-year-old photographed-with his mother.

---

his own, made a frantic bid to overpower his hijacker. The man talked about tying them up and glanced at a bundle containing clothes. As Gregsten handed it over, he hurled the bag of laundry into the gunman's face, trying to knock the gun from his hand. But in that instant the gun went off twice, killing Gregsten instantly.

MURDER, RAPE AND INJURIES

Miss Storie screamed in grief and rage: 'You bastard! Why did you do that?' The gunman, obviously nervous, said he had been frightened and that he didn't mean to kill. As he calmed her down he became more emboldened and, pointing the gun at her head, made her kiss him. Then he dragged her into the back seat and raped her. Afterwards, he made her help him drag the corpse of her lover from the car. As she wept he ordered her, at gunpoint, back to the vehicle and demand she show him how the gears worked – indicating by this, that he was a man unused to driving manual gearbox cars. Then, as she went back to grieve over Gregsten's body, he shot her several times, finally kicking her body a few times in an attempt to satisfy himself that she was indeed dead.

Convinced she was, he climbed into the driving seat and drove away. She was found shortly after daybreak by a passer-by. Valerie Storie was alive but paralysed from the waist down by a bullet that had passed too close to her spinal cord.

Police were baffled by the sheer brutality of the crime. While Det-Supt Bob Acott questioned Miss Storie in hospital, the gun was found stuffed under the seat of a London bus and the car abandoned in Ilford, Essex, far from the shooting, on the other side of the capital. An Identikit picture made up from Miss Storie's description of the murderer was circulated throughout Britain. She remembered him as having brown hair and deep set brown eyes. Acott issued an appeal to landladies to report lodgers who might be lying low or who were acting in a suspicious manner.

A break in the case seemed to come when a landlord at Amersham, Buckinghamshire, reported that a man calling himself Durrant had booked himself into his residential hotel on the day after the murder and had kept himself confined

The stranger pocketed the keys and clambered into the back seat. Initially, he robbed them of money and their watches. Then he began a rambling monologue of his life, saying that he had been in remand homes, borstals and prisons. He looked menacingly at Gregsten and said he was going to put him in the boot of the car, but changed his mind after Miss Storie pleaded with him not to do so. Then his monologue suddenly ended and he passed the keys back to his captive with instructions to drive around the northern London suburbs until he was told to stop. The courting couple and their kidnapper ended up at a lay-by on the A6 at a spot called Deadman's Hill, between Luton and Bedford.

Gregsten, obviously frightened but concerned for his girlfriend's safety as much as to his room ever since. The man was checked out by Scotland Yard and found to be one Peter Louis Alphon who was a door-to-door salesman. However, with no evidence of crime against him, the police could not arrest Alphon.

Police learned that on the night of the murder Alphon was booked into the Vienna Hotel in Maida Vale, West London. There, on 11 September, a manageress was moving furniture in room twenty-four when two spent cartridge cases fell out from a tear in the side of a chair. The woman, who had already been questioned by police about her guest, gave them to detectives straight away. Ballistic tests proved beyond a shadow of a doubt that the cartridge cases were from the weapon that claimed Michael Gregsten's life. Even though Alphon had actually slept in room six of the hotel, the police were certain that he had somehow planted the cartridge cases in the other room.

Police now set about finding Alphon again in Amersham but he had vanished. Detectives were certain they had the right

Right: *Written as he faced the death sentence, Hanratty reveals a genuine concern for, and gratitude towards, his family.*

Below: *Was Hanratty the man who hitched a lift in this Morris, then killed the driver? Police examine the car for evidence after they found it abandoned.*

As distated by inmate to R Scott off. 3/4.
In replying to this letter, please write on the envelope:—
H.M. PRISON,
ST. LOYES,
BEDFORD.

Number 3220...... Name Hanratty ....
....Prison

Dear Mum & Dad.
I am finding this letter very hard to put together. But I am going to try very hard to do everything I can to help you to recover from the terrible shock caused by all this. I am sorry I have caused you this terrible strain both you and Dad and all the family.
You have all been so brave all the way in the case, and to show my gratitude to you all, I am going to face up to it, and am going to be a son that you and Dad can be proud of. I have not been much of a son to you in the past but Mum what I am about to say to you, comes from

No. 243   (21442—3-11 42)

man in their sights. The manager of the Vienna told lawmen that Alphon had been out till 'well after midnight' on the date of the murder and had still not returned when he, the manager, went to bed in the early hours of the morning. He also claimed that when he saw Alphon the next day he looked unshaven and dishevelled, nervous about something. Alphon, using the alias Durrant, was now a wanted man and his name released to the newspapers. Even his mother had been visited and could not provide an alibi for her son. In their first interview with him, he had told police that he had been visiting her house in Streatham, but she denied this. Alphon, aware that it would only be a matter of time before the police tracked him down, gave himself up on 22 September.

There then followed a series of identity parades in which police hoped to establish beyond a shadow of doubt that he was their man. The first was before a Mrs Dalal of Richmond, Surrey, who, on 7 September, had opened her front door to a man seeking a room in her lodging house. She claimed her attacker bound her, forced her into the bedroom, lifted up her skirt preparatory to a rape attempt and whispered: 'I am the A6 killer'. He fled when Mrs Dalal screamed and she was unharmed. When Alphon was paraded with others before her he was

Above: *These women testified at Hanratty's trial. Mary Deacon, upper picture, had dated him and Ita O'Donovan worked at the hotel where police found evidence against Hanratty.*

Opposite, top: *Hanratty leaves the court and, as on his arrival, is protected by a covering blanket.*

Opposite, below: *Cleaner Harry Brookes points to the place where the murder weapon was found hidden under a bus seat.*

picked out by her as her would-be assailant. But the hotel manager failed to point him out, as did two men who had seen Gregsten with Storie and a male passenger in his car in the early hours of the day of his death. Finally, Alphon was brought before Valerie Storie at Guy's Hospital in a line-up held at the foot of her bed. When she picked out an innocent man she shouted: 'I've made a mistake! I've made a mistake!' Alphon was released, even though his own alibi for that night was questionable to say the least.

Police then turned their attention to the guest who occupied room twenty-four, where the bullet cases were discovered, that night. It was unoccupied the night of the murder but was booked out to a man named James Ryan the previous evening. The network of underworld informers soon tipped off police that Ryan was in fact

James Hanratty, on the run from his latest bungled burglary that could have landed him behind bars for a ten-year stretch.

Police began a nationwide search for Hanratty, who heard from criminal friends before the police found him that he was wanted for the A6 killing. Hanratty was terrified; true, he had been in plenty of trouble with the law, but sex crimes and violence were definitely not his trademarks. On 5 October, nervous about his fate, he telephoned Det-Supt Acott, when he explained that he was guilty of burglary but innocent of murder, attempted murder and rape. He told Acott: 'You know that's not my scene'. He claimed to have spent the night of the murder drinking with three men in Liverpool, but that he was not prepared to come to a police station because of the burglary he had commited, that would ensure another stretch inside for him.

However, on 11 October, Hanratty was recognised by two policeman as he strolled on the seafront at Blackpool and was immediately arrested. He was on an express train to London within twenty-four hours and again an identity parade was held before Miss Storie's bed. This time she asked all the men present to say the phrase: 'Be quiet, I'm thinking,' some words used

by Gregsten's killer. When Hanratty in his broad London accent pronounced thinking 'finkin' she unhesitatingly picked him out. Hanratty was then charged formally with Michael Gregsten's murder.

Miss Storie's identification of him and the fact that the gun cartridges were found in the room he had stayed in at the Vienna Hotel seemed to be the sum total of police evidence. But even that was sketchy on closer examination; Miss Storie had said that the killer had brown eyes and brown hair, which certainly matched Alphon. Her description did not fit Hanratty, who had wide, bright blue eyes and fair hair. She changed her description of the killer eight days before Hanratty was caught. There were rumours that some policemen had fiddled with the evidence of the cartridges, but these stories remained mere speculation.

Hanratty's case was heard at Bedford Assizes in January 1962. Miss Storie's evidence was the most compelling and that which ultimately damned him. In court, she swore again he was the man who had killed Gregsten and raped her. There was further identification from two men who, even though the light was bad, claimed they saw him driving the Morris car after he had killed Gregsten and left Miss Storie for dead. Hanratty's pleadings of innocence were not helped by his refusal to state

Above: *A policeman guards bags of evidence during Hanratty's trial at bedford Assizes.*

Below: *Mr Justice Gorman is welcomed at court by the Sherrif of Bedford County.*

where he was on the night of the murder.

But then, dramatically, in the second week of the trial, he blurted out that he had been at Rhyl, North Wales, where he had stayed in a guest house. He named the guest house and the landlady, but she was unable to ascertain if he had stayed with her the night of the murder, although she said he did in fact stay at her house. This also clashed with his first statement that he had spent the night of the killing with three men in Liverpool. But if an alibi was not established, neither was a motive. Hanratty, a semi-literate who had spent all his adult life in petty thievery and housebreaking, hardly seemed a contender for murder and rape, and that committed in such an unplanned manner. Nevertheless, he was convicted and sentenced to hang. The execution was set for 4 April 1962.

As the grey light of dawn shone through the bars of his dim, grey cell on the morning of his execution, James Hanratty penned his last words on this earth to his younger brother. 'Well Mick, I am going to do my best to face the morning with courage and strength and I am sure God will give me the courage to do so. I am going to ask you to do me a small favour, that is I would like you to try to clear my name of this crime. Someone, somewhere, is responsbile for this crime and one day they will venture again and then the truth will come out and then, Mick, that will be the chance for you to step in. Well, Mick, the time is drawing near, it is almost daylight, so please look after mum and dad for me. I only wish I could have the chance all

over again. But never mind Mick, as I don't know what I have done to deserve this. But, Mick, that's fate for you... Your loving brother, Jim.'

He hanged – the last man in Britain to suffer such a fate. But the battle over his guilt or innocence has raged on.

After his death there arrived on the scene a colourful character, the son of a Belgian diplomat called Jean Justice, who had an abiding interest in the law. Like a modern-day Poirot, he was intrigued by the Hanratty case and agreed with students of crime that the evidence arraigned against him was too circumstantial to be credible. Justice subscribed to the theory that the

A TALK WITH STRANGERS, NOT POLICE

On one occasion Alphon handed to Justice a detailed account of what happened on the night of the killing – not a confession and not signed in his own hand – but an account which further re-inforced Justice's view that he was, in fact, dealing with the man who should have been in the dock. Later he taped long telephone conversations with Alphon in which the suspect displayed an inordinate amount of knowledge about the route driven by Gregsten on the night he died. Justice highlighted the fact that Alphon was, by his own admittance, a

'ON THE PHONE HE COULD WORK HIMSELF UP TO TERRIBLE FURIES – AND HE TALKED IN RIDDLES, CONTRADICTING HIMSELF AND CONSTANTLY SHIFTING THE DETAILS OF HIS STORY.'

cartridge casings were planted in his room by Alphon who was the guilty party; he had already confessed as much to the unfortunate Mrs Dalal, if her identification was correct, and the first description by Valerie Storie matched his looks. Justice approached Alphon, who was initially reluctant to see him, but soon after agreed to a meeting. They were soon meeting on a regular basis and Alphon, perhaps flattered by the attention, began dropping boastful hints indicating that he was the killer and that an innocent Hanratty had gone to the gallows in his place.

poor and inexperienced driver; why would an experienced car thief like James Hanratty need to be shown the gears of a car as unsophisticated as a Morris Minor if he, indeed, was the driver that night?

In 1963, after Alphon confessed to the killing in tape recordings, Justice submitted a long memorandum to the Home Office. Part of the recording goes: 'I was there to separate a couple of people in a car. That was the motive. That is why it took five hours. Five f***ing hours it took. You've got your motive.' He said he had been paid £5,000 for his night's work. Alphon said he

Above: *Det Constable Bert Stillings, left, and Det-Con Jim Williams, who arrested Hanratty for murder.*

was a hired gun, paid for by a man he did not want to name, to separate Michael Gregsten from Miss Storie so he would return to his wife. He claimed that he wanted to frighten Gregsten and attack her, but that it had all gone terribly wrong when Gregsten attacked him with the laundry bag. In July 1963 the matter was formally raised in Parliament by Fenner Brockway MP, who argued for Hanratty's innocence and backed his arguments by reading from the transcripts of the tapes. The Home Office was unmoved; Hanratty was guilty as far as they were concerned and that was that.

Paul Foot, the distinguished campaigning journalist, remains convinced of Hanratty's innocence after many years of probing the affair. He said: 'I made contact with Alphon and then began a three-year ordeal of late-night phone calls in which Alphon taunted me with his confessions. I met him for the first time face-to-face 1969. On a cold November afternoon we walked from Brighton to Hove and back, talking all the time. He was spruce and polite – although on the phone he could work himself up to terrible furies – and he talked in riddles, contradicting himself and constantly shifting the details of his story. But in all our meetings he never deviated from his admission that he committed the murder.

'Between 1966 and 1971 I went again to Rhyl. I interviewed fourteen witnesses who supported in varying degrees of certainty Hanratty's story about his two nights there in August 1961. It is impossible, in my view, to read the testimony of these people and not to believe that Hanratty was wan-

*Above: **Hanratty's father outside Parliament handing leaflets to passers-by. He marched on Downing Street, below, with supportors to petition against the death sentence passed on his son.***

dering the streets of Rhyl looking for lodgings at the very moment the gunman was climbing into Gregsten's Morris Minor some two hundred and fifty miles away.' Foot also claims that Alphon produced proof that he had been paid £5,000, a substantial sum of money in those days.

A DETERMINED CONFESSION

The case did not end there. In 1967 Alphon, who was facing prosecution over harassment of people involved in the case, went to the Hotel du Louvre in Paris where he called a press conference on the case. He announced openly that he was the A6 murderer and later he wrote to Roy Jenkins, Home Secretary, saying he would be willing to confess to him in person. Nothing was done. In 1971, one hundred MPs signed a motion calling for a public inquiry into the case. Jenkins had been succeeded by this time by Reginald Maudling, who also refused to act. In 1974 the newly-elected Labour government commissioned

Left: *James Hanratty Snr with two other sons, Peter and Michael, arrive at court on the day his son, James, was to be sentenced.*

Below: *Mr and Mrs Hanratty have always believed in the innocence of their son. His death for a murder he swore he never committed was a bitter tragedy for the family.*

a secret report on the case from barrister Lewis Hawser – Hawser pronounced Hanratty Guilty. The government was convinced that it was time once and for all to shut the lid on the Hanratty case.

However, in 1992, film-maker Bob Woffinden tracked down Alphon, now in his sixties and living in Kings Cross, London. He still admits to the murder.

In a written statement to former barrister Jeremy Fox said: 'The crime was a result of a conspiracy that had its roots in the infidelity of Michael Gregsten with Valerie Storie. I was offered money to terrorise the couple and a criminal, Charlie 'Dixie' France provided the gun. What I thought I might do was terrorise the pair for a while, then lock Gregsten in the boot while I had some preliminary fun with the girl. I would later take him out of the boot, tie him up in the cornfield and depart with the girl.' The old man, Alphon, referred to himself in the statement as 'I, the killer'.

Right: *Police control the long queue of people trying to enter the court for Hanratty's trial.*

Below: *Mr Michael Sherrard on the right was defence counsel for Hanratty.*

Woffinden's documentary screened on Britain's Channel Four network also cast reasonable doubt on Valerie Storie's identification of Hanratty as the guilty man. The film showed that in a statement to police at the time Miss Storie had doubts before the identification of Hanratty about her ability to recognise the killer. 'My memory of this man's face is fading,' she said. 'I am so afraid that when I am confronted with the man I may not be able to pick him out.' This crucial statement was not made available to the jury at Hanratty's trial.

When Woffinden's film was broadcast, campaigners again approached the Home Office seeking a new inquiry while asking for DNA samples from Scotland Yard evidence files. If the samples were made available, a DNA match using the DNA profile of his surviving relatives could be made that might clear Hanratty. The samples of the murderer's DNA survive on clothing worn by Miss Storie on the night of the crime. Geoffrey Birdman, solicitor

Below, left: *Valerie Storie arrives in an ambulance to bear witness against Hanratty. She identified him as the man who killed her lover before raping and attacking her.*

Below: *Mr Justice Gorman who, in accordance with the law, passed the death sentence on Hanratty when the jury returned a Guilty verdict.*

for the Hanratty family, said: 'There is now overwhelming evidence to indicate that Hanratty had nothing whatsoever to do with this crime and was totally innocent.' The Home Office has agreed tentatively to look at any new evidence but has so far not agreed to a full-blown inquiry. Neither has Scotland Yard yet agreed to hand over the DNA samples or the sixteen boxes of papers collected by London detectives who led the investigation. Journalist Paul Foot who still retains an abiding interest in the case has said: 'James Hanratty cannot walk free. His will probably not be the last miscarriage of justice, but it is likely to remain one of the most shameful.'

MATA HARI
Woman of Mystery

Was Mata Hari really a spy or just the ultimate good-time girl who couldn't resist a man in a uniform? This femme fatale never made a secret of taking lovers for money but denied charges of spying. The evidence suggests that a court today would agree with her plea of innocence.

She has gone down in legend as the supreme seductress, the spy whose military lovers betrayed their nations in pillow talk. Sultry, sexy, shrouded in mystery, Mata Hari – her adopted Javanese name means 'eye of the day' – moved in the highest circles before and during First World War. However, in 1917 her sex life led her to be classified as a German spy. On 15 October, as a wintry autumn sun was just rising, she was executed by a French firing squad. Later, the beautiful body that was admired from a distance by Parisian audiences who watched her dance, and from closer range by numerous officers of both Germany and France, was dissected in medical experiments by trainee doctors.

But was she a spy? Mata Hari – real name Margaretha Gertruida Zelle – was executed at a time when the nations of Europe were gripped in a communal madness that threatened to blight Western civilisation for ever. As men died by the million in places like Chemin-des-Dames, Verdun, the Somme, Passchaendale, Vimy Ridge and Champagne, governments needed to make their sacrifices appear worthy and to prevent further bloodletting.

Spy fever was rife in the capitals of Europe. Intelligence agencies looked for spies everywhere and, if they found them, the accused paid the ultimate penalty. In wartime there is little time for balanced inquiry when the fate of a nation might depend on the secrecy of a single piece of information. But, with hindsight, it seems likely that Mata Hari died for her sexuality as much as for any state secrets – real or imagined – that she may have passed on to her alleged spymasters.

From Dutch peasant girl to a woman of beauty and intrigue was a long journey for Margaretha, born in the tiny hamlet of Leeuwarden in Holland on 7 August 1876. Her mother came from a prominent Dutch family, her father, Adam, was a business-

Opposite: *A dazzling pose from the good-time girl who was to be executed when she was accused of being most famous female spy in the world, Mata Hari.*

Below: *Mata Hari, the belly dancer, entranced her male audiences.*

Opposite, above: A Berlin newspaper reported the Mata Hari spy case and portrayed the cast of male chacters involved in the drama.

Opposite, below: Adam, Mata Hari's father, who took his young daughter to live in Amsterdam.

Below: Mata Hari also turned her hand to acting, but her fans did not appreciate her in these demure roles.

man. Her life was settled and eminently respectable until 1891 when her mother died and her father, stricken with grief, sold up in Leeuwarden and moved to Amsterdam to try his luck there. With him went Margaretha and her three younger brothers. By this time she had blossomed early into a Lolita-type beauty, advanced for her age, with an interest in men that her father felt bordered on the unhealthy. Indeed, she had to be removed from one school, where she tried to seduce the director, and was sent to live with an uncle in The Hague, who, her father and teachers hoped, would teach her some discipline.

In 1895 she answered an advertisement in a daily newspaper placed by Captain Rudolf MacLeod, a Dutch officer of Scots descent, who was seeking a wife after long overseas service in the Dutch East Indies colonies. Margaretha, who by this time had shown herself a woman whose heart beat faster for men in uniform, met the dashing Captain MacLeod after sending him a picture of herself. Within ten days they were lovers and two months later – with Margaretha pregnant – they married at Amsterdam town hall.

If Captain MacLeod was captivated by her voluptuous beauty, he was by no means so keen on her penchant for the good life. He hoped that with the birth of their son Norman on 30 January 1896, she might become more restrained in her spending habits but he was to be disappointed.

A LOST CHILD, A LOST MARRIAGE

The following year Captain MacLeod was promoted to Major and was re-posted to Indonesia, this time taking along with him his spendthrift wife. In 1898 she gave birth to a second child, a daughter named Juana Luisa, but by this time the marriage was almost on the rocks. Major MacLeod was unhappy with rumours of his wife's behaviour with junior officers. He took to drinking heavily and reportedly threatened her with his service revolver and even beat her with a whip. In 1899 he was transferred to Sumatra and his wife delayed following him for two months. When she did arrive her son Norman looked so ill that a doctor was called. The boy hovered on the brink of death for a fortnight before he died, poisoned by a bitter servant girl who thought she had suffered some slight at Margaretha's hands. The boy's death hastened the end of the marriage. In 1902, when MacLeod retired and was living back in Holland with Margaretha, she finally plucked up the courage to divorce him.

The modest allowance given to her by her ex-husband was quite inadequate for a woman with the tastes of Margaretha. After considering a career on the stage – she decided against it because she thought she would have to train for too long – she settled on becoming a dancer and moved to Paris in 1903. Supplementing her meagre allowance by working as an artist's model

Das Illustrierte Blatt

Die Wahrheit über Mata Hari?

von Harry Gordon

Mata Hari in ihrer Glanzzeit.

Gomez Carillo, Raquel Mellers Gatte, soll unverschuldet Ursache für deren Haß gegen Mata Hari gewesen sein.

Die spanische Tänzerin Raquel Meller, der man jetzt vorwirft, an der Erschießung Mata Haris schuld zu sein.

Captain Mac Leod, mit dem sich die 16jährige Margarethe Zelle (später Mata Hari) auf Grund einer Zeitungs-Anzeige verheiratet hat

„Ich ging nach Rom, getrieben vom unwiderstehlichen Drang, den Heiligen Vater zu sehen. Was ich aber von ihm erbat, hat nichts mit einer Bitte um Sündenablaß zu tun. Ich kann und darf nur sagen, daß ich den Segen des Heiligen Vaters bekam. Alles andere ist Sache m e i n e s Gewissens." Diese Erklärung der Tänzerin Raquel Meller ist von der ganzen spanischen Presse mit großer Spannung erwartet und mit großer Aufmachung veröffentlicht worden.

Es handelt sich um die tragische Geschichte der Holländerin Margarethe Zelle (Mata Hari), die einen holländischen Kolonialoffizier Mac Leod geheiratet hat, mit ihm in Holländisch-Indien ein Eheleben voller Enttäuschungen geführt hat, bis sie in Europa ihrem Schicksal überlassen wurde. Ihre Tanztalente wurden hier entdeckt, sie hatte beispiellose Triumphe, sie ließ sich aber in den Beruf der hochmondänen Courtisane abdrängen. Bekannt sind die Umstände, unter denen die Tänzerin mitten im Kriege in Paris verhaftet, von einem Kriegsgericht zum Tode verurteilt und hingerichtet wurde. Sie befand sich in Madrid. Ein gefälschtes Telegramm wurde an sie geschickt, um sie in die Falle zu locken.

Wer steckte nun hinter dieser Intrige? Die Freunde Mata Haris antworten auf diese Frage kategorisch: ein französischer Offizier, den sie verschmäht hat, und eine spanische Tänzerin, deren Eifersucht sie erweckt hat, verbanden sich, um sie zu verderben.

Der Offizier spielt hierbei keine besondere Rolle, die spanische Tänzerin aber heißt Raquel Meller. Sie habe — so sagt der letzte Verehrer Mata Haris, der ehemalige spanische Senator Junoy — Angst gehabt, ihren damaligen Gatten, den vor kurzem verstorbenen spanischen Romancier Gomez Carillo, an die Holländerin abtreten zu müssen. Sie und ihr französischer Bundesgenosse seien es gewesen, die Mata Hari zunächst nach Frankreich gelockt und sie dann ins Zuchthaus gebracht haben. Dreizehn Jahre nach der Hinrichtung ihres Opfers habe nun Raquel Meller den unwiderstehlichen Drang gefühlt, sich zu Füßen des Papstes zu werfen und ihn anzuflehen, sich ihre[r] sündigen Seele anzunehmen. Raquel Meller sagt, sie hab[e] ... gläubige Katholikin das Recht, den Weg zum Heilige[n] ... zu suchen, und der Umstand, daß sie diesen Weg be... sei kein Anlaß, sie zur Rechenschaft zu ziehen. ...

Dieser Erklärung steht die formelle, einde... Erklärung des ehemaligen Senators Junoy ... Meller verklagen könnte, entgegen. Und ... trifft, so ist die Feststellung des Gener... der ehemaligen deutschen Gegenspio... Listen des deutschen Spionagedien... nicht aus der Welt zu schaffen.

Warum mußte Mata Hari also ... werden? Kriegspsychose? Mac...

Staatsanwalt Mornet, dessen unerbittliche Strenge im Prozeß gegen Mata Hari den Ausschlag gab.

Mata Hari als Insassin des Frauenzuchthauses Saint-Lazare, von wo aus sie zur Hinrichtung geführt wurde.

Louise-Jeanne Mac Leod, die im Jahre 1919 gestorbene einzige Tochter Mata Haris.

as she sought employment as a dancer in the French capital, Margaretha became a much sought-after nude model for numerous Parisian artists. She did not want to strip but decided she had to 'for the sake of my daughter'. There are unsubstantiated stories that she also became a prostitute in a high-class brothel but no firm proof of this activity has ever surfaced.

She tried to capitalise on her stay in the East by becoming something of a woman of mystery in her dances. She dyed her skin an exotic bronze colour and dressed in flowing, oriental-style robes and veils. She adopted the name Mata Hari and soon gained a reputation in Paris that went wildly beyond the bounds of truth. Mata Hari was keen to play up the idea that she was a woman from India, a high-born aristocrat who danced to forget her broken heart. Reviews of her dances were usually pretty scathing but all critics concurred that she was, at least, pleasing to look at, her costumes revealing daring glimpses of expossed, tanned flesh. In Monte Carlo, Paris and later Vienna, her exotic 'Hindu dances' were the talk of Europe and the hazy details of her background only served to make her that much more appealing.

During this time, Mata Hari began to indulge herself in more affairs of the heart and she flitted with ease between the bedrooms of German, French and Dutch officers. By the end of 1914, when Europe was at war, she was in Berlin and had taken the capital's chief of police, a Herr von Jagow, as one of her lovers, for which she was paid the princely sum of £1,500 per year. At her trial she would later deny that she was a prostitute, saying of the financial reward: 'It was merely what I was worth!'

Mata Hari journeyed back to Paris in 1916 after visiting her homeland. She was now at the centre of the attention of French counter-espionage agents who knew of her

highly-placed German lovers (she had more than one in Berlin) and who believed she was on a mission to spy for them. Apparently one of the pieces of evidence which brought her to their attention came from the Italian secret service who reported that the previous year she had been aboard a Japanese vessel docked at Naples. Italy, a French and British ally in the First World War, reported: 'While examining the passenger list we have recognised the name of a theatrical celebrity called Mata Hari. She has it seems renounced her claims to Indian birth and become Berlinoise. She speaks German with a slight eastern accent.'

The French were also tipped off by British secret service agents who said that she had been seen on several occasions in the company of German officers in Madrid, Spain, then a neutral country and a hotbed of espionage during the war. She actually landed in England on one trip and was taken to Scotland Yard where she was accused of spying – which she denied – before being taken back to Portsmouth and put on a ship bound again for Spain.

Right: *Captain McLeod divorced his flighty wife. The stipend he gave her afterwards gave her was not enough for her expensive tastes so she went to work as Mata Hari, a 'woman of mystery'.*

Mata Hari was under the watchful eyes of officers of the Deuxième Bureau of counter-intelligence, when she travelled back to France and visited an injured Captain Marov, a Russian who had been wounded while fighting for France. They took her visit to be a smokescreen for spying on Allied airfields near Vittel and claimed later at her trial that she was gathering intelligence on the order of battle of French forces at Verdun – the worst battle of the war that eventually claimed more than eight hundred thousand French lives. More information about monies she had received from highly-placed German officers was passed from French agents in Berlin and, towards the end of 1916, Mata Hari was arrested in her hotel suite near Vittel and charged with high treason; her hearing was to be held in secret before a military court martial that was closed to both the public and press.

She was charged with seven cases of espionage. They were: that in 1916 she dealt in intelligence matters with the enemy in Spain; that in 1915 she had dealt in intelligence matters with the enemy in Holland; that in 1916 she had dealt in intelligence matters with the enemy in France; that she passed military information to German agents in Spain; that she entered the 'entrenched camp of Paris to procure information to the enemy's profit'; that she informed the enemy of a coming French offensive; that she warned the enemy of the discovery of a new chemical ink.

However, at the trial it became evident that French evidence was scanty, based more on their own fears and prejudices about her than on any solid evidence. It was based on bank receipts from her German lovers, her relationship with Herr von Jagow and a French mistrust of a woman who crossed borders with utter fearlessness during wartime. There was also more than a hint that French *savoir-faire* did not extend to her lovers in the German military. Here she is being cross-examined about Herr von Jagow:

Prosecution: But he enlisted you in the German secret service.

Mata Hari: No.

Prosecution: Do you deny that you were known as H.21?

Mata Hari: No.

Prosecution: That was your code number in the German secret service?

Above: *Mata Hari was a sensation in Monte Carlo, Paris and Berlin. Her alluring costumes were scandalous in an age when women were modest in their dress.*

THERE WAS MORE THAN A HINT THAT FRENCH SAVOIRE-FAIRE DID NOT EXTEND TO HER LOVERS IN THE GERMAN MILITARY.

*Left: **The bell at St Lazare prison tolled her death after she faced a firing squad.***

*Below: **Mata Hari dressed in furs shortly before her execution.***

made repeated calls to the German consulate at Vigo. Without hesitation Mata Hari said: 'Of course, they were my lovers of the moment!' As were, she said, Major von Specht, chief of German espionage in Amsterdam and another officer who was based in the Hague.

The French produced evidence of a telegraph cipher from Madrid about a payment of Fr15,000 made to her through a diplomatic pouch to Holland. This inordinately large sum was, they said, payment for passing on information to the Germans of a French offensive planned for the Champagne area. 'No,' cried Mata Hari. 'I... I tell you, it was to pay for my nights of love. That is my price. Believe me, be gallant, gentlemen – French officers!'

Her advocate did his best for her; a highly-placed diplomat in the French Foreign Office was called to testify on her behalf. The man, who has not been named in all

Mata Hari: Oh no. My lover gave me the sign so that he could correspond with me. He could use official methods if ordinary ones failed in wartime. Further, he could use official money to pay me.

Prosecution: You were in Berlin well away from the war. Then via Belgium, Holland and England you came to France. In wartime – why?

Mata Hari: I wished to dispose of my property at Neuilly.

Prosecution: But that only needed a few weeks and yet you stayed for seven months.

Mata Hari: I went to Vittel, to be near Captain Marov, the only man I ever loved. He was blind – I wished to consecrate my life to his welfare.

Prosecution: But while at Vittel you met many officers?

Mata Hari: Doubtless. There were officers everywhere. I like officers!

It was soon apparent to the French prosecuting team that she was exceedingly willing to be branded a harlot or a scarlet woman – but never a traitor. There was plenty of circumstantial evidence that suggested she was certainly one and possibly both. Captain Georges Ledoux testified that he had seen her in Madrid with a Major Kalle, the German military attache attached to the embassy there, Lieutenant von Krohn, the naval attaché and that she had

these years, told the court that in his 'long and intimate' acquaintance with her he had never known her to be anything other than a courtesan. Certainly she had never enquired of military secrets from him – and he knew plenty, after all.

Some of the French suppositions about Mata Hari's spying activities are so far fetched as to border on utter preposterousness. For instance, she was accused, while at Vittel, of spying out French arrangements for an attack on the Chemin-des-Dames in Champagne. How? It is one hundred and thirty miles from the scene of the planned attack (an attack, incidentally, which was a monumental failure like most of the offensives planned by the General Staff during the war). More importantly – the attack was actually over before she even went to Vittel. They accused her of reporting the French mutinies that swept through the ranks at Verdun, that threatened to break the backbone of the army and, consequently, the will of France to resist. The Germans did not learn about these mutinies until after the Armistice.

She was also accused of leaking naval secrets to her German naval attaché lover – specifically that she passed on secrets of French troopships and merchant supply vessels for enemy U-boats to sink. She did not know a single code or military cipher and post-war German naval intelligence records show that Mata Hari provided no information at all to the Kriegsmarine during its active operations.

A SUPERLATIVE FEMALE SPY

Furthermore, after the war, the Germans never acknowledged that Mata Hari – branded in the closing speeches of the court martial as 'the most dangerous and damaging female spy in the history of the world' – worked for them in any capacity at all. No file in German intelligence history has ever been unearthed that suggested she passed on anything more to her consorts than what was in the daily newspapers in the European capitals. The whole affair smacked of a witch hunt and her arrest drew protests from some of the most prominent people in Europe. The Crown Prince of Germany, son of the Kaiser, and the Prime Minister of Holland, Dutch statesman Mynheer van den Linden and the

Prince Consort of the Netherlands were among the dignitaries who voiced their opposition to her trial.

Nevertheless, she was found Guilty and duly sentenced to be executed by firing squad. After two days in a padded cell, where she was watched to see if she would try to commit suicide, Mata Hari was taken to cell twelve on death row at St Lazare jail, Vincennes. She read a Buddhist book of faith while she sat in the cell waiting for the sentence to be carried out – she claimed she had renounced all ties to any Western faith – and danced her oriental dances in attempts to forget her impending doom. One of her former lovers, a young Frenchman, planned to spring her from the jail in a dramatic and romantic gesture that came to nothing. Her execution was fixed for Monday 15 October. Dr Bizard, a police surgeon, called on her the evening before the court's sentence was to be carried out and gave her a strong sleeping draught.

Above: *Mata Hari in street clothes. She maintained that she was not interested in espionage, but she did like men in uniforms.*

'THE MOST DANGEROUS AND DAMAGING FEMALE SPY IN THE HISTORY OF THE WORLD.'

Below: *In wartime, it is usual to despatch traitors swiftly by putting them before a firing squad. This was to be Mata Hari's fate, although this is a photograph of another's execution.*

The following morning, as she was led to her place of execution in the dried up moat of the Château of Vincennes, she gaily asked a guard if she might put on a little lace corset. He agreed she could. She also put on a bright hat, but was puzzled that she could not have a pin for it; she was told pins were forbidden to prisoners in case they tried to do themselves harm.

about to kill her she said mockingly: 'What is the purpose of executing at dawn? In India it is not so; there death is a penalty that is made into a ceremony – in full daylight before crowds of guests and to the sweet scent of jasmine. I would have preferred to lunch with friends and then gone to Vincennes in the afternoon. But you choose to shoot me on an empty stomach. It is so unreasonable.'

Mata Hari was tied at the wrists to the execution post but refused the blindfold always offered to the condemned. Twelve soldiers were given the command to fire. In the split second before twelve bullets pounded into her a faint smile played across her lips. A sergeant advanced moments later to administer the *coup de grace* with his pistol in the back of her head and a doctor later testified that she had breathed her last; at least one bullet had penetrated clean through her lace corset into her heart. The beautiful, much-loved body was later cut up for use by medical students.

AS SHE WAS LED TO HER EXECUTION SHE ASKED A GUARD IF SHE MAY WEAR A LITTLE CORSET... AND A BRIGHT HAT.

Mata Hari showed bravery and gallantry in the face of death. Before she was led away she gave to Sister Leonide, a nun who was in attendance, a bunch of letters to be posted after the execution to numerous old flames and friends. 'Don't get the addresses mixed up,' she said, 'otherwise you will cause distress and upset to many, many families.' As the gentle nun began to cry, the condemned woman said: 'Since I must die, I must be resigned. I leave for the big station from which there is no return ticket. Now little mother, don't cry... how little you are. It would take two of you to make a Mata Hari.'

As she turned to the officer in charge of the firing party she said: 'I am ready, you may kill me.' When he, in turn, asked if she had any last statements to make, she replied: 'Yes. You may write that Mata Hari declares she is innocent and a victim of murder.' Scoffing at the men who were

'REASONABLE DOUBT'

Since her death the name Mata Hari has passed into legend and everyday usage. Whenever a female agent is caught or written about she instantly becomes 'the most famous spy since Mata Hari'. A woman with wiles and a feminine attraction dangerous to men is branded a Mata Hari. Those with many lovers, too, are branded with the name of the woman who died in that dusty old moat of a French château. But it is almost certain that she was not a spy – and probably, had she been tried today, her behaviour would have been questionable but the evidence would have been poor enough for 'reasonable doubt' to acquit her. A study of her trial shows at least four salient miscarriages of justice.

First, hearsay evidence was submitted that would under no circumstances be allowed in any court – military or civil – today. No proof was advanced save she received Fr15,000. The French insisted this and other payments were for her espionage activies, while she, a beautiful courtesan, maintained it was for sexual favours. Incidentally, there were plenty of precedents for the reference of the French authorities about military officials paying their mistresses out of official funds.

Second, the prosecution was unable to prove that she engaged in espionage when she came to Vittel.

Third, all the men questioned at her trial – her lovers and her confidantes – who had access to classified military information, swore that they never passed on any intelligence or state secrets. If that were the case, then what could she have passed on to her German contacts save that which was already in the public domain?

Fourth, the French alleged she was paid over the years a total of Fr75,000 for spying but they could not offer proof to counter Mata Hari's claim that this was merely income from her lovers.

In 1985 an American journalist, Russell Warren Howe, claimed that he was shown secret papers relating to the trial at Vincennes, the very place of her death. He claimed that the intelligence he received showed that she was not a German spy but a freelance operative whose sole espionage effort was in Madrid where she actually worked for the French. Howe says she seduced a German intelligence agent there, meaning to pass on the secrets he told her to the French, possibly in return for money.

Howe maintains she did give the Germans who became her lovers information on the French war effort – but she used stories that were culled from newspapers and street gossip. She was never in a position to jeaopardise whole offensives, nor learn the secrets of chemical ink, as was ludicrously stated at her trial. But the French in 1916, having suffered appalling losses throughout the war and major mutinies in their ranks at Verdun which literally threatened to smash the national will to fight on, were looking for a scapegoat. It is fair to comment that it was easier to blame a treacherous woman spy than incompetent generals.

If she was a spy, then she broke every cardinal rule ever laid down for practitioners of that sly, dark world. She was high profile, remained high profile, never met with her contacts in any places other than top European hotels or at magnificent country estates. Historians who have studied her case over the years think it inconceivable that she had the political skill or motive to have contributed to the deaths of hundreds of thousands of allied servicemen, as was alleged at her trial.

In the Fifties, one historian wrote of her: 'Mata Hari was not a sympathetic character; there can be no question of presenting her as a romantic heroine. But a courtesan – even a spy – is entitled to justice. The atmosphere of the hour must be taken into account. The influence of defeat and mutiny must have militated against impartial judgement for Mata Hari appeared as one of the reasons for the current distress. No court is infallible. It may be that the French have more definite proofs of the woman's guilt than they have ever made known, or that were produced at the trial. If so they should be revealed. There can be nothing secret about them after such a lapse of time. If not, there is a case for the complete re-examination of the Mata Hari affair.' He wrote further observations about the case. 'She was no Joan of Arc, but her claim to justice is just as strong. The French need have no fears. It is not a sign of weakness but of strength to admit that you may have been wrong. Until a formal re-assessment is made possible, I imagine that many people will favour the old Scottish verdict of "not proven".'

IT MAY BE THAT THE FRENCH HAVE MORE DEFINITE PROOF OF THE WOMAN'S GUILT THAN THEY HAVE EVER MADE KNOWN.

Below: *Many accused spies were summarily shot during the Great War. They were put against a cross as they faced the bullets. Mata Hari showed great courage in the face of death, and wore a cheeky corset and pretty hat for her execution.*

STEFAN KISZKO
A Malicious Prank

How does a gentle tax clerk get locked away as a brutal sex-murderer in modern Britain? Stefan Kiszko spent sixteen years in prison as a result of a malicious prank. The system that is meant to protect ordinary citizens failed with frightening ease.

Prison, with all its punishments, menace and stigma, is bad enough at the best of times. To live within its walls as a rapist or, worse, a child molestor, is hard indeed; yet this was what simple-minded Stefan Kiszko endured for sixteen years. For he was trapped in a nightmare of Kafkaesque proportions; an innocent man in jail for the brutal sex killing of an eleven-year-old girl.

Finally, from the shadows of this monstrous injustice, Stefan emerged blinking into the sunlight of freedom in February 1992. Waiting for him, as she had waited every day was his mother, the courageous-woman who believed he was innocent and who took on the full majesty and weight of British law to prove it.

Charlotte Kiszko was fifty when police called on her modest home in Rochdale in 1975 to say that her son Stefan was wanted for questioning in connection with the murder of eleven-year-old Lesley Molseed. Little Lesley was found on a lonely Yorkshire moor in October 1975. She had been abducted while out shopping on an errand for her mother and her violated body found on moorland near to Rochdale. She had been dragged from a car, stabbed and sexually assaulted. Her clothes were stained with semen and these stains would prove vital both in Stefan's conviction and later to prove his innocence. These moors were notoious because Hindley and Brady buried their child victims there.

'My first thought,' said Charlotte in a voice strongly accented by the gutteral tones of her own native Slovenian language, 'was that the police only want to talk to Stefan. They asked him to go to the police station and he drove there in his own car. He never came back.

'When I begged them to let me speak to him or to just give him a message that I was all right, they refused me even that. I didn't think you could get solicitors on a Sunday, but then I wasn't prepared for that, we have never been in any kind of trouble before. You don't know what to do for the best when it comes along.' It was 21 December 1975.

Stefan, a tax clerk, was regarded in his town as a kind of gentle-but-dim bachelor; overweight, an obvious introvert who was clumsy with girls. His life seemed to revolve in turns around his mother, his Hillman car which she had bought for him and his job. He was neither a drinker nor a gambler, and had a limited social life.

HORMONAL MEDICATION

The first time he had come to the attention of the police was just weeks before Lesley's body was found. Local girls in Rochdale trooped into a police station to report Stefan for exposing himself to them. Much later they admitted that they had made the allegation up 'for a lark'. They thought Stefan 'stupid' and all had a good laugh at his discomfort at the thought of the police interviewing him.

The police interviewed him three times and discovered two things about him: that he was infertile and that he was taking hormonal medication to ease his condition. One of these crucial factors remained hidden at his later trial for the murder of Lesley Molseed.

Around the time of the killing Stefan was receiving injections of the male hormone testosterone to combat his medical condition of hypogonadism, the root cause of his infertility. The drug was meant to increase his sperm count and thereby his sexual drive. Four samples of semen found on Lesley's battered body were analysed at a forensic laboratory in Harrogate, Yorkshire, by Peter Guise, a specialist forensic scientist working for Ron Outteridge, a distinguished forensic expert

Opposite and below: *Stefan Kiszko, a shy and gentle soul, weeps with relief after his sentence was overturned. He was suspected of sexual deviancy only after some schoolgirls – for a laugh – gave the police a false report that the clumsy batchelor had indecently exposed himself.*

HIS LIFE SEEMED TO REVOLVE IN TURNS AROUND HIS MOTHER, HIS HILLMAN CAR WHICH SHE HAD BOUGHT FOR HIM AND HIS JOB.

for the police in Yorkshire who had handled literally thousands of cases.

Guise found that the semen on Lesley's clothing contained 'sperm-heads', medical proof that her killer was a fertile man. Further examination revealed that the sperm count was, however, perculiarly low, in the bottom twenty-five per cent of sperm density. Armed with this information the police officers in charge of the case – tough Yorkshire coppers Detective Chief Superintendent Jack Dibb and Detective Superintendent Dick Holland – went in search of Stefan Kiszko.

For two days Stefan, the simple-minded tax clerk was subjected to intense interrogation. He was not allowed access to a

Below: *Stefan Kiszko with his loving mother, Charlotte in the happy days before he was wrongfully arrested for the murder of a little girl.*

solicitor and was unable to successfully give himself an alibi for the time of the murder. Mrs Kiszko said later: 'They [the police] regarded Stefan as some kind of village-idiot. I think they had already made up their minds about him before he was even in the police station.'

On the second day of Stefan's confinement in custody he signed a detailed confession to the murder that, sixteen years later, would be proved to be totally forced and false. Stefan would tell how the statement was in fact written by a police officer and that he signed it 'because I was scared'. He was a timid man of low intelligence.

The statement was enough to secure his conviction.

His trial in July 1976 was a farce of circumstantial evidence, forensic tests on some fibres found on Lesley's clothes and Stefan's own confession. The fibres had supposedly come from a carpet square in Stefan's home – a carpet that was one of the top-selling brands in the north of England and probably was in thousands of homes. The fibre evidence was used as damning testimony.

RE-INVESTIGATION OF THE CASE

Dr Edward Tierney, a police surgeon, carried out a test on Kiszko and found him to be suffering from hypogonadism. Tierney said: 'My physical examination confirmed that he indeed suffered from this affliction. I did not know of the discrepancy between Kiszko's and the killer's semen until after the Home Office ordered a re-investigation of the whole affair.'

What happened, in fact, was that the tests taken by Guise were not mentioned during the trial and Stefan Kiszko was framed. Outteridge, Guise's boss, submitted a statement to the trial referring to the semen stains on the girl's body, but did not mention the discrepancy between the sperm-heads found there by his junior and Stefan's inability, backed up by Dr Tierney, to produce sperm.

His solicitor was David Waddington, QC, now Lord Privy Seal and leader of the House of Lords. He advised his client to run a defence of 'diminished responsibility' on medical grounds and claimed that the testosterone injections he was receiving had boosted his sex drive in

some uncontrollable way. By a 10-2 majority verdict Stefan Kiszko, condemned for a crime he never committed, was consigned to the miserable prison life of a sex offender.

In Wakefield prison he was put on Rule 43, the segregation policy practised in jails to keep sex offenders safe from vengeance. Year after year his mental condition deteriorated until he was diagnosed as an acute schizophrenic. Meanwhile, his mother was battling for him in a fight that seemed hopeless but would one day lead to victory.

Charlotte, a widow, always refused to accept the verdict and knew in her heart of hearts that her son was no sex killer. She says: 'I knew he hadn't done it. When you see a child grow up and you are very close to them you can spot the changes in them. I know my son was having a course of testosterone injections around the time of the murder and a lot of people liked to say they turned him into a monster, but that was all just rubbish.

'The first solicitor I went to wouldn't help. He didn't bother about witnesses or evidence. My sister and I went to him and told him that the poor girl had eleven stab wounds on her body. So why didn't they find blood on my son's clothes or body or in his car? And he said to me that all the blood went inside the girl's body. I told him that I had grown up on a farm and that when you kill a chicken there is blood. He called me a hysterical woman and assured me that there was nothing to be done. I always remember his words: "That is the law of this country and that is the end of it."

'But I knew he hadn't done it. On Saturdays and Sundays my son never left me alone for longer than half an hour and the Sunday of the murder was no different. We went to the cemetary together to put flowers on my husband's grave. I remember very well coming home because there was a fire in the street – then Stefan took the car to the car wash and went to see if his aunt Freda needed anything. They didn't think a mother knew if her son had just popped off and turned into a murderer in ten minutes? I knew he hadn't.'

Above: *The murdered child's family wept when they learned that the wrong man had been imprisoned for the crime. Her sister, Julie Crabb is supported by her father, Fred Anderson on the left, and her brother, Fred Anderson Jnr.*

'THEY DIDN'T THINK A MOTHER KNEW IF HER SON HAD JUST POPPED OFF AND TURNED INTO A MURDERER IN TEN MINUTES?'

She had neither the money nor the public support to bring pressure for a re-investigation of the case. But five years ago, with her solicitor Campbell Malone, and a dogged private eye called Peter Jackson, she took on the establishment to save her son from his living hell.

Jackson, a former RAF policeman, turned up the clues which finally led to the shameful miscarriage of justice being exposed. Jackson thought of the case initially as a routine investigation but 'I became alarmed as I looked further into the case. In my view the police and the defence were both at fault. I wanted it all to come out so that no other poor devil could ever fall into the same trap.'

When he began investigating nobody knew about the forensic evidence on the semen samples, long forgotten in police files. Jackson discovered that Stefan remembered being in a corner shop on the Sunday of the murder and he heard a row between customers. Jackson did establish from other witnesses that the row had taken place and that Stefan had been present.

FOUR WITNESSES SAW A RED CAR, STEFAN'S CAR WAS BRONZE

Jackson also sought to destroy the credibility of Stefan's 'confession'. A witness said she had seen Lesley Molseed on the day of the murder in a white car with red markings around the wings. Three other witnesses had also reported seeing a similar car near to the murder scene. Stefan's Hillman car was bronze coloured.

All this evidence was sent in a file to the Home Secretary who ordered an internal inquiry of the West Yorkshire police force. That inquiry turned up the 'missing' slides with the semen samples that could have proved Stefan Kiszko innocent all those years ago. They proved it now. Three appeal court judges ruled in February 1992 that he was a wrongly convicted man. Quashing the conviction Lord Lane, the Lord Chief Justice, said: 'The result is that this man cannot have been the person responsible for the ejaculation and, consequently, cannot have been the murderer.'

Stefan was forty when he walked free from jail with the lost years behind him. He was a broken man in many ways, suffering from chronic schizophrenia brought on by his imprisonment. He said: 'My years inside were a hell and a nightmare, but I never lost faith that I would be acquitted. I always believed the courts would come on my side. But I always believed in my own innocence.' Smiling broadly, he turned to his mother, kissed her, and said: 'Mum has given me every confidence. What would I have done without her?'

So what went wrong with British justice? An inquiry has been ordered by the Home Office into why the scientific evidence wasn't available at the trial and its outcome is still a considerable way off. The people involved now hold some of the highest positions in the land but will still have to account to the Lancashire police carrying out the inquiy. Peter Taylor, the barrister who led the prosecution of Stefan – and who is now the Lord Chief Justice – will be asked if he knew why the key evidence regarding Stefan was not produced at his trial. The same will be asked of Lord Waddington and Dick Holland, who now works as a security expert. Chief Superintendent Kenneth Mackay, who is heading the inquiry, said: 'I will need to talk to a lot of people. They will all be interviewed in time.'

Campbell Malone believes it is 'most unlikely' that the evidence of a semen mismatch was contained in the bundle of papers handed to Taylor and Waddington as they prepared for Kiszko's trial. He says he has seen most of the papers made available to the lawyers involved in the case and claims that there is only one paragraph which mentions semen, saying it was impossible to identify the attacker's blood group by testing the sperm found on the girl's body. Dick Holland has made a statement saying that he did not see written documents suggesting samples from Kiszko and from the body were incompatible. He added that, at the time of the arrest, he was not informed, that there was a mismatch. Did a clerical slip-up condemn Stefan?

Charlotte Kiszko, happy that the long crusade is over, hopes that the inquiry will also re-examine the original defence process at her son's trial. She is angry that Lord Waddington, a proponent of the death penalty, chose the defence he did for Stefan. She said: 'Suppose if we had capital punishment, would Stefan be dead now? I would like to string Waddington up by his

SHE TOOK ON THE ESTABLISHMENT TO SAVE HER SON FROM LIVING HELL.

THAT INQUIRY TURNED UP THE 'MISSING' SLIDES WITH THE SEMEN THAT COULD HAVE PROVED STEFAN KISZKO INNOCENT ALL THOSE YEARS AGO.

'MY YEARS INSIDE WERE A HELL AND A NIGHTMARE, BUT I NEVER LOST FAITH THAT I WOULD BE ACQUITTED.'

feet for an hour until he saw sense. Capital punishment is too barbaric an idea for a civilised country like this.

'They are talking now about compensation for what has happened, as much as half-a-million pounds, possibly. But how can any amount of money compensate for sixteen years spent in prison? I just want Stefan home, back where he belongs. If there is some money, perhaps he will go and visit his uncle in Australia. All I hope is that he will be well enough to live a normal life with me here. But we have to wait a few weeks to find out the truth of that.

'But you know what I think would be nice? I think if someone, somewhere, could give me an official apology for the terrible thing that happened to my son. No one has said sorry properly to me yet. Stefan tried very hard over the years to be positive and it is much easier for him to forgive than for me. It is in his nature. My main faith has always been him and I would have done anything to clear his name. I kept thinking through the years about his office colleagues, good state workers, and how they must have felt working alongside a murderer. I had to prove to them that he wasn't. Stefan's sentence was a life sentence for murder. I would have fought for ever if it had taken that long.'

Campbell Malone, to whom she owes so much, is not sure that the inquiry will ever bring out the full facts into this gross miscarriage of justice. He is not sure it was deliberate. He said: 'The police are very keen to get to the bottom of it because they feel it is a slur on the professionalism of all the police forces. But a lot of time has gone by, one of the most important people in the case, Jack Dibb, is dead and people's memories play tricks. What is certain is that anything that could go wrong with this case did go wrong.'

Above: *Charlotte Kiszko kisses the son who was so cruelly snatched from her after a tragic miscarriage of justice.*

ALFRED DREYFUS
A Shameful Case

All Alfred Dreyfus wanted was to serve his country, France. The establishment repaid his loyalty by branding him a spy, imprisoning him for five years and subjecting him to three rigged trials. The case still arouses both shame and passion.

Like no case before it or after it, the Dreyfus affair – or 'L'affaire', as it became known – shattered the morale of France and left a lasting stain on the national character. An exemplary French officer, Captain Alfred Dreyfus, attached to the French General Staff, was accused in 1894 of selling secrets to his nation's enemy, Germany.

In a grotesque frame-up, made all the more sinister by blatant religious bigotry because Dreyfus was a Jew, he was court martialled, stripped of his rank and sentenced to Devil's Island, the notorious disease-infested penal colony where death was the only release. At one time Parisian mobs clamoured in the streets and screamed for his execution as Dreyfus fever gripped every strata of society.

Only world opinion and the strivings of a few good men, spurred on by an unbending belief in his innocence, finally secured justice for Dreyfus and eventually succeeded in reversing a great miscarriage of justice. But what happened to Dreyfus sank deep into the French consciousness and it remains a national shame that the society that proclaimed liberty, brotherhood and equality in the 1789 revolution will never entirely shrug off.

Alfred Dreyfus was born into a wealthy family in Mulhouse in the French region of Alsace-Lorraine, on the borders with Germany, on 9 October 1859. His father was a textile merchant who had created a fortune and, through shrewd management and investments, ensured that Alfred and his other sons would be well looked after in life, no matter what careers they choose.

For Alfred, however, there was only ever one love in his life – the military. His sense of the greatness of France, 'La Gloire', motivated his desire to serve as an officer in its army, and, in 1880 he entered the 14th Regiment of Artillery as a 2nd Lieutenant after a stint at a military college. By this time France was licking her wounds, the nation still in a mortal state of shock, after the war with Prussia in 1871 which led to the humiliating defeat of France and the abdication of Emperor Napoleon III. In a lightning war which routed the French forces, Prussia took over Alsace-Lorraine and with it Dreyfus's home city. Determinedly, almost obsessively French, Alfred and his family moved to Paris after the defeat rather than live under the Hohenzollern eagle.

Opposite: *Alfred Dreyfus with his two young children. He was both an honourable soldier and family man, but he was also a Jew and for this, he was besmirched and damned.*

Below: *The famous newspaper article by the author, Emile Zola, that shamed the French Army and the government into the reinstatement of Dreyfus' honour and good name. The photograph shows Mathieu Dreyfus, Alfred's brother who fought relentlessly to prove his innocence.*

HIS SENSE OF THE GREATNESS OF FRANCE, 'LA GLOIRE', MOTIVATED HIS DESIRE TO SERVE AS AN OFFICER IN ITS ARMY.

anti-Semite who despised what he perceived as the aloofness of Dreyfus on the staff, claimed the letter had been recovered from the wastepaper basket of Lt Col Max von Schwartzkoppen, military attache at the German embassy in Paris, by a cleaner named Bastian who was one of Henry's own spies. The letter was in French, torn in four and detailed information on several military matters, including the hydraulic braking system of a 120mm gun, new artillery tactics and French troop strength on the island of Madagascar.

Anti-Semitism in France at the time was rife; several prominent Jewish politicians had been involved in a scandal surrounding the bankruptcy of the Panama Canal company. In such a climate of hysteria and loathing it was awkward to be a Jew in the army. Alfred Dreyfus was a man in the wrong place at the wrong time. Suspicions that he may have been the sender of the *bordereau*, because he was an artillery

As a young artilleryman, Dreyfus rapidly proved himself a military talent destined for great things. By 1889 he had achieved the rank of Captain, married a woman called Lucie Hadomard, to whom he was devoted, and become the loving father to two children. He had an austere bearing, although not given to too much close intimacy with his brother officers, he was kind and considerate, an officer and a gentleman in every way who devoted himself to his country, his work and his family.

Above: *Officers parade the accused Dreyfus into court.*
Below: *Scenes from Zola's trial for libel.*

A MODEL OFFICER

He was nominated for an attachment to the General Staff. The staff was the highest accolade for an ambitious young officer, the pinnacle of the French military machine that was seeking ways to restore the morale, reputation and, more importantly, the fighting effectiveness of the army after the debacle of 1871. He joined as a probationer on 1 January 1893 and for more than a year served as a model officer. But during this year there were alarming, ever increasing leaks of information about new weapons, defensive forts and tactics to the enemy across the Rhine. Dreyfus's life collapsed with the discovery of a memorandum, or *bordereau* which inexplicably turned up in the offices of the Statistical Section of the War Ministry offices in the Rue St Dominique on 27 September 1894.

Just five officers served in this small ministry, including Major Hubert Henry of the French Intelligence Service. Henry, an

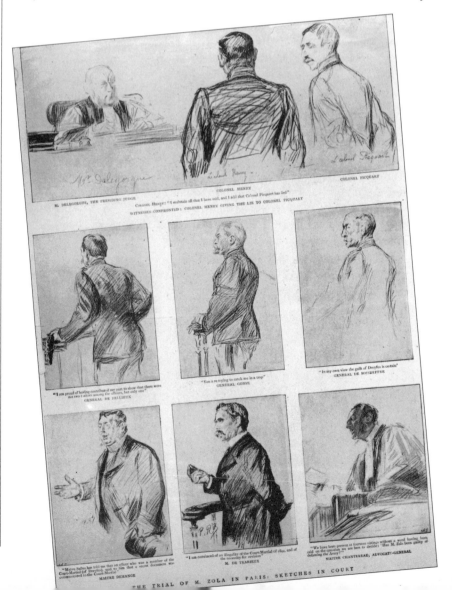

THE TRIAL OF M. ZOLA IN PARIS; SKETCHES IN COURT

expert who had access to the information contained in it, soon became accepted fact without any proof at all. He was blamed because of his distance from his fellow officers, his lack of humour, because of his Jewishness and because he was the odd man out. Soon all the less-than-circumstantial evidence was believed to point to Dreyfus as the guilty party. Handwriting experts – all associates or friends of the

---

GUTTER NEWSPAPERS TOOK THE OPPORTUNITY TO USE THE PANAMA SCANDAL AS REASON TO CALL FOR THE REMOVAL OF ALL JEWS FROM PUBLIC LIFE IN FRANCE.

Charged with high treason, the family of Dreyfus, who never wavered in their belief of his innocence, cast about for the best lawyer they could find. They settled on Edgar Demange, an elderly, highly respected Catholic lawyer who told them: 'Should I find the least reason to doubt his innocence I shall not defend him. This will be known and commented upon. In fact, I shall be his first judge.' When he saw that all the evidence amounted to one *bordereau*, and the petty suspicions of the General Staff of a man they considered to be 'outside the fold' he was dumbstruck. He was confident that he could tear their case to shreds in a court of law.

On 18 Deceember 1894, the night before his trial began, Dreyfus wrote to Lucie, saying: 'Tomorrow I shall stand before my judges, upright and at peace with myself. I have nothing to fear.'

But the madness of mob hysteria was already gripping France and right-wing newspapers ran editorials pleading for the death penalty before his case had even been heard. In such a climate Dreyfus went

General Staff officers – concluded that a handwriting specimen from Dreyfus matched the writing on the *bordereau,* although even to the untrained eye they were patently very different.

Dreyfus was arrested and imprisoned on 15 October 1894. His chief inquisitor during preliminary investigations was Major Armand-Auguste-Ferdinand-Marie Mercier du Paty de Clam, an officer every bit as pompous as his lengthy name would suggest. Louis Snyder, in his scholarly study of the Dreyfus affair 'The Dreyfus Case', said: 'A cousin of the chief of staff, he was a blundering and erratic busybody who felt himself honoured by the assignment. A man of fertile and cruel imagination, he had the soul of a medieval inquisitor and was a violent anti-Semite.'

For seventeen days he continued a baffling and perplexing interrogation of Dreyfus, the man he considered the 'outsider within the fold' because of his Jewishness. 'That my brain did not give way,' Dreyfus wrote, 'was not the fault of the Commandant du Paty.'

*Above, top: **The case was revised in 1899 at this court in Rennes. This revision was as unjust as his trial.***

*Above: **The fake letter that was the chief evidence against Dreyfus and some of those involved against him.***

to trial the next day at the Rue Cherche-Midi, near the prison where he was held.

Seven officers were elected as judges at the court martial that the defence tried but failed to open to the public. Dreyfus knew it was in his interests to have the press and public there but he was powerless to bend the will of the court. Dreyfus set out his testimony: that it was impossible for him to

Henry, who was a relative of the courtroom judge, suggested that he, Henry, be called with some new information. Taking the stand, he said he had received information the previous March, and again in June, from a man he called 'impeccable' but whom he refused to name that there was a traitor on the General Staff leaking secrets to Germany. Turning to Dreyfus with a theatrical flourish he pointed and said in a booming voice: 'There is the traitor!'

THE SECRET IDENTITY OF AN INFORMER

In plain violation of Article 101 of the Military Code which stipulated that an accused man had the right to know the identity of his accuser, the judge ruled that Henry did not have to name the person who had supplied him with this dubious intelligence. All Henry said was that it was a 'person of integrity' and, touching his hat, added: 'There are secrets in the head of an

have the information on the hydraulic braking system mentioned in the incriminating *bordereau* because he had never had access to it; that he knew nothing about Madagascar and that he was completely happy to serve the French army patriotically and undemandingly. He was rich, and did not need to sell secrets for money, and that if he had preferred the army of the Kaiser to that of the Second Republic, he would have returned to his native Alsace.

Three handwriting experts were summoned as the first witnesses. Two said the handwriting in the memorandum matched correspondence taken from Dreyfus's home, a third launched into a preposterous, totally bewildering account of how he had determined by scientific processes – which no one present could possibly fathom – that Dreyfus had merely disguised his handwriting in the *bordereau* to look different, but that it was really his. The evidence was looking so thin, so flimsy, that one senior War Ministry official reported to his superiors that it seemed likely that Dreyfus would be acquitted. That is, until the infamous Major Henry stepped in to nobble Dreyfus permanently with what has proved historically to be one of the most pernicious lies ever told in a courtroom.

officer that are kept even from his kepi.' Adding insult to this injury was a letter handed to the judge by the pompous Major Mercier du Paty de Clam who detailed within it his interrogation results. It was a document filled with lies and innuendoes, claiming that Dreyfus had been disloyal in the past and had, while at Bourges military academy, sold the Germans secrets of a new explosive. What he failed to say was that the Germans had been given the secrets of the new melanite shell before Dreyfus even attended the academy. Again, the contents of this appalling document were denied to his defence lawyer.

On 22 December, four days after the kangaroo court began sitting, the accused was led out of court for the reading of the verdict. He was found Guilty of treason and condemned to dishonourable discharge from the army, deportation from France and exile for life 'in a fortified place'. Demange, the honourable lawyer, wept with the injustice of it all.

Following his conviction came the public humiliation for Dreyfus. The press whipped the mob frenzy to fever pitch and thousands gathered in the great cities of France for weeks in rallies to demand his execution. He had become the scapegoat for all ills, including the French loss of the 1871 war, even though he was just twelve at the time of the French defeat. On 5 January 1895, at the Champ de Mars, the parade ground of the Ecole Militaire, a great crowd gathered, chanting 'Death to the Jew' as Dreyfus was led out before men representing each regiment in Paris. General Darras of the French Cavalry announced: 'Alfred Dreyfus, you are unworthy of carrying arms. We herewith degrade you in the name of the people of France.' With that a giant sergeant walked up to Dreyfus, tearing the epaulettes of rank from his shoulders, shredding the red stripes denoting his attachment to the General Staff from his trousers and snapping his officer's sword in two.

In desperation Drefus cried out, 'Soldiers! An innocent is dishonoured. Long live France!' From the mob which had poured into witness this spectacle came an answering roar: 'Death to the Jew!' As he was paraded before the soldiers and the mob he stopped before a cluster of newspapermen and said to them in a soft voice: 'You will say to the whole of France that I am innocent.' On 17 December, after contemplating suicide in his cell over his hopeless situation, he was shipped off to Devil's Island, the former leper colony, but by now a remote, brutish hell-hole of a prison off the coast of French Guiana.

On Devil's Island he was forbidden to work, write and receive letters and even forbidden to look upon the sea, lest he somehow should contrive a means of toss-

> DREYFUS CRIED OUT, 'SOLDIERS! AN INNOCENT IS DISHONOURED. LONG LIVE FRANCE!'

Above: *The military prison in Rennes where Dreyfus was held.*

Left: *Captain Dreyfus on the left, leaves the War Office in Rennes during preliminary investigations before his trial. He is with an unidentified officer.*

Opposite, above: *Dreyfus stands before the tribunal in Rennes.*

Opposite, below: *Emile Zola, the author who fought to free Dreyfus.*

ing a bottle or some other message out on to the waves. Not even his guards were allowed to talk to him. In France his name was never mentioned in the Chamber of Deputies and Jews, who continued to suffer increased public persecution, all blamed the despicable actions of Dreyfus.

A single courageous French officer, Lt Col George Picquart, was determined never to forget the memory of his friend. He always believed in his innocence and was determined to find the guilty cuplrit.

Below: *The military paraded in honour of Dreyfus' re-instatement in 1906, but he had suffered the shame of having his sword broken and his freedom taken.*

In March 1896, fifteen months after Dreyfus was sentenced, a second torn note was again found in the German embassy, this one addressed to a Major Ferdinand Walsin-Esterhazy. Esterhazy, a French-Hungarian nobleman was a brave officer who had served with distinction in the war against Prussia, but was a reckless gambler who had squandered most of his family's fortune. Esterhazy was chronically in debt and almost always involved in one shady business deal after another; Picquart vowed to keep an eye on him. The torn letter was not proof of treason – it contained no military references – but its arrival and its source convinced Picquart that he had found the real traitor.

Picquart had been present at the Dreyfus trial but had been denied access to any written document other than the *bordereau*. He wanted to get hold of a handwriting sample of Esterhazy's – and good luck came his way when a month later Esterhazy, ambitious for more rank, status and money, applied for a position on the General Staff. Comparing his application to the notorious *bordereau*, Picquart discovered that the handwriting on each was almost identical. He showed it to several senior members of the staff who scrutinised it in turn. One, General de Boisdeffre saw it, saw the original memorandum which condemned Dreyfus, heaved a sigh and said: 'Well, we were wrong, weren't we?'

A HUMILIATING ADMISSION OF FAILURE

But it was by no means the end of the ordeal for Dreyfus. Esterhazy was a close friend of the despicable Major Henry, the man who had testified at the trial about a trusted stranger who had whispered of treachery, and whose name he could not reveal. It was becoming plain to Picquart that Major Henry had probably recognised the identity of the *bordereau's* author all along, and that he had framed Dreyfus in order to save his friend the gambler, Esterhazy. When Picquart confronted him with the handwriting Henry accused him of trying to stir up trouble to save 'that damn Jew'.

And that was the attitude of his superiors, too. In their view, the Dreyfus case was closed. The *bordereau* belonged to the Dreyfus case. If Esterhazy was found guilty

Soon the newspapers were clamouring for more blood and the French high command had no choice but to put Esterhazy on trial. As the Dreyfus hearing was a mockery of law, so was that afforded to his brother officer – only the outcome was different. In a two-day hearing on 10 and 11 January, 1898, Esterhazy was cleared of all charges by a corrupt court that again sat in secret and steamrollered all rules and protocal, including the right of Dreyfus' attorney to sit in and listen to the evidence. It became abundantly clear, even to the staunchest defenders of France's military clique, that something was rotten with the very fabric of the army.

The verdict in the court martial exploded in an historic front page of the newspaper L'Aurore on 13 January, 1898, written by the eminent novelist Emile Zola. Entitled 'J' Accuse' – 'I Accuse' – he risked criminal charges by publicly denouncing the military men, the system they shielded behind and calling for all Frenchmen in the abysmal case to stand up and be counted.

of peddling military secrets in the future then he would be tried. But not on the evidence that convicted Dreyfus. The military caste wanted to preserve their reputation and they could not suffer the humiliation that an admission of failure in the case of Dreyfus would bring upon them. Picquart was dumbstruck and vowed, in a shouting match with one superior, that he would never rest until Dreyfus was cleared.

Esterhazy was silenced by being sent out of France on missions, including examining the intelligence services on France's eastern border. They were assignments intended to stop him from rocking the cozy, closeted world of the staff any further. Major Henry went so far as to forge more crude letters, allegedly traitorous missives signed by the hand of Dreyfus, which mysteriously turned up. But Mathieu Dreyfus, the imprisoned officer's brother, learned of Picquart's discoveries and publicly denounced Esterhazy.

Above: *Colonel Schwarzkoppen (top), who was supposed to be Dreyfus's German spy master and journalists at the trial .*

Addressed to the President of the Republic, it read in part: 'A court martial has but recently, by order, dared to acquit one Esterhazy – a supreme slap at all truth, all justice! And it is done; France has this brand upon her visage; history will relate that it was during your administration that such a social crime could be committed. Since they have dared, I too shall dare. I shall tell the truth because I pledged myself to tell it if justice, regularly empowered, did not do so fully. My duty is to speak – I have no wish to be an accomplice.'

He went on to denounce Mercier du Paty de Clam and the military who had dragged France's name through the mud, condemning their secrecy and their passionate, obstinate protection of their own kind at the expense of an innocent man locked in a hellish jail thirteen thousand miles from France.

Left: *The hut and guard tower on Devil's Island where Dreyfus was held.*

Centre: *Devil's Island in relation to its neighbours.*

Below: Bernard Lazarre, centre, was a staunch supporter of Alfred Dreyfus.

Nevertheless, the military tried again, with the connivance of government officials, to put Dreyfus on trial one more time. His family and supporters were convinced that this time he would be exonerated and the shame of his conviction and banishment lifted for good. Once more, however, the shallow, evil but powerful men triumphed over the good.

Dreyfus arrived back in France, his sentence quashed and in the uniform of an artillery captain, to stand trial again in a court martial convened at Rennes. This time it was public, it lasted for thirty-three days, heard one hundred and fifteen witnesses and still regarded the litany of lies told by senior staff officers as the truth. At the end of the trial Dreyfus said in an impassioned speech: 'I only want to say to the country and the army that I am innocent. I have endured five years of horrible martyrdom to save the honour of my name and that of my children. I am certain that through your honesty and your sense of justice I shall succeed today.' Two hours later, by a verdict of five to two, he was again found Guilty of high treason but, due to 'extenuating circumstances', he was ordered to serve ten years instead of life.

A shocked world reacted with a barrage of outrage against France. In America the

Zola concluded: 'I have one passion only, for light in the name of humanity, which has borne so much and has a right to happiness. My burning protest is only the cry of my soul. Let them dare carry me to the court of appeal, and let there be an inquest in the full light of day! I am waiting.'

The force of the Zola article reverberated through the corridors of power. His masterful attack was called by the author Anatole France 'a moment in the conscience of mankind' as it sought to reverse the great injustices heaped upon the unfortunate Dreyfus. But before there was justice, there was revenge. The establishment closed ranks against Zola, charged him with libel, struck his name from the roll of the Legion of Honour and drove him into exile in London for a year. Their revenge was petty and short lived; soon the cause of Dreyfus was taken up by other important intellectuals and writers, among them Leon Blum, Jean Jaures and the man who would one day be premier of France, Georges 'The Tiger' Clemenceau.

On 19 September, 1899, Dreyfus left prison and the last stage of the campaign to clear his name began in earnest. In May 1906, the appeal court judges in Paris finally quashed the conviction of the court martial at Rennes, saying they were convinced that Dreyfus had been framed all along. He was restored to full rank in the army and his named was – rightly – added to the roll of the Legion of Honour.

On 22 July 1906, a military parade took place as he was given the award, France's highest for merit. Troops who twelve years before had paraded as his sword was broken and his rank badges stripped from him, now stood in salute. A huge crowd of two hundred thousand gathered spontaneously in the streets, screaming 'Long Live Dreyfus! Long Live Justice!' Tears of relief and joy streamed down his face as Dreyfus clutched his son Pierre to him.

Esterhazy, the villain of the piece, retired to England where he lived in poverty and shame in a slum area of London. He was spurned by the country he betrayed and died in poverty in 1923, having confessed

French flag was burned in the streets, a movement was started to boycott the great exhibition scheduled for the coming year. Queen Victoria was not amused and expressed publicly her hope that next time the poor martyr Dreyfus would be able to appeal to better judges.

The president of France wanted to pardon him, but Dreyfus and his supporters knew that a pardon would be an admission of guilt; to be pardoned of something you had to have done something in the first place. But his mental and physical state weakened, Dreyfus accepted the pardon, issuing the following statement: 'The government of the Republic gives me back my freedom. It means nothing to me without honour. From today I shall continue to seek reparation for the atrocious judicial error of which I am still the victim. I want the whole of France to know by force of final judgement that I am innocent. My heart shall be at peace only when there shall not be a single Frenchman who can impute to me the crime which another committed.'

Above: *The guard of dishonour as Dreyfus is led to prison. The troops turn their backs because they are forbidden to look at the traitor.*

Above, top: *An elderly but honoured Dreyfus can be seen weeping at the funeral oration for Zola.*

to a newspaperman that he had been the author of the infamous *bordereau* all along. Dreyfus served gallantly in the First World War, earning decorations for his actions at the Chemin des Dames and Verdun. He died after a long illness in bed on 11 July 1935, his legacy was the courage he displayed; his life was proof that an individual can take on the madness of wholesale corruption and triumph.

JOHN DEMJANJUK
Ivan the Terrible

Is the retired car-worker from Cleveland really Ivan the Terrible, the butcher of Treblinka? How would it feel to stand before an Israeli court accused of the most terrible crimes of the century? The jury is still out on John Demjanjuk.

Treblinka. To the very few who survived it, the name of the Nazi death factory is enough to bring back the most terrible memories, for it was one of the extermination centres designed to process those considered enemies of the Third Reich. Between 1942 and 1943, when the camp was razed to the ground in favour of the more efficient camps Auschwitz and Maidanek, Treblinka 'processed' nearly one million souls.

These so-called enemies of the Reich, brought from all over the conquered territories, were unloaded from cattle wagons and driven into the gas chambers filled with carbon monoxide gas from massive petrol engines. On their path to oblivion stood a man whose sadism has been described by one survivor as 'something so terrible, so inhuman, that he could not be called a creature of this planet.'

As the naked women filed into the death chamber this man hacked off their noses and their breasts with a sword. He casually bashed in men's skulls with lead piping and flayed prisoners with a whip knotted with iron balls. On his tour of the camp huts, where the living dead were kept working for the Reich for as long as it suited their masters, he drilled into men's buttocks with a carpenter's tool and shot the agonised victim if they cried out. The prisoners called him Ivan the Terrible.

Investigators came for a retired car factory worker called John Demjanjuk in 1981 after several years investigation by America's Immigration and Naturalisation

Service. Demjanjuk was a pillar of his community in Cleveland, Ohio, where he had lived since 1952 after arriving from war-torn Europe in search of a better life in the New World.

In August 1952 Demjanjuk – his first name is Ivan but he changed it upon his entry to the USA – was hired for the princely sum equivalent to 90 pence an hour working on the production line at the Ford Motor Company plant. After toiling in the engine department of the factory he was promoted to a foreman's job. His wife, Vera, found work at a local General Electric plant and both diligent workers would stay with their respective employers until the day they retired.

The Demjanjuks had a son and a daughter – John Jnr and Irene – and lived in the Cleveland suburb of Parma before they saved enough money to move to the more affluent neighbourhood of Seven Hills. Every Sunday morning was spent at St Vladimir's Orthodox Church, the core of Ukrainian ex-patriate life in Cleveland. To

'SOMETHING SO TERRIBLE, SO INHUMAN, THAT HE COULD NOT BE CALLED A CREATURE OF THIS PLANET.'

Opposite: *John Demjanjuk who may be the victim of a ghastly KGB frame-up that branded him as a monster from the concentration camps.*

Below: *A pass that was supposed to have been issued in 1942 by the Nazi SS was used to identify Demjanjuk some forty years later.*

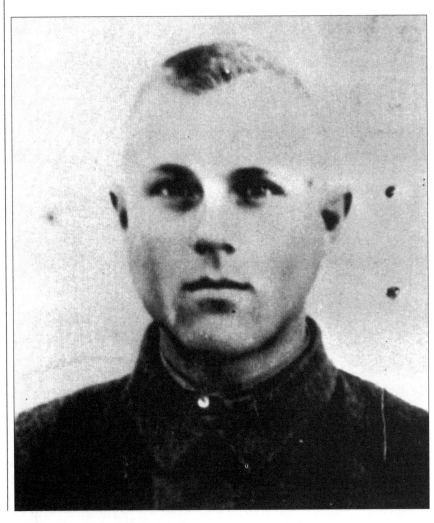

West believe him to be the victim of an old-style KGB frame-up; a frame-up designed and executed in the days before the collapse of communism. The people who believe in his innocence say that the evidence against him is circumstantial at best. Those who believe he is guilty are relying on the testimony of people who witnessed crimes committed fifty years ago. The fact that the Israeli Supreme Court is now giving credence to Soviet files – files released after the fall of the Communist system in Russia – means that doubt has been cast on his wartime role and upon the conviction. For the readers of this volume, here is the challenge of the evidence as presented on both sides – you be the jury on the most controversial war crime trial that has been staged since the end of the Second World War.

THE CASE FOR THE PROSECUTION

Ukrainian-born Ivan Demjanjuk first came to the notice of the US Justice Department in the late Seventies when a pro-Soviet journalist from the Ukraine arrived in New York brandishing a list which he said contained the names of more than seventy Nazi collaborators from the war years who now resided comfortably in America. The journalist handed the list to the Immigration and Naturalisation Department which went through its files on the people named. The list alleged that one Ivan Demjanjuk had

all who knew them and befriended them, the Demjanjuks were the perfect family.

But the FBI came for John Demjanjuk and shattered this harmless life. They came for him on the pretext that he had entered the country illegally. He had: he lied on his documentation that he was Polish and not Ukrainian, fearing, he said, that he might be sent back to the USSR of Stalin. But the INS were not really interested in a small lie on paper three decades before. They came for him because they believed he was Ivan the Terrible, the monster of Treblinka.

John Demjanjuk was tried, convicted and sentenced to hang by an Israeli court for his role in the biggest mass murder in history. At the time of writing, his conviction is still under appeal. It is too early to say whether or not he is guilty – but some of the most distinguished legal minds in the

served as a guard at the Nazi concentration camp of Sobibor. The INS in turn sent the picture taken of Demjanjuk at the time of his entry to the United States to Israeli police, along with the photographs of fifteen other suspects.

Ivan Demjanjuk was born on 3 April 1920, in the Ukraine village of Dub Macharenzi. Both his parents were disabled – his father from wounds received in the First World War and his mother from pneu-

Opposite, top: *The defence claimed this was an authentic photo of Demjanjuk, a policeman not an SS guard.*

Opposite, below: *Demjanjuk in handcuffs charged as a war criminal in Israel.*

later artillery training. He was wounded in fighting near the Dnieper River by a German shell and needed emergency treatment to remove a large sliver of shrapnel from his back. By 1942 he was fighting in the Crimea where superior German forces captured him and his unit. It is this point that the two versions of what happened to Ivan Demjanjuk part company.

The prosecution contend that he was taken to a POW camp at Rovno –

monia. Life was hard in the Soviet dominated republic where there was never enough food and schooling was limited. He moved to Moscow as a boy when Stalin's agricultural collectivisation policies created a famine that killed ten million people, but soon he was back in his village after his father failed to find work. 'My father sold his house for the equivalent of eight loaves of bread,' he said, 'and we went to Moscow. We ate the bread and were forced to return to nothing.' Luckily, in his teens, he gained employment as a tractor driver on one of the state farms and in 1938, in a bid to increase his chances of promotion, he joined the Komsomol, the Communist youth organisation.

In 1941 Hitler launched Operation Barbarossa, the conquest of the east. Demjanjuk was called up, given basic and

Above: *A US immigration photo of Demjanjuk dated 1951 (left). On the right, a photo said to date from 1947 and taken at Flossenburg, East Germany. There is dispute that both of these are images of the same man, Demjanjuk, the alleged 'Ivan the Terrible'.*

THEY CAME FOR HIM ON THE PRETEXT THAT HE HAD ENTERED THE COUNTRY ILLEGALLY.

Demjanjuk himself confirms this – where he willingly volunteered to serve the Nazis. It is to the eternal shame of the Ukrainian people that her citizens were found, by the Nazis, to be among the most willing servants of the Reich. Ukrainians were found guarding the concentration camps, operating the gas chambers, enforcing Jewish round-ups in ghettos across the conquered territories. The prosecution contended that he was taken to a Nazi training camp at Trawniki, near the Polish city of Lublin, where he was issued with a uniform, a rifle and given SS identification in the form of a Wehrpass, or identity card. His blood group was tattooed under one arm, standard SS procedure. He was recruited for the sole task of service in the death camps.

From Trawniki, the prosecution contends that he moved to Treblinka where he

Right: *The many faces of Ivan the Terrible according to the prosecution: from top left, as Red Army soldier; camp picture, Trawniki; Flossenburg 1947; wedding picture 1948; immigration image 1951; daughter's wedding 1981 and at his trial in Israel.*

Below: *An electronic image mixing Trawniki photo of Demjanjuk with a current photograph.*

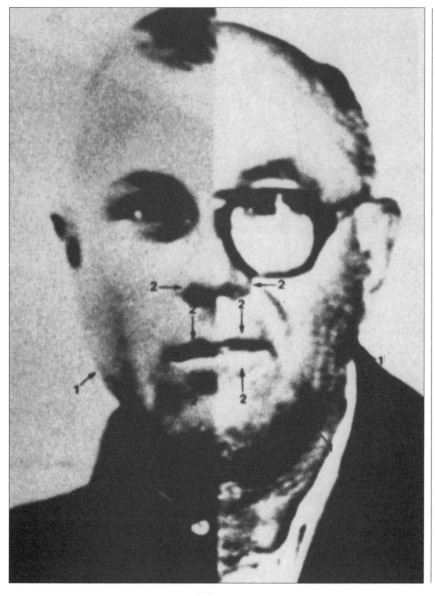

operated the machinery of death that 'processed' eight hundred and fifty thousand human beings. Here he excelled in pain and suffering, inflicting cruelties on his fellow-man that made his Nazi superiors baulk. They say that his limited intelligence was fuelled by rampant anti-Semitism – his birthplace was a known centre of anti-Jewish feelings.

After his immigration photo was sent to Israel it was shown to potential witnesses. After several positive identifications, an advertisement was placed in Tel Aviv newspapers seeking survivors from the camps of Sobibor and Treblinka to come forward. The Israeli authorities also asked for similar assistance in identifying another war crimes suspect from Miami, one Feodor Fedorenko, who later admitted he had served as a guard at Sobibor, albeit a reluctant one, and denied that he had ever taken part in atrocities. (Later Fedorenko was acquitted by a Miami judge of war crimes at his denaturalisation trial on the grounds that Jewish survivors were 'coached' into identifying him. Ultimately, however, a new hearing on appeal returned Fedorenko to the Soviet Union where he was executed by firing squad for war crimes. America, with its powerful and large Jewish population, among them survivors of the Nazi terror, intensely dislikes war criminals in its midst.)

After the Jewish survivors had identified Demjanjuk as their tormentor inside

Treblinka, he was interviewed by the Cleveland US Attorney's office to give a statement which he declined to do on the advice of his lawyer. A year later, after weighing up the Israeli evidence which included verification of an SS identity card, the Justice Department stepped in and filed a federal complaint against him.

In 1981 he went on trial to be denaturalised as a citizen, the first step in deporting him either to the Ukraine or to the Israeli authorities who now viewed him as a major war criminal. In June 1981, after hearing heart-rending testimony from survivors who swore that the man before them was Ivan the Terrible, Judge Frank Battisti ruled that 'the defendant was present at Treblinka in 1942 and 1943 and should therefore be stripped of his citizenship.'

Judge Battisti singled out the evidence of a man called Otto Horn, the only German SS man who stood trial for war crimes at Treblinka after the war to be acquitted. Horn, a humanitarian, served there as a nurse tending to SS staff and took no part in the massacres, although, controversially, some eyewitnesses claimed he took part in torturing inmates. American special investigator Norman Moscowitz showed him pictures of John Demjanjuk; he identified him as Ivan the Terrible.

AN INVESTIGATION OF PREJUDICE

On 18 October, 1983, Israel issued an arrest warrant for John Demjanjuk and a month later requested his extradition from America. Demjanjuk, fearful that he might be summarily executed if he was returned to the Soviet Union like Fedorenko had not thought of the possibility of facing justice in the Jewish homeland. For years he fought through every court in America. Appeal and counter-appeal failed until, on 28 February, 1986 he was flown to Tel Aviv to stand trial.

While he was held in an Israeli jail a crack team of Israeli prosecutors was assembled to methodically build the case against him. One of the men who would give evidence against Demjanjuk was Pinchas Epstein, a Jew in a working party at Treblinka who escaped in a revolt in the summer of 1943. In his shocking testimony, which he would later recount to the court, he said: 'I have nightmares... to this very

day. One day a living little girl managed to get out of the gas chambers. She was alive. She was speaking. A girl of about twleve or forteen. People who took the corpses out of the gas chambers made her sit down on the side, and this little girl, her words ring in my ears still, she said: 'I want my mother'. Ivan took one young man from among us whose name was Jubas. He struck at him brutally with his whip. "Take your pants off" and with that he ordered him to rape the girl. This act was not performed and she

was shot instead.'

When Ivan came to trial in 1987 there were four other survivors who took the stand after Epstein. Eliyahu Rosenberg's testimony was the most gripping. He described the terrible horrors he witnessed, the savagery with which Ivan hacked off pieces of bodies, of beating to death people with lengths of piping. When he came to identifying Ivan in the courtroom, Rosenberg said: 'Ivan. I say so unhesitatingly and without the slightest doubt. This is Ivan from the gas chambers. The man I am looking at. I saw his eyes. I saw those

'THE DEFENDANT WAS PRESENT AT TREBLINKA IN 1942 AND 1943 AND SHOULD THEREFORE BE STRIPPED OF HIS CITIZENSHIP.'

Above: *Demjanjuk during his internment in Israel while the prosecution tries to prove that he is Ivan the Terrible from the Treblinka concentration camp. But the accused man insists that he is innocent.*

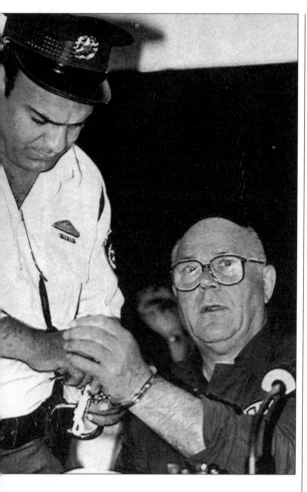

in Hebrew for his death.

THE CASE FOR THE DEFENCE.

ON TOP OF THE TEARFUL
IDENTIFICATIONS WAS THE
ONE KEY PIECE OF PHYSI-
CAL EVIDENCE – THE SS
CARD BEARING A PHOTO OF
THE YOUNG IVAN.

Left and below: *The verdict was Guilty and the old man – Demjanjuk was seventy-two-years old at the time – was sentenced to death by the Israeli court. He was an ill man, and had to be wheeled into court. The verdict is still under appeal, and there is increasing evidence that Demjanjuk has been mistakenly identified and wrongly accused.*

John Demjanjuk argued an entirely different scenario to that offered up by his Israeli prosecutors. He agrees with events only as far as his capture in the Crimea. Then, he says, he was taken to the Rovno camp in Poland and transferred a few weeks later to the POW camp for Red Army captives in Chelm, Poland. Here, he claimed, he was put to work digging peat and moved on from there to another POW camp in Graz, Austria. It was at the Graz camp, he claimed, that he was given the tattoo under his arm to indicate his blood group – not, he said, because he was in the SS.

In 1945 he claimed the Germans offered him and his fellow Ukrainians the chance to join the Russian Liberation Army, an anti-Stalinist cadre. Because he, like other Ukrainians, felt little kinship for the Bolsheviks in Moscow, he says he agreed to join up, escaping at the end of the War to the west where he had the tattoo removed, an operation which left scar tissue. In 1945 he ended up at a displaced person's camp in Landshut, Germany, where he met Vera Kowlowa whom he would later marry and

murderous eyes. I saw that face of his.'

The evidence of the eyewitnesses made moving testimony – testimony that defence lawyers for Demjanjuk were unwilling to call into question because of the enormity of the witnesses' suffering. But on top of the tearful identifications was the one key piece of physical evidence – the SS card bearing a photo of the young Ivan. Fully fifty days of the trial were spent assessing its authenticity, coming as it did from the Soviet Union which, in its time, pulled some mean stunts against enemies real and imagined. In the end the court decided that the card was authentic.

Judge Zvai Tal, handing down the ultimate penalty in May 1988, said: 'Demjanjuk served as a chief hangman who killed tens of thousands of human beings with his own hands. These crimes can never be forgiven in the minds or in the hearts of men. These crimes can never be obliterated from memory. It is as though Treblinka continues to exist, as though the blood of the victims still cries to us.' As the manacled Demnjajuk was led away the hysteriacl crowd was chanting ecstatically

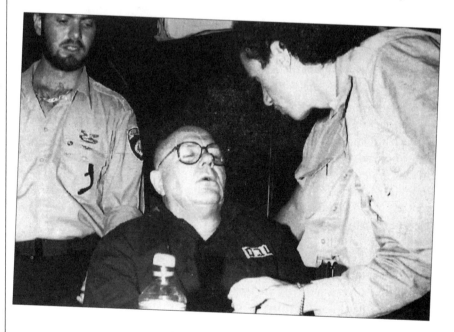

take to America for a new life.

On the stand at the trial his defence lawyers were hampered by their own inexperience in handling a war crimes trial and by Demjanjuk's inability to recall accurately his whereabouts in wartime. The SS identity card, he claimed, was a forgery –

as indeed, upon closer scrutiny, it might well be – and the eyewitnesses were mistaken over traumatic events that took place half-a-century earlier. Uneducated, still barely able to manage much English after close to four decades in America, his lawyers put down his inability to form a coherent defence to the charges to his lack of intellect. Either way, John Demjanjuk did not cut a convincing character in the dock and there were few surprises when he was found Guilty. But it seems, on appeal, that the case might finally swing his way.

It is thanks to the determined efforts of his son, John Jnr, and his son-in-law Ed Nishnic, that he might shake off the death sentence and prove beyond doubt that he is not Ivan the Terrible – even though it is conceivable he did work for the Nazis. After learning of their sleuthing through Kremlin files (which had become more accessible under glasnost and finally totally accessible after the fall of Communism in the summer of 1991), Gitta Sereny, the influential Italian journalist has pointed out: 'It is conceivable that the Israeli Supreme Court may now have to be content with Ivan the Less Terrible.'

'My father,' said John Jnr, 'was just your typical immigrant who came over on the boat trying to escape Communism and make a better life. Go into any Serbian or Ukrainian church and you'll meet a hundred like him. He is not a mass murderer. I would not give up my life for him if I ever thought he was.'

Thanks to amazing detective work – and some help from insiders on the government team who were sympathetic to the Demjanjuk side – John Jnr and Nishnic built up a credible dossier for his acquittal. One employee of the Office of Special Investigations, which carried out the Justice Department probe into Demjanjuk's life, went through garbage every week from the OSI bins. It was pieced together painstakingly by the two men in the basement of Demjanjuk's home. They learned, for instance, that Horn, the acquitted SS man, initially did not pick out Demjanjuk, then identified someone else and was then shown pictures selectively in a fashion calculated to make him point out Demjanjuk.

The appeal was put back eighteen months due to the suicide of one of his lawyers and an acid attack on another. But in that period Nishnic and John Jnr were not idle. In September 1990, John Jnr trav-

Above: *Demjanjuk is embraced by his son during the Israeli trial. His children have stood by Demjanjuk throughout and have even rallied tremendous support in the American Ukrainian community for their father. They are sure he is not Ivan the Terrible. Meanwhile, Demjanjuk (left) continues his brave battle to clear his name.*

elled with Yoram Sheftel, Demjanjuk's fierce and brilliant new lawyer (who was rewarded for his efforts to defend Ivan the Terrible with acid in his face that nearly cost him his sight) to the Crimea, in search of answers to riddles that took place a long time ago. They were promised the KGB file on the trial of Fedorenko... but then the KGB refused to hand it over. Ultimately, however, they contacted Alexander Yeemetz, a sympathiser in the Ukrainian Parliament who obtained a KGB file containing twenty-one confessions of former Treblinka guards – all of them Soviets – taken between 1944 and 1961.

Each statement identified Fedorenko.

Each statement said that the gas chamber was operated by Ivan the Terrible.

Each statement said that Ivan's surname was Marchenko.

In August 1991, after much legal wrangling, the file was accepted into evidence for the defence. Also accepted into evidence were the names and statements of a further forty Soviet guards and underlings of the Treblinka camp – each one of whom testifies that a man named Marchenko was the operator of the gas chamber. One of the statements is from a Nikolai Shelayev, who admitted to being one of the gas chamber operators along with Ivan Marchenko. He

---

'IT'S LIKE THEY CAN'T GET HIM ON ONE THING SO THEY WILL FISH AROUND UNTIL THEY GET HIM ON ANOTHER.'

Below: *John Demjanjuk has been away from home for over ten years, his life with wife and family shattered. Yet his case is seen increasingly as a dreadful error by the Israeli authorities, compounded by the fact that dubious KGB files have been used as evidence.*

says that in June 1943 he and Marchenko were moved to Trieste in Italy to guard political prisoners and that he last saw him the following year when he defected to communist partisans fighting for Tito in Yugoslavia. Shelayev was shot by the Soviets in 1951. He died without ever mentioning the name Demjanjuk.

More significantly, in documents obtained under America's Freedom of Information Act, Demjanjuk's crusading family learned that the Justice Department knew back in 1978, via a Soviet official called Pavel Leleko, that the duo who operated Treblinka's gas chamber were named Nikolai and Marchenko, and that Marchenko had a brutal penchant for severing women's breasts. This information on the man that the Demjanjuk family contend is Ivan the Terrible was never followed up.

Last year Nishnic went to the Ukraine in search of clues as to the background of Marchenko. He found his widow's apartment but was too late – she had died forty days before his arrival. His daughter in the city of Kryvy Rog said her father had gone off to war and had never come home again; she had never known him beyond infancy. But she promised to try to find a photograph of him; it was handed over to Nishnic in January 1992. When placed alongside Demjanjuk's picture the similarities are striking. Now the defence team are confident that the Guilty verdict can and should be overturned.

WHICH CRIMINAL? WHAT CRIME?

But Demjanjuk is so vague on his wartime record – and new files are being unearthed monthly – that it is likely that, although he will escape the death penalty, he may be punished for crimes he may or may not have committed. Israel has never gone after camp guards, the 'small fish' who were not involved in wholesale mass murder. But confronted by the new evidence which suggests that he is not Ivan the Terrible, prosecutors seem intent on making him guilty for other, unspecified crimes. For instance, if the SS identity card is genuine, it lists him being at Sobibor, another death camp. A Sobibor guard has sworn in a statement that he knew a Demjanjuk there.

Other documents from what was East Germany show that a Demjanjuk served at

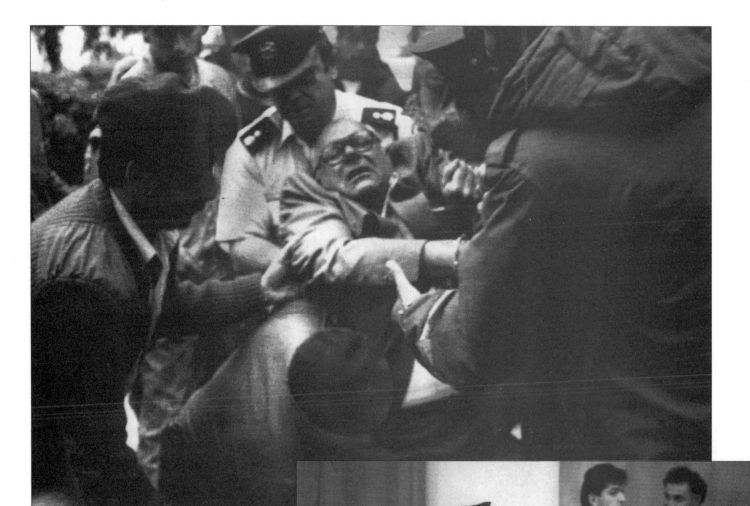

the Flossenburg concentration camp with the number 1393 – the number he was allegedly given at the Trawniki camp. However, nothing exists to link him with mass murder at these places. Dov Freiburg, one of only twenty living survivors of Sobibor, said: 'He must have been small fry otherwise I would have remembered him. If he had been one of the big-timers destroying people, I may have remembered him. It was all along time ago.'

Assistant prosecutor Dafna Bainvol seems to sum up the Israeli attitude when he said: 'We are going to prove to the Supreme Court that he is a Nazi who was at least in Sobibor and Flossenburg.'

At least – they are two words which smack of vengeance. However much the souls of the Nazi concentration camp victims cry out for it, justice is what is needed to preserve the memory of the Holocaust, not mindless vengeance.

John Jnr is outraged that his father should now face a different set of charges. 'It's like they can't get him on one thing so

Above: *In April 1988, John Demjanjuk had to be carried into court as his back was so very weak and painful. In court, he had had to listen to allegations that he was responsible for gassing more than 850,000 Jews and torturing countless more.*

they will fish around until they get him on another,' he said. If his father did admit to being a guard, and not being Ivan the Terrible, he says he could forgive him. He added: 'Would he have been morally wrong at the time, to choose the option of living over dying? Would he be any more culpable than the Jew who worked for the Nazis pulling gold teeth out of the mouths of victims after they had been gassed? I

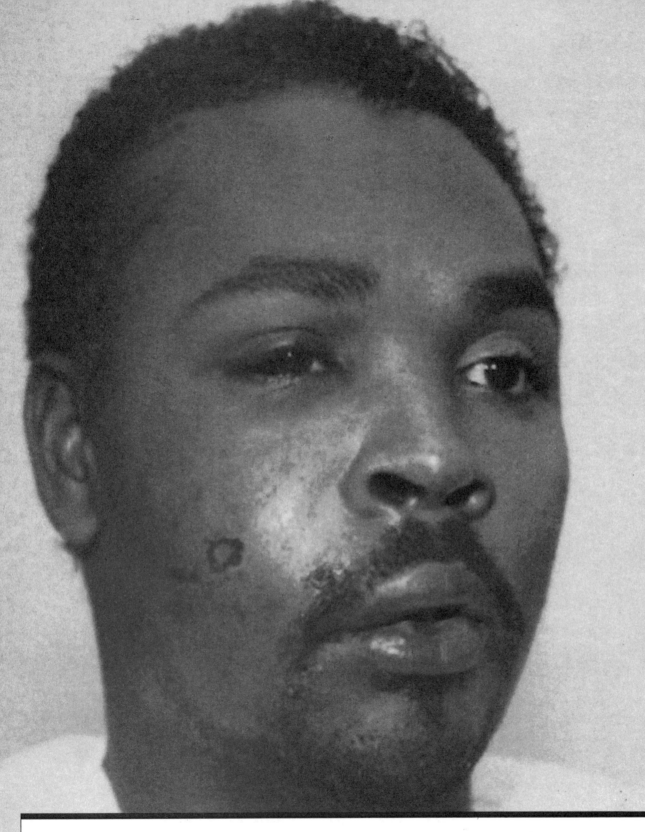

RODNEY KING
Denial of Evidence

When a jury refused to believe their own eyes, they set off a riot which left Los Angeles burning for days. The video tape of the vicious beating Rodney King received from the police had been broadcast around the world. Why were the policemen acquitted?

In his masterpiece '1984', George Orwell depicts a nightmare world of Big Brother, thought police and hate-ins, where his hero, Winston Smith, works in the Ministry of Truth where he re-writes history to suit his masters. Things that took place are altered so they never happened, black becomes white, white becomes black. Something frighteningly similar happened for real in Stalin's Soviet Union: subscribers to Russian encyclopaedias regularly received correspondence telling them to rip out the biographies of generals or statesmen who had been purged from the hierachy and officially no longer existed in the consciousness of the state.

The West has long held up such pernicious practices as the ultimate evil of authoritarian, communist tyrannies. But in May 1992, in America, the guardian of the free world where the rights of man are contained in a written constitution, it seemed that Winston Smith and his Ministry of Truth could have been at work in a courtroom north of Los Angeles.

In this courtroom, a jury decided that a videotape, which showed a black man being beaten and kicked repeatedly by police officers in a shocking orgy of brutality, was nothing more than 'legitimate force'. They ruled, with classic Orwellian logic, that the black man – motorist Rodney King – was 'controlling the situation' because of his attitude even as he lay helpless under the rain of blows. With the acquittal of the four police officers charged in the incident came the aftershocks of disgust and indignation. President Bush in the White House could not believe it and ordered FBI enquiries to bring fresh, civil rights violations against the accused policemen. But shock and outrage were not enough for the oppressed minorities in the ghettoes of LA who rose up in a two-day orgy of looting, burning and murdering. The City of Angels turned into a battleground as the fury over the King

verdict spilled on to the streets and against the police who were vindicated in a case where modern technology, in the form of a video camera, should have ensured there could be no vindication. At the end of the rioting – which spread to other cities – LA's South-Central district was a smoking ruin, swarming with armed troops and National Guards. Was there one justice system for whites and one for everyone else?

A BLACK MAN BEING BEATEN AND KICKED REPEATEDLY BY POLICE OFFICERS IN A SHOCKING ORGY OF BRUTALITY, WAS NOTHING MORE THAN 'LEGITIMATE FORCE'.

Above: *The acquittal of the policemen who beat King sparked riots and looting in Los Angeles.*

Opposite: *The bruised and beaten face of Rodney King after he encountered policemen who tried to stop him speeding in his car.*

The officers ultimately responsible for turning LA into a charcoal pit with 51 dead and billions of pounds worth of damage, couldn't have known what they were getting into when they stopped Rodney Glen King in his car on the night of 3 March 1991. King, no angel when it came to the law, was stopped for speeding. A convicted armed robber, a drug abuser, a man, in that classic phrase 'well known to the law', led officers of the Los Angeles Police Department on a terrifying, sometimes life-threatening high-speed chase on the freeway network of LA At times King was driving close to 100 miles per hour and there were real fears that he would kill innocent people if he lost control of the vehicle. Finally, King was forced to stop in a suburb of Los Angeles and surrounded by over a dozen cops from several squad cars, all with their guns drawn. King was a lethal suspect who had terrorised a corner store owner with a knife – the incident which led to his armed robbery conviction – police had every right to be wary of him. He was obviously drunk – and, for all the police arresting him knew, maybe stoned on drugs

> HE WAS RECORDING A SLICE OF VIOLENT HISTORY THAT WOULD BECOME EVERY BIT AS IMPORTANT TO THE CIVIL RIGHTS MOVEMENT IN AMERICA AS THE BIRMINGHAM BUS BOYCOTT.

Below and opposite: *An amateur cameraman filmed a nasty scene of police brutality as the law officers beat and kicked King. The policemen claimed that they used only 'reasonable force' to subdue the man.*

like LSD or PCP, the latter known as 'Angel Dust' and a drug capable of giving a person superhuman strength combined with a loss of the sense of reality.

Rodney King's arrest would not even have made the newspapers had it not been for thirty-one-year-old plumbing store manager George Holliday who was on his balcony after midnight. Unable to sleep, he was experimenting with his new video recorder to see how it worked in poor lighting conditions. Suddenly, as he panned his camera around, he switched on the zoom lens as he caught sight of the police cars with their lights flashing. Illuminated in the headlights of the cars was a black man, his hands above his head. George Holliday did not know it at the time but he was recording a slice of violent history that would become every bit as important to the civil rights movement in America as the Birmingham bus boycott or the shooting of Martin Luther King.

His camera rolled for seven minutes – but it was eighty-one seconds from that seven minutes that shocked the world when George sold it for less than £300 the fol-

lowing day to a local TV network. In that eighty-one seconds, Rodney King, twenty-five, was subjected to over eighty-five blows from the batons of the police officers. At 12.52 am, roughly thirty seconds into the beating, King is seen struggling to his knees, his arms raised apparently in a gesture which says 'no more, no more'. He was hit twice by Taser stun-guns, which deliver 50,000 volts of electricity. At 12.53am he is seen still writhing under a rain of blows. Officer Theodore Briseno has his boot on King's neck. Ten seconds later he is motionless and *still* receiving blows from batons and kicks. Finally he is cuffed and dragged into a police car. He has sustained a broken ankle, skull fractures, a permanently damaged eye and needed two days of hospital treatment. 'What happened to you?' one doctor reportedly said to him. 'Fall down a set of stairs in the police station?' It was a throwaway line, but one with sinister overtones of what might happen to minorities if they fall into the hands of brutally and illegally violent LAPD police officers.

Newscasters at a TV station in Los Angeles where George Holliday sold his tape could not believe the explosive materi-

al delivered into their hands. Clearly this was some of the most sensational amateur footage of a crime being committed – committed by the personnel entrusted to defeat and prevent crime – ever taken. When it was screened the effect across America was explosive. Coast to coast, civic leaders stepped forward to condemn what happened while the embattled Los Angeles Police Chief Darryl Gates struggled to put

TEN SECONDS LATER HE IS MOTIONLESS AND STILL RECEIVING BLOWS FROM BATONS AND KICKS.

Above: *Rodney King did not testify at the trial but in the wake of the verdict he stepped forward to deliver a halting, impassioned plea for peace as the city of LA burned.*

'IT WAS A WIERD FEELING AND I WAS TRYING TO THINK: "WHAT COULD HE HAVE DONE TO DESERVE THIS?"'

some kind of explanation to what was rapidly becoming an indefencible incident. Gates, a figure of controversy for many years – he once claimed blacks died in police choke holds because their physical make-up was different from that of whites – was even disowned by Los Angeles Mayor Tom Bradley. Bradley, a black man who was a former police officer, voiced the disgust and indignation of an enraged nation when he said: 'Clearly there will have to be an investigation so far reaching and so wide that no aspect of this disturbing and unsettling affair can be left unaccounted for. This is something we cannot and will not tolerate. I am as shocked and as outraged as anyone.' At first Gates suspended the four officers who dealt out the beating, but when it became clear that public outrage would settle for nothing less than criminal charges, the LA district attorney handed down charges.

The shadows who wielded the batons that night were identified as career officers. Sergeant Stacy Koon, forty-one, was in command that night. He was charged with assault with a deadly weapon, excessive

force by an officer under colour of authority, filing a false police report and being an accessory to assault. Koon served in the Air Force and joined the LA police department in 1976. It would later come out that he shot and wounded a suspect who had fired on police after a drive-by shooting in 1989. The police commission commended him for his handling of the incident, but they were not so proud of his disciplinary hearings for excessive force while on the job. Married with three children, he plans to write a book about his experiences on patrol with the LAPD.

THE POLICE LOSE CONTROL

Theodore Briseno, thirty-nine, would later break ranks with his fellow cops during the trial and blame them for the beating. 'I just thought the whole thing was way out of control,' he claimed. Married with two children, he was charged with assault with a deadly weapon and excessive force by an officer under colour of authority. Theodore Briseno has been twice commended for bravery while on duty.

Laurence Powell would come to be painted as the bogeyman during the trial because he delivered most of the blows to King – thirty-three in all. When he was initially arraigned he said he thought King was on drugs and that 'I was completely in fear of my life. I was scared to death.' Powell, son of a Los Angeles Marshall, was twenty-nine at the time of his arrest and has been in trouble before with the force for excessive use of force. Salvador Castaneda, thirty-six, a robbery suspect, had his arm broken after being struck five times by Powell's baton. He was awarded £40,000 in a civil suit settlement last year. A police officer since 1987, Powell was charged with assault with a deadly weapon, excessive force by an officer under colour of authority and filing a false police report.

Timothy Wind, a thirty-two-year-old probationary cop, was the fourth man arrested and was fired by Chief Gates in the weeks following the beating because he did not have a contract with the city due to his rookie status. Accused of aggressively beating and kicking King he was also charged with assault with a deadly weapon and excessive use of force by an officer under colour of authority. He became a policeman a decade ago in Kansas and had only been in the LA force a short time when the King beating happened. He is also a married man with a young child.

George Holliday became a nationwide celebrity and appeared on TV talk shows with the regularity of a film star. He described how he was experimenting with his new camera on the terrace of his home twenty miles from downtown LA when he witnessed the dramatic end to the police chase. He couldn't believe his eyes when he saw the beating begin. He said: 'Before they started hitting him he was pretty much co-operative. It was a weird feeling and I was trying to think: "What could he have done to deserve this?"' Another eyewitness, Eloise Camp, said: 'I never saw him offer any resistance.' A third eyewitness, Dorothy Gibson, a fifty-two-year-old nurse, added: 'I could hear him pleading: "please

Below: *Righteous anger gave way to gratuitous and wanton destruction of property all across the city. Other racial tensions were expressed as blacks burned down Asian owned shops and homes.*

stop, please stop." He put his hands over his head to try to cushion the blows. After the beating was over the policemen were all just laughing and chuckling like they had just had a party.' The incident triggered a slew of instant TV and newspaper probes into previous allegations of Los Angeles police brutality. For once the mainstream media was alert and listening to numerous cases of brutality allegedly committed by police officers – most of which had gone unpunished. The accusations of inbred racism in the eight-thousand-four-hundred strong police department were further

Below and opposite:
Rodney King presented a dignified, yet emotional, public face. His obvious distress at the burning of his city touched many as he pleaded on television 'Can't we all just get along?' He became a symbol for something better than either the law or the mobs.

strengthened by the release of computer message transcripts sent from the police involved in the beating back to their headquarters that night. There were references to 'Gorillas in the Mist' and other racial slurs which only served to fuel the growing anger and resentment just bubbling beneath the surface of the population.

Karol Heippe, executive director of the Police Misconduct Lawyer's Referral Service, a national watchdog body which monitors incidents of police violence, said of the videotape: 'It's horrible. It's horrible, but I must say that we receive complaints in this office of that kind on a weekly, if not a daily basis. The difference is that this time there was somebody there to video-

SLICK LAWYERS WHO ARGUED SUCCESSFULLY THAT WHAT THE JURY SEES ON THE TAPE IS NOT WHAT ACTUALLY HAPPENED.

tape it.' For the first time in American judicial history a videotape would be offered up to a jury as the only evidence for the prosecution. The camera couldn't lie, mused prosecutors, and they felt certain that a conviction for all four police officers was assured. But they hadn't reckoned on three things – a change of trial venue outside LA, a jury that was ready to side with authority rather than a convicted criminal and slick lawyers who argued successfully that what the jury *sees* on the tape is not what actually *happened*.

The trial was switched at the last moment to the Los Angeles suburb of Simi Valley. A judge decreed that switching the trial away from Los Angeles, where feelings were running high, would ensure a fairer trial. What in fact it did was to weigh the scales of justice heavily in favour of the defendants. By ordering the trial to take place in Simi Valley the judge was effectively placing them in the hands of jurors drawn from a suburb that is largely white, largely middle class and, crucially, drawn from a community that is the residence of choice for many LA police officers. The result was indeed a jury with just two ethnic minorities sitting on it and no blacks. Another factor was that the jurors had little awareness of how violent were racial confrontations between public and law officers had become in the big city where the very concept of law enforcement took on insidious and brutal connotations. The trial gave the cops the edge from the word go.

PLAY IT AGAIN, AND AGAIN, AND AGAIN

The trial opened a year after the assault – a year in which the wedge between black and white in Los Angeles was driven wider and deeper. All four officer pleaded Not Guilty to all the charges and it immediately became apparent that their defence strategy was going to be that they were within the law to use force to subdue their suspect. The video, now shown hundreds of times on TV, was about to be dissected and microscopically analysed by their lawyers – planting in the minds of the jury that the apparent random use of force against the hapless Mr. King was nothing of the kind – that it was in fact sustained, measured and controlled violence as laid down by the

LAPD guidelines for dealing with potentially violent prisoners. Michael Stone, the attorney for officer Powell said: 'When I first saw the tape my knees were shaking. I thought the frames, particularly those where King is on the ground and he is still being hit, put us in a terrible hole. But then I realised that there were positive things to point out. I figured with the other lawyers that the officer clearly complied with rules for escalating degrees of force. Police are trained to use their batons to cause pain. That usually stops a suspect. If it doesn't they are allowed to increase the level of pain and that's what these officers did. King is a big man and these officers were not going to allow him to get into a position where he could stand up again and perhaps pose an additional threat to them.'

NO EXPRESSION OF PAIN OR FEAR

Lawyer Darryl Mounger, himself an ex LA cop for ten years who was representing Sgt Stacy Koon, said: 'A little pain is a great incentive. When you get hit with a metal baton by someone who knows how to swing it, you're supposed to do what they say so they don't hit you again. The officers simply did what they are trained for, using the tools that they are given. A picture is worth a thousand words, but a lot of times it takes a thousand words to explain a picture. What you think you see isn't always what you see. King had a look of determination in his eyes. He did not have a look of pain or fear on his face.'

This was where unreality seemed to take over during the proceedings as the jury was, in the eyes of trial critics, literally brainwashed into thinking that the beating was exactly what King deserved, despite the fact he offered no resistance and posed no threat. The line of defence was that the police thought him capable of posing a threat to them and were correct in subduing him before that threat materialised. To many this was the equivalent of 'shoot first and ask questions later'. When it came to explaining why Officer Briseno had his foot on King's neck his lawyer John Barnett said: 'He may actually have saved King's life. Briseno isn't really attacking him but keeping him on the ground for his own good. In this late stage of this highly-charged confrontation maybe he could have

> 'THIS WAS CALIFORNIA, WITH IT'S EQUALITY LAWS AND ITS POSITIVE THINKING AND ITS INGRAINED, INBRED SENSE OF FAIR PLAY.'

got shot if he didn't stay down. That was what my client was doing.'

Despite the arguments from the lawyers it is fair to say that an air of inevitability hung over the courtroom. President Bush, who had already instructed FBI officers to look into possible civil rights violations, seemed as convinced as anyone of the outcome of the trial. The men were facing up to seven years each in jail, but it was likely that they would probably get a couple of years a piece, some of it suspended. There had developed in the psyche of the American public a belief that justice, in lib-

eral, progressive California, would be done in the shape of Guilty verdicts on all four men. 'This was not some redneck trial taking place in Alabama or some other deep south hell-hole where nigger-lynching was an accepted part of folklore,' wrote columnist Peter Melnitch. 'This was California, with its equality laws and its positive thinking and its ingrained, inbred sense of fair play. Nothing could prepare us for the verdict when it came down.'

The verdict came down on Wednesday 29 April 1992 and America – and later the world – was shaken to the core by it. The men were all found Not Guilty on all counts, save for officer Powell. The jury were deadlocked on one count of use of excessive force. Winston Smith and his Ministry of Truth had won – what had happened that night hadn't actually happened and what was seen on the video wasn't what actually had taken place. The jury had bought into a jargon-ridden defence which honoured the violence as being an 'acceptable' part of police procedures. The effect of the verdict was both instantaneous and

appealed for calm, admitted he was as staggered as anyone by the verdicts; even President Bush had to admit his surprise. But words were no longer sufficient for a mob who saw the acquittals as tacit approval for the LAPD to beat black men as and when they liked.

Throughout that first night LA burned as never before as the police totally lost the

Above and opposite:
Fires burned out of control and hard-pressed emergency services struggled to cope. LA was blanketed in a thick layer of soot. Planes could not land and many people suffered respiratory problems. And race relations were exposed as taut and hostile. The city has yet to recover from the physical and spiritual damage of those days.

tragic. The president in his Oval Office in Washington was informed immediately just as the flames from the first riots began to level whole sections of the City of Angels.

Soon America would witness scenes it hadn't seen on national television in decades. The all-consuming rage of a population in the ghettoes of Los Angeles, ground down by poverty and drugs, hopelessness and murders, rose up in fury at the 'white man's justice'. Whole city blocks in the South-Central district of the city, the teeming quarter that is home to blacks and poor Latinos, were consumed in the flames of madness. Tom Bradley, the mayor who

streets. Mobs screaming 'no justice, no peace!' marched on City Hall, on the courthouse, looting, torching and attacking any white face they saw. Although no justification can ever be found for the way the mob behaved, their spontaneous outburst of anger at so grotesque a miscarriage of justice jarred the nation to its roots. LA became a city under siege as the notorious gang-members in South-Central joined forces to wage war against cops and the city was placed under a dawn-to-dusk curfew. Still the fury wasn't played out and by dusk on the second day the city glowed anew with thousands of fresh fires. Mostly confined to the black ghettoes and downtown Los Angeles, the rioting spread to posh residential districts and many whites joined in the trouble which flared with the rapidity of a brush fire.

The fringes of Beverly Hills, one of the richest square miles of real estate on earth, was targeted by looters who ransacked a gem store, a clothes shop and torched a gym and there was also sporadic looting in wealthy upper-crust Westwood.

President Bush appealed for calm as the rioters continued to loot and destroy their ghettoes and areas near the downtown section of the city. Horrified TV viewers were stunned at the sight of marauding black lynch mobs stopping cars at random on the streets to drag the white occupants out for brutal beatings.

In perhaps the most graphic TV scenes a truck driver was pulled from his cab and his head smashed in with a tyre iron. As innocent Reg Denny staggered on to his hand and knees another black youth came by and kicked him with all his might in the head. Another stole his wallet as one of his assailants punched the air with glee. A helicopter-mounted TV camera captured the scenes of appalling brutality as the man staggered back into his truck and drove it for two blocks before he collapsed. Another man was seen with a pump-action shotgun peppering any passing cars that came within his field of fire.

The murderous rat-tat-tat of automatic weapons and the report of shotguns echoed throughout the night. Hospital emergency rooms were swamped with victims, many of them caught in cross fire. Twenty five primary school children were trapped in their classroom overnight as the flames from petrol bombs made them prisoners in the school at the heart of South Central Los Angeles. Many Korean stores – the resentment between blacks and Koreans has been simmering for years in American inner cities – were targeted by the mobs. Black shopkeepers, desperate to save their properties, hung signs saying 'black owned' in a bid to save them from the petrol bombers. By the time National Guardsmen and regular troops hit the streets LA looked like a war zone. There were fifty-one people dead, hundreds of injuries and property damage close to a billion and a half pounds. The city looked like a war zone.

> THE MURDEROUS RAT-TAT-TAT OF AUTOMATIC WEAPONS AND THE REPORT OF SHOTGUNS ECHOED THROUGHOUT THE NIGHT.

> AS INNOCENT REG DENNY STAGGERED ON TO HIS HAND AND KNEES ANOTHER BLACK YOUTH CAME BY AND KICKED HIM WITH ALL HIS MIGHT IN THE HEAD.

The jurors, many of whom sought police protection, justified their verdicts in anonymous interviews afterwards. Appalled by the mountain of indignation and scorn heaped on them, they claimed they were merely doing their duty within the framework of the law. One said: 'The only input I had was what the judicial system, the judge, the defence attorneys, the prosecutors gave me to work with – the law's the law.' Another said: 'The video was ludicrous. Clearly Rodney King was controlling the whole situation.' The disbelief that had settled in America over the acquittals went to the highest levels. President Bush announced shortly afterwards that the men would be back in court to face charges that King's civil rights were violated in the attack; clearly he was as outraged at the verdict as some of the people who took to the streets in the blood disturbances. At the time of writing the four accused have not yet had their second day in court.

Mayor Bradley spoke for all when he said: 'The jury's verdict will never blind us to what we saw on that videotape. The men who beat Rodney King do not deserve to wear the uniform of the LAPD, nor do any others who think what they did was right. The system failed us. We must do our best to ensure that it never fails us again.'

SIMON HAYWARD
An Officer And A Gentleman

Simon Hayward was a dashing Guards officer, the last man anyone expected to be involved in an international narcotics ring. He was jailed for five years but was it the right Hayward brother who was put behind bars? And where is brother Christopher now?

For newspaper reporters, it was a story too good to miss. When the first wire reports came through from Stockholm on Saturday, 14 March 1987, with their story that a British army officer, who used to guard the Queen on ceremonial duties, had been arrested near the Swedish capital and charged with drug running, Fleet Street dispatched hordes of newshounds to cover the unexpected case.

Simon Hayward, a dashingly-handsome career officer with a brilliant future ahead of him in his chosen regiment, the Guards, had seemingly thrown it all away for one hundred and eleven pounds of high-grade cannabis resin worth over £250,000 at street value. The cannabis was discovered by Swedish police hidden in false panels inside a Jaguar car. On the surface it seemed, to use a well-worn police phrase, that Simon Hayward was caught 'bang to rights'. In July that year in a Swedish court he was found Guilty of smuggling and sentenced to five years jail. But behind the simple act of smuggling lay a story of international intrigue, brotherly betrayal and a murderous international syndicate.

Simon Hayward is out of jail now and still sticking to his story that he was the innocent dupe of his wayward brother Christopher, a man with a history of drug use and abuse; a modern day Cain who betrayed his brother and never lifted a finger to help him when he became the fall guy. Sweden is a democratic country with fair laws and a judiciary independent of political control. And yet there are many who feel that Simon Hayward was a victim of a miscarriage of justice... and that, if Christopher Hayward ever reappears, he could be the man who could clear his brother's name.

Before he was branded a drug runner Simon Hayward had everything to live for. A captain at thirty-three, his rank and his charm gave him an entrée into the world of debutante balls, society dinners and exclusive holidays. A product of Wellington College in Crowthorne, in the heart of the English countryside, his masters knew from an early age that he was destined for great things. The son of an RAF officer who left the service to fly for a commercial airline, Simon Hayward was driven by two firm principles – honour and duty. He betrayed neither in the long years with the army and was entrusted with guarding his monarch when Simon was a resplendant horseman vigilant outside Buckingham Palace. It was a moment that Simon wished his father could have seen, but his mother Hazel held enough pride for the entire family.

> SIMON HAYWARD WAS DRIVEN BY TWO FIRM PRINCIPLES — HONOUR AND DUTY.

Opposite: *Simon Hayward, a guardian of the Queen and part of the military elite, was an unlikely drugs-runner. He was, it seems, framed by his own brother.*

Below: *Simon Hayward freed from prison is embraced by the women who believe in his innocence, his fiancée, Sandra Agar on the left and his mother.*

The same values were shared by his elder brother David. But the same could not be said of Christopher, the black sheep of the family, whose devotion seemed to be only to himself and his hedonistic ways. In 1968 he left school after a dismal performance where he was constantly compared

unfavourably with his brothers. The Sixties, with its revolution in dress, music and taste, claimed Christopher. He became enmeshed in eastern philosophy and religion and a devotee of the mind-altering drugs espoused by many disciples of this 'alternative' lifestyle. Like many of his generation, who questioned the rigidity of the class system they were brought up in, he decided to go off in search of himself on the hippy trail to the Far East.

Christoper journeyed through Afghanistan, Thailand, India, becoming lost in clouds of smoke from marijuana that was plentiful and cheap. In 1971 his wanderings took him to Ibiza, the Spanish Balearic island that still retained its peace and charm; it had not yet been invaded by the hotel developers who would destroy much of its old world beauty. In Ibiza, Christopher fell in with a hippy crowd in the village of Santa Gertrudis, later moving to San Carlos on a remote headland where

SIMON HAS ALWAYS
MAINTAINED THAT HE KNEW
NOTHING ABOUT
HIS BROTHER'S
NEFARIOUS ACTIVITIES.

he bought a fishing boat and earned a few pesetas ferrying tourists through the crystal clear Mediterranean waters. With a plentiful supply of cheap hashish from Morocco that was landed in secret coves and inlets, Christopher had his own chunk of paradise far away from the rigidity of his upbringing in chilly England.

While Simon trained hard, he always had time to keep in touch with Christopher by mail. Although the brothers were, on the face of it, as different as chalk and cheese, they had a genuine affection for each other. From Ibiza, Christopher wrote to tell him that he had fallen in love with a hippy friend, a Swiss-born upper-crust young girl named Chantal Heubi. At twenty-two, she had also turned her back on the conventional life. Christopher explained to his brother how Chantal had lost their unborn baby the previous spring. It had devastated her at the time but further cemented the bond between the couple.

On 12 August 1972, he came back to London from Ibiza with her and married Chantal at Fulham register office – an occasion none of the officials forgot in a hurry as both bride and groom donned flowing red robes as favoured by members of the Bhagwan cult of eastern mysticism. The marriage lasted for two years during which time she produced a son, Tarik, by Christopher. Although they parted, they remained on good terms.

A BREAK IN THE SUN

The baby would later play a major part in the destruction of Simon Hayward.

While Christopher continued his lotus-eating lifestyle in sunny Ibiza, Christopher plunged into an army career. His talents marked him out for service with the Special Air Services Regiment, the feared and famed SAS, in Northern Ireland. In long, covert tours of duty in the bandit-ridden border country of Armagh he waged the war against the terrorists that his training had equipped him for. Every man in his unit knew what the IRA did if they captured an SAS man. Both sides played for keeps and the strain of duty told on every man. In March 1987 he felt it was time for a holiday and what better place to spend it than with his brother in the sunshine of the Mediterranean on the island of Ibiza?

Within days, Simon was lazing in the sunshine, drinking by the poolside while he stored up his energy for nights in the discos. Tourism had come with a vengeance now to Ibiza. After nearly two decades living there Christopher Hayward classified himself a native as much as anyone. He had learned Spanish, bought a bigger boat for tourist excursions and had invested in some property. He drove a Jaguar, a luxurious symbol of success.

But did Simon Hayward really know then what the police in Sweden would later allege he knew? That his brother used his catamaran Truelove for more than innocent excursions; that, in fact, he was a key member of an international drug smuggling cartel that bought top grade cannabis in Morocco? That he regularly sailed to Moroccan ports to pick up the consignments? That the drugs were then processed somewhere on mainland Spain before being distributed across Europe?

Simon has always maintained that he knew nothing about his brother's nefarious activities. But Interpol certainly did know and, if Captain Hayward has been telling the truth, he became caught like a fly in a spider's web that he never saw.

Simon was relaxing on holiday but eighteen hundred miles away in Sweden's second city, Uppsala, a high-level meeting between drugs squad officers in the city police and a drugs task force in the capital

Left: *The home of Hayward in Walton Street, London. It is the address of a man who had no need to indulge in squalid drug deals.*

Below: *The Jaguar that Hayward drove as a favour for his brother, Christopher. The car was packed with illegal substances.*

resin, destined for the students of Uppsala. Again the question must be asked: did Simon know when he made the offer what was in the car's fake panels or was he an innocent 'mule' whom the organisation was willing to sacrifice if things went wrong?

If Simon Hayward thought the instructions for the rendezvous with the man he was to contact in Sweden regarding the sale of the car bordered on the dramatic, he did not say so. His brother told him to drive to the railway station of the lonely town of Linkoping, one hundred and twenty miles from Stockholm, where he would meet a man called Lokesh.

Sure enough, at 10pm on 13 March, after a journey that had taken him across the continent, he met Lokesh who climbed

was taking place. They met to discuss the details of a two-year operation planned to smash the international drugs syndicate of which Christopher Hayward was part.

Uppsala, an old academic town with a five-thousand-strong university population eager to get its hands on cheap narcotics, had been the target for large-scale drug peddling by the syndicate. Intelligence told narcotic squads that the next consignment was due in March. Christopher Hayward had been under intense surveillance for months, but there were still no clues as to how the drugs might be couriered into the country. As these officers discussed the fine-tuning of the drugs bust, Christopher put a proposal to Simon his brother.

Midway through the first week of March he was joined in Ibiza by Sandra Agar, his beautiful society girlfriend from London, who was there to hear the proposition put to Simon. Christopher said he wanted to sell his British Racing Green Jaguar XJ6 because it was unsuitable for the winding, narrow roads of Ibiza. He said he had a buyer ready for it in Sweden and would Simon mind driving it to that country as part of his holiday?

Simon jumped at the offer, relishing the prospect of enjoying driving the high-performance car through some of the loveliest scenery in Europe. It was, of course, the car in which Christopher Hayward would plant one hundred and eleven pounds of cannabis

Above: *A good-looking and dashing young army officer, Simon Hayward was also a great party-goer. Before his arrest in Sweden, he was at a ball with Susan, left, and Tracey Woodall.*

Above, top: *Simon Hayward with Sandra Agar, the woman who loves him and believes him. She is convinced he was part of a ghastly frame-up.*

into the front seat of his car. Lokesh was a hippy name that the man had adopted on the island as part of the drug culture he was involved with. In reality he was Scottish-born Forbes Cay Mitchell, a man whom Simon had met briefly once on the island; a veteran drug smuggler who was assigned to get the car to the safe house where other syndicate members would strip it of the drugs. Simon Hayward still maintains he was, as far as he knew, taking the car to be sold. After that he would return to England and his regiment. But he would see neither again for several years. As they drove to the safe house they were arrested by Swedish police who had been planning the bust for nearly two years.

It did not take the police long to locate the drugs. First the elegant Jaguar was weighed and its manufacturer's weight compared with the police scale. It was found to be about one hundred and eleven pounds heavier, and it didn't take long to find the drugs hidden in secret panels in the doors; bag after bag of drugs was laid out on the floor of the Swedish police garage.

Pictures taken of Simon Hayward at the time and that appeared in British newspapers certainly conveyed the impression of a man in total shock, unable to believe what had happened to him. He protested his innocence and told police the whole story as he knew it. He vehemently denied being a drug runner and having anything to do with drugs at all. He was, he said, set up, and once his brother realised the predicament he was in he would step forward to clear his name. Five years on, he is still waiting for that to happen.

DABBLING IN A DANGEROUS GAME

Jan-Erik Nilson is a towering giant of a man, a police officer over six-foot six-inches tall, who, with prosecutor Ulf Forsberg, assembled the case against Simon Hayward. He briefed journalists assembled in Uppsala to cover the story of the shamed soldier with the following story. Cay Mitchell, Nilson said, had squealed on Christopher Hayward while in custody and explained why his brother was chosen to drive the drugs into Sweden. Cay Mitchell said that it was usually a man called Macundo who delivered the illegal cargoes, but his nerves were gone. Significantly, Cay Mitchell said that Simon Hayward knew what he was bringing in, that he was excited by the prospects of dabbling in such a dangerous game and that he was due for a handsome, unspecified reward for his efforts. 'He knew what he was doing,' said Nilson. 'We believe that Captain Hayward entered into this conspiracy willingly. He was not an innocent dupe in our opinion.'

Simon pinned his hopes on Christopher contacting him. Courageously and honourably, he refused to disown his brother even though it seemed, to those who believed his story, that he had been the vic-

> 'WE BELIEVE THAT CAPTAIN HAYWARD ENTERED INTO THIS CONSPIRACY WILLINGLY. HE WAS NOT AN INNOCENT DUPE IN OUR OPINION.'

tim of a frame-up. Police said they hoped to make contact with Christopher, believing that he might want to cut some sort of deal for leniency. If he held the key to identifying the top men of the syndicate, it would have gone a long way into getting a reduced sentence for both brothers. But by the time that his brother had been thrown to the police Christopher was already on the run; a price had been put on his head by the syndicate bosses who believed he had botched the job.

A newspaper has since confirmed that while Interpol was searching for Christopher, he had docked Truelove, his fifty-seven-foot catamaran, in M'diq, scene of so many of his illicit deals. Here he had a secret re-union with his son Tarik. The

Above: *A grim-faced Simon Hayward is driven off to begin a five-year sentence for a crime he protests he did not commit.*

love of his son convinced him that he could not help his brother. Christopher had been told that Tarik would be murdered if he cut any kind of deal with prosecutors in Sweden. Later, Christopher phoned his mother in England. He said he was sorry for what was happening to Simon, but that if he came forward to speak he would be killed and so would Tarik, and he said he was not prepared to let that happen. He was sorry for Simon, but that was the it was. Tarik meant more than Simon.

Cay Mitchell got seven years. At his trial he once again reiterated what he had already told police under interrogation: that Simon Hayward knew everything about the drug running operation and that he was an enthusiastic collaborator in it. Things looked bleak for the disgraced officer at his trial.

His lawyers emphasised the fact that Hayward had never been in trouble before and was merely helping his brother out when he agreed to drive his car. But why, then, asked the judges, was the rendezvous with this car buyer in the car park of a lonely railway station at the dead of night? How come the screwdriver which fitted into the specially-designed holes securing the hollowed out door panel was inside the car? Surely the good Captain must have known of this? What about an overheard conversation that Cay Mitchell alleged Simon had with his brother in which he jumped at the chance to courier the drugs into Sweden? The only defence Simon had, and which he maintains to this day, is that he was tricked by someone he believed in absolutely. While the court recognised his excellent career, his unblemished character and his stoic defence of his brother, it nevertheless found him Guilty and sentenced him to five years.

Events after he was sentenced cast an even more favourable light upon his plea of innocence. Shortly before the verdict in July, Christopher's ex-wife Chantal telephoned Mrs Hayward at her London home. Mrs Hayward, who had lost her husband, one son in jail and the other on the run, was astonished to hear her claim that she had evidence who was behind the drugs run. She told her that it was neither Christopher nor Simon. She refused to reveal the name over the phone but promised to fly to London from Ibiza to speak with solicitors. Mrs Hayward urged her to make the journey as soon as possible but just days before she was scheduled to arrive she was found dead with a needle in her arm.

THE RIGHT-HAND TURNS SINISTER

An autopsy showed that she had died from heroin and other drugs mixed together in a lethal cocktail. But Chantal's friends all knew her as a woman who had dabbled in marijuana but had never, ever fallen into hard drug use. And more mysterious was the fact that the needle was plunged into her left arm even though she was left-handed. It begged the question: why did a girl unused to injecting drugs use an unfamiliar hand to do so? Her death coming just days before she was due to arrive in London led Simon's supporters to believe the poor woman had been murdered.

A court has to prove guilt 'beyond reasonable doubt'. Simon Hayward continues to maintain his innocence, even though his sentence is behind him. He does not know of the whereabouts of his brother, or even if he is still alive. But the ingrained decency in Simon Hayward has given way to a bitterness towards the brother who condemned him to a prison term. He says: 'Ninety-nine per cent of me believes that Christopher stitched me up. Only that other one per cent clings to the fact that he is my brother, that he couldn't have done. But ninety-nine per cent screams out that he did. One thing is very obvious. Whether he did or he didn't, whether he is genuinely terrified of something or somebody thát I know nothing about, there must have been some way for him to get a message or information through to clear me. He has not done that and for that I will never forgive him.' But where is Christopher?

Below: Simon Hayward published a book about his ordeal. There is still no trace of the whereabouts of his brother, Christopher, who seems to have been responsible for his brother Simon's arrest and imprisonment.